DATE DUE

DEC 1 4 2007			
FEB 15 2013			
MAY 1 4 2015			
GAYLORD			PRINTED IN U.S.A

Lives and Letters

LIVES AND LETTERS

A. R. Orage
Beatrice Hastings
Katherine Mansfield
John Middleton Murry
S. S. Koteliansky

1906-1957

by
JOHN CARSWELL, 1918 -

A NEW DIRECTIONS BOOK

Manufactured in Great Britain

First published by New Directions in 1978

Library of Congress Cataloging in Publication Data

Carswell, John. 1918-
    Lives and Letters.
    (A New Directions Book)
    Bibliography: p. 294-297
    Includes index.
    1. Authors, English—20th century—Biography. 2. Orage, Alfred Richard, 1873-1934. 3. Hastings, Beatrice. 4. Mansfield, Katherine, 1888-1923. 5. Murry, John Middleton, 1889-1957. 6. Koteliansky, Samuel Solomonovitch, 1880-1955. I. Title.

PR106.C37   820'.9'00912   77-15986
ISBN 0-8112-0681-5

New Directions Books are published for James Laughlin by New Directions Publishing Corporation, 333 Sixth Avenue, New York 10014

Nous sommes les petits, les obscurs, les sans-grade

L'AIGLON

Contents

[1] I owe this chapter heading to Mr Rayner Heppenstall's memoir of Middleton Murry in *Four Absentees* where he records misreading the notice on Murry's farm announcing The Adelphi Herd.

Illustrations

PLATES

between pages 160 and 161

FIGURES

Preface

This book is neither a straightforward biography nor a work of literary criticism. A word of explanation is therefore needed.

The first twenty years of my life were spent in a household where the names and sometimes the presence of the people in this book were an everyday matter. Like them, my parents were literary freelances. Long before I knew anything of literature itself I had sensed literary life—the impact of publication, the comings and goings, the half-caught murmurs from my parents' room immediately below that reached me as I lay awake at night. I recall Lawrence, gaunt and auburn-bearded yet to me by definition benevolent and a family hero; the wide smile and tousled blonde hair of Frieda; the nimble, and then much later the placid form of Edwin Muir; known long before I had an inkling of their works.

Then, as a result of the war, my life took a different turn. My parents Catherine and Donald died, and I adopted a salary-earning existence.

But I remained attached to the freelance philosophy. I had always known that these literary people had little to do with 'Bloomsbury', which they respected for its success and comfort but despised for its comfort and success. My choice of the main characters in rediscovering this freelance world was to some extent haphazard, and I had no idea of the central position Katherine Mansfield would prove to occupy.

I have been lucky in gaining a great deal of help, especially from those who remember the people in this book. I have been able to draw on the recollections of Mrs. Jessie Orage, the late Philip Mairet, Mr. Maurice Reckitt, Miss Ruth Pitter, Miss Dilys Powell, the late Mrs. Ivy Litvinov, Mr. David Garnett, Mr. Martin Secker, and Mr. Hugh McDiarmid. Mrs. Mary Middleton Murry and Mr. Colin Middleton Murry have kindly allowed me to quote

Preface

copyright material relating to their husband and father respectively; and Mrs. Catherine Stoye has generously given me access to the papers of S. S. Koteliansky in her possession.

I am grateful to many others: among whom are Mr. John Bunting, who kept on coming up with most remarkable material about Orage and Beatrice Hastings; Professor Wallace Martin; Professor Sam Hynes; Mr. Miron Grindea; Mrs. Bryna Davis, who found out a great deal about the family of Beatrice Hastings in South Africa; the Principal and Vice-Principal of Culham College; Mr. Arthur Crook; Miss Geraldine Conroy; L.M.; the *New Statesman*, which fortunately incorporates the *Athenaeum*; the Library of the Society for the Propagation of the Gospel; the Alexander Turnbull Library of Wellington, New Zealand (especially for the right to quote from Koteliansky's letters to Waterlow); the University of Sussex (for Koteliansky's letters to Leonard Woolf); the University of Urbana, Illinois; the University of Victoria, British Colombia; the Municipal Library of Port Elizabeth, South Africa; the British Library (including its Colindale Annexe); the Library of the Department of Education and Science and the London Library.

I am indebted for the Orage portrait of 1932 to Llyle Stuart; for the Modigliani portrait of Beatrice Hastings to the Art Gallery of Ontario; for the photographs of Katherine Mansfield and of Murry at Sierre to L.M.; for the portrait of Murry in 1935 to Mrs. Middleton Murry; and for the wedding picture and the photographs of Koteliansky and of the Thursdayers to Mrs. Catherine Stoye.

A very special debt is due to Inge Goodwin. Her verve in following every trail and her support to me at every turning made the book possible.

J.C.

February 1977

14

The Schoolmaster

Fenstanton is on the Roman road joining Cambridge to Huntingdon, rather nearer Huntingdon than Cambridge: still a quiet place
with fewer than a thousand inhabitants, and in the early 1870s still
governed by squire and parson with the reservation that the squire,
Thomas Coote, though a J.P. and a Deputy Lieutenant, was a
Nonconformist.

Among the inhabitants of this village which retained so much of
the atmosphere of *Tom Jones*'s early chapters was a widow living on
an income of about fifty pounds a year, Mrs. Sarah Anne Orage
(or Orridge) and her four children Florence, William, Edith and
James Alfred, the last of whom had been born on 22 January 1873.
The father of this family, William Orage, had been a native of
Fenstanton, but after failing there as a farmer he had taken to teaching, and later to drink. His last post had been in a school at Dacre
near Pateley Bridge, on the edge of Nidderdale and about twenty
miles across the dales from Bowes, where Dickens had placed
Dotheboys Hall. There James Alfred had been born, and there, in
the following year, William Orage had died, leaving his widow to
return with her four young children to Fenstanton.

Sarah Orage was not from Huntingdonshire stock: she was almost
certainly Irish, for her maiden name was McGuire. She and George
Hicks, the village schoolmaster of Fenstanton, were the dominating
influences on the boy's early years, and James Alfred prospered,
both mentally and physically, despite a serious accident at the age
of eight, when he fell from a hay-wain and broke his thigh. Hicks
encouraged him with private tuition and modest prizes, and he
shone in the school play.

For some reason, even at school, the boy was known neither as
Alf nor Jim, but as Dickie, and later on he was to drop the James
altogether in favour of Richard, making the celebrated initials

'A.R.O.'. And this was not to be the only juggle with his name when he had left Fenstanton behind. However the name Orage was spelt in Huntingdonshire it was pronounced to rhyme with 'porridge'. Bernard Shaw used to insist on the Huntingdonshire pronunciation, well knowing Orage's preference for making his name sound like the French for 'storm', which he buttressed by vague suggestions of Huguenot origin.

Mr. Hicks and the vicar of Fenstanton saw young Dickie in much the same light as the teachers in Ripley, Derbyshire, a decade later, were to see young David Herbert Lawrence: as a future teacher. The new battalions of teachers required by the Education Act had to be sought in the schools of villages and slums, for the possessing classes were neither numerous enough nor willing to see their children take up teaching on weekdays. The process was at work all over England, with immense social consequences, for it created, in three decades, a large and unprecedented social category, more than half of which consisted of women. In 1870 there were not quite 3,000 teachers in training, and nearly 2,000 of them were men. By 1900 the number was almost twice as great in total, and three-fifths were women. Between the two dates the force of teachers had built up from 14,000 to over 100,000, three-quarters of whom were women. Here was the rank and file of the movement for women's rights, and a public for progressive journalism on a scale never known before. The teacher training programme not only gave Orage his first career: it gave him the audience for his second.[1]

He remained at school at Fenstanton beyond the normal leaving age of twelve with the aspiration of progressing through the grades of pupil teacher and teaching assistant towards a college place and qualified status. It was not easy for Sarah. The little capital producing the £50 a year which her husband had left her had been embezzled by a fraudulent solicitor. After two years of keeping her clever youngest son at school she appealed to the manor house for help, otherwise, she declared, he must go out to work like the other children. And some help was given, both in cash and kind. The effective force in the Coote family was now the old squire's twenty-one-year-old grandson Charles Harold, who had been to Rugby and

---

[1] Source for these figures and subsequent quotations will be found at the end of the book.

the University of Neuchâtel, and he took an interest in the boy. There were visits to the library at the manor and French lessons at the vicarage, where Alfred was given a grounding in the classical eloquence of the seventeenth-century Bishop Massillon, and in Chateaubriand. He tramped to the Cambridge Art School, ten miles in each direction, for drawing lessons, and with the help of his sister Edith compiled a calendar of extracts from the improving weekly *Great Thoughts*. At sixteen he began to teach as a pupil teacher, and at eighteen took the Queen's scholarship examination, obtaining a second class.

It took him to the austerely Anglican Culham College, near Abingdon, one of the oldest of the church training colleges. It then had about a hundred students under a discipline which had recently been somewhat relaxed on the arrival of a new and milder Principal, the Revd. W. F. S. Long, but was rigorous none the less. The students rose at six a.m. and the first lecture was administered before breakfast. Until quarter to ten in the evening, which was bed-time, every week-day hour was timetabled, and no less than thirty hours was assigned to lectures. Many of these must have been delivered by the versatile G. H. Fathers later Vice-Principal, who at different times taught French, Latin, Divinity, history, drawing, science, reading, recitation, political economy, and teaching method. Orage carried into later life something of this great teacher's flexible omniscience. At Culham, also, Orage was probably introduced to Plato, whose work was the greatest and most lasting influence on his intellect; and there was a debating society in which he undoubtedly took part. He was an assiduous and successful student, being placed first in the Certificate of Education examination, and first in Divinity, at the end of his first year.

Culham also gave him his first experience of journalism. Within two months of his arrival he was sub-editor of the college magazine, the *Culhamite*, and in his second year he was editor, transforming (as he said later) 'an infant into a child'. His 'causeries' and editorials have the affectation which is so common in student magazines, but the didactic yet smooth style that he was to make famous is already perceptible in a trifle which appeared in the *Culhamite* for November 1893, called 'Thro' a Ring of Smoke'.[1]

[1] I am indebted to the Principal of Culham for much of this information.

Only a few years earlier a Culham student had been rusticated for 'talking to a woman on Saturday evening in Abingdon'. The new Principal was not quite so severe (or perhaps not so well-informed) and Orage, who was unusually attractive, acquired a girl-friend. Who she was is not recorded, except that she was a student of the Royal College of Art in Kensington, and lodged with a fellow student named Jean Walker, daughter of a hard-working Scottish Inspector of Schools named Alexander Walker. On an illicit trip to London, possibly the first he ever made, Orage met Jean, who quickly replaced her fellow student. It was the beginning of a long series.

In September 1893, at the age of twenty, Orage qualified as a teacher and entered the employment of the Leeds School Board at Chapel Allerton elementary school with a salary of eighty pounds a year. Even at the height of his fame as editor and oracle his income was not much more than twice this. Finance interested him, but not money. In 1894 Jean joined him from Glasgow, and it appears that they got married.[1]

Leeds was one of the most progressive education authorities in England, and in the two decades since the introduction of compulsory education it had conquered the problem of school attendance and built forty-five new schools. Such of them as survive today are no doubt gaunt and forbidding, but for those who built them they were brand-new not only in fabric but in purpose. Education had been a political battlefield in Leeds, with Anglican 'voluntarists' pitted against Liberal, Nonconformist supporters of state education at a succession of hard-fought School Board elections in which, on the whole, the Liberals triumphed. In School Board elections every ratepayer had a vote—even illiterate Irish labourers, even women. For years the Liberal champion in the educational battle against the Anglican cause in Leeds was a Mrs. Catherine Buckton.

The year 1893, when Orage established himself in a cottage at Ingle Row, Chapel Allerton, was also the year of the formation of the Independent Labour Party. The preceding decade had seen the celebrated division of English socialism between the Marxists, led by the uncompromising H. M. Hyndman, and the Fabians pinning

[1] Careful searches, however, have failed to trace the record.

their faith in bureaucratic domestication of the economic system. Hyndman stood for revolution, the Webbs for penetration. The I.L.P., which was discountenanced by both, aimed at socialist transformation of the working class by propaganda. This movement, of which Keir Hardie was the hero, was Orage's first contact with socialism.

From the first he was a socialist with a very great difference, for his mind was reverberating with the doctrines of Plato. The notion of a reality beyond appearances, of an inner knowledge that might be attained by mental struggle, never left Orage, and was to lead him into some strange morasses. Plato also sharpened his powers of disputation, both in speech and in writing, which were altogether beyond the ordinary. 'Do you speak?' G. D. H. Cole once asked him, when Orage offered to appear on the platform to support Guild Socialism. 'Do you write?' was the editor's reply.

The young schoolmaster spoke at street-corner meetings for the I.L.P. and contributed little essays to Keir Hardie's *New Leader* for five shillings a week. But he had a strong empirical streak, despite his Platonism, and there was never anything sectarian about his socialism. He quickly grasped the fact that even in its infancy socialism was producing almost as many variations as there were socialists; and that the doctrine which elevated collectivism was held most enthusiastically by people who, in doing so, vigorously asserted their own individuality: as indeed, he did himself.

His mother died at the end of the year he started teaching at Leeds, and very soon came the end of his relationship with Fenstanton and all it stood for in the way of roots. The spring after he went to Leeds he came back to the village and shocked the whole family, who were still in mourning, by his bright red tie and scoffs at conventional observances. By that time he had met Tom Mann, the Labour leader, at a meeting in Sheffield, and was becoming known himself as a platform speaker well beyond Leeds. His marriage to Jean Walker was the last straw. The Cootes thought it grossly premature and irresponsible, and a suggestion that they should finance an undergraduate course for him at Oxford was decisively declined. Long afterwards Beatrice Hastings said that no one could understand Orage who did not know the passion with which he had rejected his village origins.

In the cottage at Chapel Allerton he was exposing himself to a cascade of powerful influences. The socialist primary-school teacher was poring over the *Bhagavadgita* and the *Mahabharata*: and, still more puzzling, over the outpourings of the theosophist Madame Blavatsky—*Isis Unveiled* and *The Secret Doctrine*. That extraordinary woman, to whom the Society for Psychical Research had paid a grudging tribute as a skilful and unblushing impostor, had recently died, leaving an inheritance that was strongly disputed among rival sects of disciples. But one should not be wholly surprised at Orage's lasting and omnivorous interest in the occult. It was not unusual. Socialism had not yet established itself as a faith in its own right, and the great explanations of psychology were still to come. The gigantic and pervasive forces of organised religion were still able to demand that even those who rejected their doctrines and discipline (as Orage already did) should formulate some other supernatural synthesis; so socialism was not uncommonly found in association with theosophy. The period between Marx and Freud, which was also the period of decay in English institutional Christianity, was a kind of Thebaid filled with seekers and pedlars of new, quasi-religious formulations: a period of intense speculation, and some gullibility.

In Leeds and its neighbourhood Orage gradually acquired a local reputation as a skilled controversialist, whether in public or private meetings. His knowledge of Plato undoubtedly helped, and so did his appearance:

> In appearance Orage was tall, and, at this time, slim and dark-haired, and he dressed conventionally, except for a soft felt hat, then unusual. . . . It was usually worn on the back of his head. He wore a plain hand-woven silk tie, sometimes blue, but oftener an orange or flame colour. His hair was worn short except for a long tuft which sometimes strayed over his forehead. His eyes were hazel, lively, and challenging, and in moments of excitement they seemed to emit a red glint. It was a feline face and there was something cat-like in his movements. He walked as though he were going to pounce on something, much as his mind pounced upon an idea or an opponent. His expression was earnest without being solemn. There was wit in his poise and manner

and he was good to look at without being good-looking. But he did not impress by his features so much as by that which was outside and beyond features. You were conscious of his aura; you felt his presence so much that you forgot details, even the vague birthmark which broke into his complexion like an irregular sunburn, and seemed to become deeper when he was bored or out of humour.

The birthmark, to which no other description of Orage refers, was on the left cheek, so that most portraits of him are in profile showing the right side of the face, which is massive, with somewhat deep-set eyes below heavy eyebrows, and divided by a strong, prominent nose. No doubt the physical characteristics were an important part of the power he seemed to radiate. But in the end it can only be defined by the tributes of those who fell under his spell—his 'peerless conversation', his 'immediate warmth', his gift of conveying integral interest in the person he was with. It never left him.

Orage was no doubt one of the liveliest and best-informed primary school teachers in grimy, industrial, slum-cursed Leeds during the last decade of the century. He was the focus of a Plato Group, which met in his tiny rooms, and of a Theosophy Group. But he had not yet encountered one of the most formidable influences on his generation, that of Friedrich Nietzsche, whose work was slow to reach England in translation.[1] Jean Orage had read some Nietzsche in French, but it was not until he was lent a copy of an English translation of *Also Sprach Zarathustra* in 1900 that he was stormed by the energy, insight, and prophetic fervour of that extraordinary mind.

The man who had lent him *Zarathustra* was a young lace merchant of progressive views called Holbrook Jackson, whom he met in a second-hand bookshop. Their friendship ripened quickly in long fireside conversations, of which the first had ended with an exchange of the *Bhagavadgita* for *Zarathustra*. Orage read it in a single night, returning next morning—a Sunday—to Jackson's house at Headingly, with the red glinting in his eye. It was the first time that a new doctrine had overwhelmed Orage at the same moment as a new friendship. It was not to be the last.

[1] *Also Sprach Zarathustra* was composed in 1881. The authorised translation by Thomas Common under the editorship of Oscar Levy (one of the most regular contributors to Orage's *New Age*) did not appear until 1909.

Jackson was considerably better off than Orage, had some experience in business, and what was more had access to homes and interest in middle-class Leeds which was denied to an elementary schoolmaster of socialist principles. But of the two minds Orage's was undoubtedly the stronger. They not only exchanged books and fireside debates but conducted a more formal written exchange. It is still preserved in a stenographer's notebook which passed by post from Headingly to Chapel Allerton, each debater adding his successive contribution on the question whether a critic should be impartial or committed. In this rather mannered debate Orage took the more difficult side in favour of commitment, and won hands down. His neat rounded handwriting moves effortlessly without a correction from argument to insinuation—'Examples of so-called impartial impersonal criticism you can find in the leading articles of the *Daily Mail*—your favourite organ is it not?—or in any of the columns of the vapid anonymous press . . .' while Jackson's replies are increasingly cramped, spotted with corrections and marred by false starts deleted in favour of second thoughts. At last, driven into the corner of saying that criticism should be as impartial as mathematics and as logical as Euclid, he receives the full force of Orage's Socraticism, and breaks off the discussion with such dignity as he can muster.

The manuscript is interesting, as showing the clear-headed side of Orage, which prevented even his worst-judged enthusiasms from falling into intellectual sloppiness. He concedes instantly to his 'deluded friend' that a critic should give his reasons for expressing a preference, but then in the last resort taste is beyond reason. What the critic is doing is to express taste plus reason: 'but that does not make it *impartial* criticism, merely because it is superior to taste without reason'. 'There is no definite rational standard in matters of taste. You cannot reason a man into loving a picture by Whistler, or out of adoring Beardsley . . . emotion and reason are in two different worlds . . . your so-called impartial critic is *reasoning* about a thing on which other people feel. And *because* he reasons instead of feeling, *you* call him impartial. . . . Our perfect critic both feels *and* reasons. But notice, notice, he reasons no further than he feels,—not even as far.'

The date must be about 1901. The document shows Orage's zeal to get ascendancy in argument and his ascendancy over Jackson. At this point he also gained influence over another mind, representing a very different, yet complementary strain of intellectual development.

Among the visitors drawn to Orage's Plato Group was a young architect named A. J. Penty, practising in his father's firm at Knaresborough. Two years younger than Orage, Penty was in the tradition of William Morris, captivated by the fellowship of skill, by craftsmanship, and by the dream of guilds as a fraternal basis for society. He was an outdoor man, a hiker, a believer in the simple life and a few warmly-felt ideals which led to socialism, though by a grassy path. Later his romanticism was to lead him into paths far from socialism—admiration for kingship, and even for Mussolini.

This was the diversely socialist trio on which the Leeds Arts Club was built. The venture was a bold one, and went far beyond the Platonic and theosophic gatherings Orage had organised before. He was the moving spirit, and the idea of calling it the William Morris Society, which was suggested by Penty, was firmly rejected by Orage. Prosperous citizens of Leeds were canvassed and placed on the committee; and the subscription was half a guinea a year. The manifesto is unmistakably the work of Orage:

> The object of the Leeds Arts Club is to affirm the mutual dependence of art and ideas. The separation of use from beauty or beauty from use proves in the long run disastrous for both; and only their union in a single clear purpose can restore to us the value of either.

It was a great success. The Club had exhibitions of art and of craft and of fine printing; brought the works of Edward Carpenter, Chesterton, and Shaw to the Leeds bookshops; and eventually produced the very men to give lectures. The proceedings were widely reported in the local papers, and there was a Fabian section under the direction of Holbrook Jackson. As a result Orage himself became even more widely known, and was in strong demand as a lecturer all over Yorkshire, astonishing audiences with his expositions of Nietzsche and Ibsen. One of his most devoted admirers was a wealthy Pudsey coal merchant named Joseph Smith, who used to attend Orage's lectures in a state of silent wonder. Some of the women members of his audiences were more forthcoming. 'Do what you will', he urged them, 'and you will find out how little you can will. Till you have the courage to take your own way, you can't know what it is.' 'At least', said one girl after the lecture, 'I have always tried to do my duty.' 'What a pity,' said Orage.

The provincial offensive against Victorianism was under way. Orage had met Shaw in 1898[1] and on St. Valentine's day 1905 Shaw himself, with two plays in rehearsal at the same time in London, came to Leeds to lecture to the Arts Club on 'What is the use of an Arts Club?'—a title more artfully chosen than appears on the first reading. The swirl of ideas on which Orage was now being carried could not be better summarised than in a letter Shaw wrote about the current intellectual scene only a few days before the lecture which marked the Arts Club as the leading edge of progress in the East Riding: '... the last quarter of the nineteenth century, especially as to the Collectivist movement in politics, ethics and sociology; the Ibsen–Nietzschean movement in morals; the reaction against the materialism of Marx and Darwin ...; the Wagnerian movement in music; and the anti-romantic movement (including what people call realism, naturalism, and impressionism) in literature and art'.

Orage already saw wider horizons. He had visited London at the expense of a wealthy theosophist banker, Lewis A. R. Wallace, and the meeting with Shaw in 1905 made him still bolder. In October of that year he wrote to H. G. Wells enclosing a cutting from the *Leeds Mercury* reporting his address 'before a crowded audience' of the Leeds Arts Club on the topic 'Practical Imagination'. It contained warm references to Wells's three recent works on 'imaginative sociology'.[2] The covering letter expressed the hope that 'you will gather from it that I—and a good many others here as well— think no end of your ideas'. Now the admiring coal merchant, Joseph Smith, provided him with sixty pounds to start a new career. That summer he had resigned his safe job with the Leeds School Board, and in November 1905 he stayed briefly with a theosophical acquain-

[1] 'I have known the Shaws well', Orage told C. S. Nott, 'for many years. I was with them the day before they were married' (C. S. Nott, *Teachings of Gurdjieff. The Journal of a Pupil*, p. 30).
[2] *The Discovery of the Future* (1902); *Mankind in the Making* (1903); and *A Modern Utopia* (1905).

tance in Harrogate, where he left an entry in the visitors' book. Under 'Where to' he wrote 'God only knows', and under 'Remarks', 'Over a precipice. How far to the bottom?'. Very soon afterwards, accompanied by Jean, he was in London.

It was a heavy risk, even with Smith's sixty pounds and the literary and theosophical connections he had formed. Weekly incomes were measured in shillings, not pounds, and literary work might command half a guinea a column if it could be placed at all. Except for the few journalists who were regularly employed on major papers the absence of any settled income and often extreme poverty, was the rule. Credit was out of the question. The population of the world Orage had joined lived in rooms over shops in Fulham or in obscure, inaccessible cottages in Bucks, and took their meals in Express Dairies and A.B.C.s. The arrival of as much as three guineas, let alone the acceptance of an entire book for an advance of twenty-five pounds, represented a *coup* which put the struggling author and perhaps a crowd of needy friends in funds of a kind for weeks. Many reached the point which Johnson had described in his *Life of Savage* more than a century earlier—'at last he wanted bread'.

Socialism was in fashion, and Orage was a socialist, though a romantic, arty socialist rather than a social engineer. In some ways the many voices of socialism in his time sound surprisingly like those of today: there was the same abundance of doctrine ranging from the moderate to the most extreme, there were many of the same phrases. But there was one immensely important difference. There was no such thing in the world as a country which had professedly adopted socialism as its comprehensive system of organisation; and therefore no centre of political power to which socialists could look for their terms of reference or opponents of socialism for proof of its dangerous effects. On the contrary, the whole world seemed to be dominated and permeated by the military and industrial power of Western Europe, and above all by Britain. The Englishman who adopted socialism as a criticism of the society in which he had been brought up found it no easier than the Indian Civil Servant or the village postmistress to imagine the absence of the security that his seemingly powerful society provided. It was possible perhaps, to be even bolder in one's expressions simply because of this. The probability of ever being called to account for them was remote. The tide was a long way out.

We do not know the expectations with which Orage came first to London. But no sooner had he arrived than there was a general election, and to the astonishment of everyone the Conservatives, who had governed with only a brief interregnum for twenty years, were swept from office and the Liberals were installed with an unprecedented majority. And it was a new Liberalism, far removed from the Gladstonian party which had foundered on Home Rule in 1886. In that long interval socialism had taken shape and force. The old Parliament had contained eleven members described as Labour; the new one had fifty-five. For tens of thousands of younger people the general election of 1906 was the greatest and most liberating political experience of their entire lives. The walls of Jericho seemed to have fallen. The political public itself, everyone suddenly began to realise, had changed. Those born in the last quarter of the previous century, and exposed to primary education and (in large numbers) to secondary and teacher education, were not going to behave like their parents: and large numbers of them had not had votes in 1906. In 1903 Mrs. Pankhurst had launched the Women's Social and Political Union, and two years later propelled it into militancy.

Even the first generation of Fabians—Shaw, the Webbs, the Blands (two women, in this group of five)—were having to face a challenge, though through the genius of Shaw they survived it. That summer H. G. Wells had launched his celebrated attack on 'the old gang' in the Fabian Society and his own bid to capture the leadership of the society, which in his view 'ought to have 7,000 members instead of 700, and everything else to scale'. That winter saw considerable manoeuvring at excited meetings of the 'Fabian', as a result of which a committee, with Wells as its leading spirit, was set up to review the whole scope of the Society's activities. The struggle was by no means over, but for the time being it was the policy of Shaw and his allies to give Wells his head.

Orage, of course, as a provincial schoolmaster, was far from the centre of all this, but there can be little doubt that he knew of it. Holbrook Jackson, his closest friend, was an active Fabian; and although Orage's own mind was not in the traditional Fabian cast, the combination of literary and political power exercised by Shaw, and now being attempted by Wells, was peculiarly attractive to him. He had a wide foundation of reading—wider probably than most university-trained men of his time; and he had no doubts now about his personal powers. At any rate this was the equipment, and the hoped-for sponsorship, with which the Orages took up a share of a flat with A. J. Penty off the Goldhawk Road.

❧ 2 ❧

The Moon-girl from Port Elizabeth

Penty's modest Hammersmith lodgings were at 57 Weltje Road. There Orage probably finished his little book introducing the philosophy of Nietzsche which appeared in 1906, and did his best to get himself known as a journalist and lecturer. At one meeting of the Theosophical Society for which the advertised lecturer had failed to appear he volunteered from the audience to take his place, and it may have been on this occasion (certainly it was at a Theosophical Society meeting) that he found himself involved, after the lecture, in conversation with a green-eyed young woman called Beatrice Hastings. She was lively, dark, and outspoken; and remarkably well-read. The acquaintance developed, and by 1907, as Beatrice later put it, 'Aphrodite amused herself at our expense.'

Her name was not really Beatrice Hastings but Emily Alice Haigh, born in 1879 in Hackney, where it seems that her parents were on a visit from Port Elizabeth, Cape Colony, where her father kept a store. Much of the early part of her life had been spent in the small-town atmosphere of Port Elizabeth or the wide spaces of its hinterland, in the shadow of the Stormberg range, and very early she had felt a sense of unjust inferiority and rebellion:

She looks at me: and I don't like her. She has a white dress on, but I find her ugly.

'Pooh!' I *see* her say to my pinafore, full of *beautiful* things: my shining, smooth marbles, my glass bottle with a hole in the top to let in sand, my ever so many bits of glass. 'Pooh!' in recording now I can feel how my fatness quivered under the insult.

'We were a big family', she wrote elsewhere in her autobiographical 'Pages From an Unpublished Novel', 'yet I was always solitary.' She conducted imaginary orchestras, and failed to fit into a series of

schools. For her parents she seems to have had no strong feelings—
she never mentions her father, and her mother only gleams with a
kind of remote benevolence. She resented the tallness of grown-ups
and their power, frequently exercised, to force her to do things.

When she was about twelve she was brought back to England
and sent to a small boarding school in Kent. It was at Pevensey,
near Hastings, where there were many such schools, and it seems
likely that it was from Hastings, rather than any subsequent marriage, that she took the surname she ever afterwards used.[1] As for
the Christian name, she had already substituted Beatrice for Emily
Alice, much as Orage had substituted Richard for James. It expressed her independence.

She hated the school at Pevensey as she had hated all the others.
She 'wickedly' caught flu and gave it to everyone else; and was
bullied by the headmistress's husband, 'an orange-coloured little
man with tight bird features and a great mass of oily ringlets'. But
she had done well as a pupil. 'My divine memory, though abused
by the pedagogues, never allowed me to fail when the facts were
asked for. I never in my life failed under examination.' Her gifts,
especially for words, were indeed not inconsiderable, and she had
a very high opinion of them.

In or about 1893 she was taken back to South Africa by her elder
sister, and there spent her adolescence. The business at Port
Elizabeth was making the Haighs prosperous, and for the rest of her
life Beatrice, like her future friend and enemy Katherine Mansfield,
was to be able to rely in the last resort on the fortune of a prosperous colonial father. When the South African War came her
adored elder brother Richmond Haigh served under Sir George
White in the defence of Ladysmith, and in due course became something of an expert in African affairs. So indeed, during what seems
to have been a happier period of her life, did Beatrice. She had
adventures with Kaffir children, caught the speech of the Boer
ostrich-farmers which she was later to reproduce in *The Maid's
Comedy*, and developed a strong feeling for the rolling, lonely

[1] There is an unproved suggestion that she married a boxer named Hastings
in South Africa. There is no trace of this marriage or of the divorce which would
have been needed to enable her, when still a young woman, to marry (as she
certainly did) one Lachlan Thomson, also described as a boxer. And few
women go through life after a second marriage using their first husband's name.

country that looks down on Port Elizabeth, peopling it with quixotic and semi-Arthurian beings conjured out of her extensive reading and strong imagination.

She must have left South Africa for ever before she was twenty, and for the next six or seven years—that is until her meeting with Orage at the Theosophical Society lecture—we have only her own word to go by, and with Beatrice unsupported statements are often not only unreliable but positively false. Perhaps, as she is recorded as saying, she came to England as a nurse on a hospital ship. She hinted that she had visited the United States. She somewhere married, and parted from, Lachlan Thomson. And she often spoke violently (though to some minds unconvincingly) of the horrors of maternity, and of having lost her child. What is certain about Beatrice in 1906 is that she was twenty-seven, unencumbered, and consumed by literary ambition.

Faith in the overwhelming power of reason jostled in her mind with a kind of transcendental idealism; and this in turn coexisted with a strong turn for iconoclasm. This contrariness showed in both her opinions and her style, but these were supported by such a massive vocabulary and such unflagging industry that they were to make her a formidable, if unpredictable journalist. Her life was a dream of which she was the heroine, and although like many people of this kind her instincts were often destructive, she had insights which were denied to more sober and calculating personalities. Beatrice was good at paradox and exposure of the conventional. She could crusade with passion, and floor the most impressive adversaries orally or on paper. But she often overdid it, and when she tried to write poetry it was a disastrous failure, with one single exception. And even 'The Lost Bacchante' her best-known poem, of which she was excessively proud, collapses after the first few lines.

Neither of the new allies, Orage and Beatrice, had a job, but Orage's little book *Nietzsche, the Dionysian Spirit of the Age* was published towards the end of the year. He sent a copy to H. G. Wells, expressing the hope that if he cared at all for it he would 'say so in the right place'; and it did quite well, with Shaw saying in the *Fabian News* that 'Mr. Orage's statement of Nietzsche's position is just what was needed'. Just the same the strain must have been heavy, and then there was Beatrice. It was all too much for Jean Orage. This was not the kind of life for the daughter of the Divisional Inspector of Schools for northern Perthshire, which Alexander Walker now was. She left Orage for Holbrook Jackson, a change which lies with some importance in the background of the two men's journalistic careers in the next year or two. But she refused to divorce Orage.

Jackson had followed Orage and Penty to London, and the three of them quickly became involved in the current controversies of the Fabian Society, where the 'Old Gang' led by Shaw and the Webbs was defending itself against Wells's plan for turning the Society into a political party. The Leeds trio were on Wells's side, and the announcement of a 'Fabian Arts Group' (FAG) with Jackson as its secretary, coming just before the Fabian executive elections of February 1907, was regarded with profound suspicion by Shaw and the Webbs. This was a long way from the moral improvement by administrative action for which they had always stood. They were still more concerned when some of the lectures given at FAG's hired room in Fleet Street were given by people who were hardly socialists at all—by G. K. Chesterton, for instance, Hilaire Belloc, W. B. Yeats, and the English pioneer of psychoanalysis, Dr. M. D. Eder. They also disliked other ideas which Orage was peddling at Fabian meetings and behind the scenes. In the summer of 1906 he had been trying to start a 'Gild Restoration League', for which the notions had clearly come from Penty. It called for the replacement of Trade Unions by Craft Gilds, and 'opposed the nationalisation of all industries as proposed by Collectivists'.

The main objection to Socialism [Orage wrote to Wells enclosing this scheme] which I have found amongst the middle classes is to its materialism. This, of course, is due to the accident that socialism has been largely bound up with Trades Unionism, which in its turn has been necessarily an economic protestant movement. Thus the real obstacle to the middle class conversion to socialism is the fear that it may involve government by Trade Union officials.

What was needed, he argued, was a fusion of the Trade Union and Craft approaches, and this was the cause he would like to see the

Society take up: 'but I am afraid that the major part of the Fabian is too rigidly bound to the collectivist formula to make such a hope practicable'. It is clear from this letter that Orage had not so far met Wells, but was still relying on his Pudsey coal merchant, 'who has recently written to you on my behalf'.

Gilds came to nothing (for the time being), and the foundation of FAG was probably the modest substitute. Soon afterwards Penty, disgusted by the philistinism of the Fabians,[1] departed for America, but FAG for a time retained an importance in Fabian politics. Jackson was a candidate for the Fabian executive, and although he was careful to explain to Wells that FAG was not entirely at his disposal 'the Arts Group has a measure of independence that may be useful to you and Orage and I will be glad to help. If I am elected I shall of course be with you in the new spirit of the executive.'

Jackson was not elected and although Wells came fourth in the poll his campaign fizzled out. The political skill of Shaw, combining opposition in public with disarmingly candid relations in private, outmanoeuvred Wells and preserved the ascendancy of the 'Old Gang'. But from Shaw's point of view additional precautions were desirable. He saw a genuine need and a political advantage in providing a safety valve for the younger generation of Fabians. He also saw an opportunity of making a diversion from the Fabian rumpus.

There was a dying radical weekly called the *New Age* edited by a socialist and High Anglican (eventually a Roman Catholic) called Joseph Clayton, from a back room off Chancery Lane. The title went back a long way, almost to Chartist times. In number 659, published on 25 April 1907, there appeared:

> Arrangements for the future of THE NEW AGE now being complete, we have pleasure in informing our readers that on and after the next issue of May 2 THE NEW AGE will be jointly owned and edited by Mr. A. R. Orage and Mr. Holbrook Jackson.

Orage often told his friends how he had received by the same

[1] It is said that Penty finally lost faith in Fabianism when he discovered that the Webbs and Pease (the secretary of the Society) had awarded the prize for the design of the London School of Economics entirely on the basis of minimum cost per usable foot of floor space. He parted with Orage during a walking tour from which the two 'returned by different routes' after a profound difference of socialist principle.

post, while living in the rooms he now shared with Jackson behind the Middlesex Hospital, the two cheques totalling £1,000 which had made this great venture possible. One was from Shaw, the other from Orage's old backer the Leeds banker and theosophist, Lewis Alexander Wallace. Shaw had been applied to first, and had made his contribution of £500 on condition that a second contributor should be found for the same amount. Wallace, who had turned from medical studies to banking, had retained an interest in the human psyche and was to contribute to the paper for many years to come, both as an 'angel' and as a contributor of copy under the pseudonym of 'M.B. Oxon.'. Indeed his work, now unread, was to have some remarkable consequences.

S. G. Hobson, an Ulsterman who had worked for the *New Age* under Clayton and was to play a great part in it under Orage, described his first meeting with the two new editors at a Fabian meeting in June 1907. They were standing near the door, 'two tall men, dark-haired and noticeable in any company'. They were both 'upstanding and lithe', but while Jackson was clearly the decisive Northerner, Orage, Hobson noted, 'had a touch of wistfulness both in his eyes and voice'. He gave the impression of having had 'an esoteric experience' of which his Yorkshire friend was slightly contemptuous. Orage, as Shaw put it, was 'a mystery man'. Shaw's own motives, however, were no mystery. He wanted to see a weekly paper in which all sorts of socialists could knock their heads together under mildly Fabian auspices. That the two editors he had helped to instal were out of sympathy with his particular kind of socialism (Orage, as long ago as 1896 had said, in the *Labour Leader* that 'The spirit of Captain Cuttle is in every Fabian tract'[1]), hardly mattered.

Orage and Jackson were not the only people associated with the new periodical from its beginning. S. G. Hobson was one; Beatrice Hastings, bursting with journalistic fervour, was another; and yet another was Clarence H. Norman, originally an Old Bailey shorthand writer. As such he had acquired some knowledge of the law and a profound hatred of judges. For years he was to be a thorn in their flesh, denouncing their hard-heartedness. He was a tireless accumulator of facts that would support his view of a case, and

[1] The reference is to Captain Cuttle's favourite aphorism, 'When found make note.'

developed considerable skill in working up a correspondence with his targets for subsequent publication. He was also a kind of protégé of Shaw, acting as shorthand writer for Shaw's lectures, and an unofficial channel between Shaw and Fleet Street. Not long afterwards—early enough to be counted among the founding fathers—came A. E. Randall, literary critic in his own name and dramatic critic in that of 'John Francis Hope': a slaughterman under both, yet with a great reputation for learning, 'gaunt and tallowy' with bulging eyes. These, with the later additions of Dyson and Kennedy, made up the core of what Selver called Orage's skewbald witenagemot'.

The office of the *New Age* was in an upstairs room in a passage called Tooks Court, which curls between Cursitor and Furnival Streets, just to the east of Chancery Lane. It consisted of two small rooms, the inner of which was occupied by the editors, a large roll-top desk, and two chairs. The outer room was later occupied by a devoted and defensive secretary. But the real business of the paper was not carried on in the office but in the basement of the A.B.C. café across the road, where on Monday afternoons Orage was always to be found surrounded by his contributors clearing the proofs in preparation for Thursday, when the paper appeared. Towards six, with the proofs settled and the paper sent to bed, they would adjourn, perhaps to Orage's shabby flat at the upper end of Chancery Lane, where he was now living with Beatrice, perhaps to cafés and restaurants further afield. But the tea-shops—A.B.C.s, the Kardomah round the corner in the Strand—with their green and white tiles, heavily aproned waitresses and harmless beverages, were the usual background for the ranging speculative discussions that kept the *New Age* alive.

Orage needed neutral ground against which to exert his extraordinary power of eliciting the ideas and enthusiasm of others, and he was not much of a host in his own home. Of course he could hardly afford to entertain on any scale, and Beatrice was a terrible hostess. A young recruit to the paper rather later on, C. Bechhofer Roberts, has described how he was asked by Beatrice, after a weekend at Orage's cottage in the country, to make a contribution to the housekeeping expenses. At first Orage had hesitated to introduce her to the staff gatherings at the A.B.C., and when he did she quickly made an impression that was not far short of awe for the sharpness of her tongue. As she said herself, 'I had a temper not to be trifled with.'

The first number of the *New Age* to appear under Orage's management makes its Fabian auspices clear. It contains messages of support from nearly the whole Fabian establishment—with one exception: from Pease, the secretary of the Society, Sidney Webb, H. G. Wells, Granville Barker, Hubert Bland, and his long-suffering wife 'E. Nesbit'. The exception, of course, was Shaw, who had contrived the whole thing. The editorial manifesto contained a significant broadening of the paper's terms of reference. 'In place of the sub-title "A Democratic Review",' wrote the editors, 'we have substituted the significant sub-title "An Independent Review of Politics, Literature, and Art". Disavowing any specific formula, whether of economics or of party, the NEW AGE will nevertheless examine the questions of the day in the light of the new Social Ideal; an ideal which has owed as much to the aristocracy of Plato, the individualism of Ibsen and Goethe, the metaphysics of Schopenhauer, the idealism of William Morris, the aestheticism of Ruskin, as to the democracy of Whitman and Carpenter.' Orage did not quite get so far as mentioning Nietzsche; and the absence of emphasis on democracy is interesting.

There was nothing eye-catching about the *New Age*—that was part of its success. In format it resembled one of the established weeklies such as the *Spectator* (the organ of conservative clubmen and clergy) and the *Athenaeum* (the organ of dons and established literary men). From the first it assumed a confident, even jaunty air of complete authority, whether the subject was politics (the first half of the paper) or literature (the second half). As a result the magazine extended, for the price of a penny a week, the stimulus of an apparently classic weekly to a new, literate, but relatively unprivileged public; while at the same time filling a void in journalism. The earlier radical press, though it had a genealogy stretching back to Leigh Hunt and Wilkes, had been strident, scandalous, seditious, and above all sectarian. The *New Age* was as much a journal of ideas as of comment, and it chimed with the aspirations of thousands of individuals and small groups throughout the country who were uncommitted, progressive and for the most part young.

The paper's records no longer exist (if they ever did) and its finances are impossible to reconstruct in detail, but certain features of Orage's system are clear. One was subsidies. Shaw, despite applications for more money, did not repeat his donation; but 'M.B. Oxon.' who, unlike Shaw, was happy to pay to appear in print, went on paying, and later the death of the Pudsey coal merchant brought a legacy. But on the whole Orage worked to the principle that good copy could be had for nothing. Unknowns were delighted to see themselves in print, and even the famous would provide free copy if they were allowed to say exactly what they liked. In dealing with his contributors, therefore, Orage exercised two arts. With an unknown author he took immense pains, encouraging him, improving him, building up his confidence. This literal contribution to the writings of subsequently famous authors is immeasurable, and as he once said, he wrote writers. For the famous he organised spectacular controversies which they could not bear to keep out of. The success of this policy was remarkable. He published Shaw, Wells, Chesterton, Belloc, Bennett, at the height of their fame and prosperity, without paying them anything; and he introduced to the public for the first time Ezra Pound, Katherine Mansfield, Edwin Muir, T. E. Hulme, Ruth Pitter, Richard Aldington, 'Michael Arlen', Herbert Read, and Dylan Thomas.

Several of these—Muir for instance—owed their reputations not only to the notice of Orage but to his direct tutorship. His methods can be glimpsed in his handling of Ruth Pitter's early work, which began to reach him in the summer of 1911 through her father George Pitter, who was a typical *New Age* reader, being a socialist school teacher in Ilford. He was a fellow Culhamite into the bargain. The poems by his schoolgirl daughter (Ruth was then fifteen) were greeted enthusiastically at Cursitor Street, but before very long the tutorial process had begun. 'We all like Ruth's new poems', Orage was writing in April 1912:

> the prose rather less so . . . Ruth is too much of a poet to make fanciful prose . . . by the way, would the young lady deign to change a single word in the *Song*? Verse i line 3 *amorous* kissed.[1]

[1] The advice was accepted. The word 'amorous' became 'silently' ('Song', *New Age* 23.5.1912).

The attribution of human emotions . . . to natural objects is fancy
not imagination. Do ask Ruth if she will find the right word to
take its place.

Ten years later it was the same gently chiding yet forceful note
with Herbert Read, who as a subaltern had shocked the officers'
mess by reading the *New Age*, and after sending a war story to the
paper (which was rejected) was encouraged to write reviews. In
due course he was promoted to the main literary column 'Readers
and Writers', but with Orage at his elbow. 'Not *articles*', urged the
mentor, 'but causeries on topical literary debates and similar
material.' A month or two later Orage was telling him to

Beware of the valueless business that insists on *essay* in place of
causerie. 'Everything divine runs on light feet'; and I will take
the liberty of saying this. The discussion Romanticism v. Clas-
sicism is just a little on the scholastic side. The conclusion, however, in all these things is neither subject nor treatment in the
abstract—but one's relations with one's readers. *Provided* they
are interested, *provided* they are kept in hot pursuit—anything is
permissible. Au contraire, nothing is justified in writing that is
not read. I gently recommend you to cultivate your divination as
regards your readers. . . .

The voice—and it is a voice rather than a pen—is almost the same
as in the youthful exchange with Holbrook Jackson more than
twenty years earlier.

Although Orage depended on charm, bluff, and hard work, money
was never his object. As Shaw said long afterwards, this 'desperado
of genius did not belong to the successful world'. Since he could not
put his heart into developing the advertising revenue of his paper,
virtually the only source of funds apart from sales was an associated
publishing house, the New Age Press, which was also an enterprise
of Jackson's and at one point had a not inconsiderable list of
pamphlets by well-known names.

From the first the pages of the new paper were open to contributions from women: Beatrice, of course, under her own name and
a fistful of aliases; 'E. Nesbit', now best remembered for her children's stories, contributed sentimental poems; there was a stern

feminist called Teresa Billington-Greig; and Florence Farr, at whose salon in Hammersmith Shaw was introduced to Yeats as the latest addition (Shaw's words) to the hostess's 'Leporello List'. But Beatrice covered more columns than all the rest, and her peculiar style can be detected over the initials E.H. and B.L.H. in some of the earliest numbers on such widely separated topics as Kipling and the Servant Question.

Orage at once steered his paper into the great dispute that was still convulsing the Fabian Society: should Fabianism continue to be a generalised pressure group for socialism, or should it try to develop into a socialist party? Wells, the great proponent of the second of these policies, started the ball rolling with an article on 13 June 1907 called 'The Socialist Movement and Socialist Parties', which was answered, in the manner Orage made famous, by another Fabian, Cecil Chesterton, defending the idea of an organisation separate from the Trade Union movement and devoted to doctrinaire socialism. The battle gave Orage the chance to make the point, in an editorial, that since socialists were not agreed on anything except the economic undesirability of private property, 'a free platform for socialist discussion must be kept open at all costs'.

By the end of 1907 the circulation had been raised to 5,000 copies which, allowing for newsagents' profit, brought in about £1,000 a year: hardly enough to pay the printer, let alone salaries for the staff. Holbrook Jackson, Fabian though he was, was also a business man, and he pressed for expansion of the advertising side of the paper, which was bringing in almost nothing. But Orage was simply not interested. His ostensible reason—that he could not spare the time and energy to drum up advertisements—is not convincing, for there was an 'advertising manager', Frank Palmer, who was later to play a not unimportant part in the history of the paper. It is difficult to doubt that the real reason was the growing sense of power in himself, his pen, and his paper, which made Orage indifferent to most other things, and impatient with a colleague. He and Jackson parted company, and in the first issue for January 1908 Orage's name appears alone as editor.

3

The Rise of the *New Age*

1908 was the golden year of the *New Age*. In the previous November there had been an article by a new recruit to the paper, Arnold Bennett, under the title 'Why I am a Socialist'. The main theme was that the Conservatives were the unintellectual, stupid party, and that no thinking man could opt for anything but socialism. Just before Christmas Hilaire Belloc, then a Liberal M.P., was induced to contribute reflections on the paper's first six months. It is a rather dreary, pernickety article with the cloudy title 'Thoughts about Modern Thought', but on these two contributions Orage managed to fan up a second controversy which provided some of the best things he ever printed and made the paper famous.

A small announcement in October 1907 had said that next year the *New Age* would be enlarged to provide scope for articles by 'leaders of thought'. And the mast-head was silently changed to replace the word 'socialist' with the innocuous word 'weekly'. Orage kept his promise to the readers. In the first number for 1908 he printed a piece by G. K. Chesterton under the heading 'Why I am not a Socialist'. It was a coruscating reply to Bennett. The pleasure of giving and taking, said Chesterton, was greater than the pleasure of sharing: 'I for one should greatly prefer that world in which everyone wore someone else's hat to every Socialist utopia that I have ever read about.' Ownership was one of the deepest desires of mankind; and just as individualism with its concomitant horrors of Victorian industrialism, had been imposed on people by a clique of Manchester merchants, so the people were now threatened by the imposition of Socialism at the hands of 'a handful of decorative artists, Oxford dons, journalists, and Countesses on the spree'. Chesterton tried with some success to root his position in the genuine virtues and forgivable weaknesses of ordinary people, and to insinuate that the socialists, especially the Fabians, were unsympathetic, puritanical snobs.

This last point, with its hint that a socialist would scruple to stand his friend a glass of beer, became the centre of the controversy. Chesterton had taken standing a round of drinks as an example of human pleasure in giving and receiving; and Wells, who was the next to enter the lists, fell straight into the trap by denouncing the sordid commercialism of the brewing trade and saying every beer-drinker would be happy if he had a well-organised fair share of beer. His stronger point, which was to confront his opponent with the choice between plutocracy and socialism and defy him to offer a third way, was trodden down in the scuffle. Chesterton made mincemeat of him in the next number, by concentrating on beer.

Circulation was soaring when a further champion, Shaw, was brought on in February under the title 'Belloc and Chesterton'. This famous article is not really fair, but it is very very funny. It poked fun at Chesterton and Belloc for pretending to be English, while being in fact foreigners. Chesterton, said Shaw, was clearly French. As for Belloc, 'You cannot say he is wholly French . . . but still he is not English. I suspect him of being Irish.' It then went on, with banter that hurt, to insinuate that Chesterton had concentrated on rounds of drinks because he ate and drank too much. But it contained the passage that made the controversy famous. Shaw compared his two opponents to a pantomime elephant, 'The Chesterbelloc', which claimed to be the *Zeitgeist*. 'To which we reply, bluntly, but conclusively, "Gammon".'

Though Shaw had rescued Wells he had done less than justice to Chesterton, who had tried to put the discussion on a theoretical basis and to avoid questions of what could or could not be done in practice. His refreshing paradox, 'If socialism is established, you may not fulfil your practical proposal. But you will certainly fulfil your ideal vision' had the effect of forcing his opponents to talk about what they really wanted; and it enabled Belloc, as the series developed, to demand why it should be supposed that a social system in which the legal control of modern means of production was widely distributed among the citizens should not endure. Wells could only reply that this was the American system, and in modern conditions it put the managers in charge.

During the six months of the Chesterbelloc controversy Orage had done a great deal more than just promote the heavyweights. Helped by the youthful Clifford Sharp as literary editor, he had managed to attach Arnold Bennett (under the alias of 'Jacob Tonson') for the weekly book column 'Books and Persons'. He had printed articles by Galsworthy, Havelock Ellis, and Anatole France, besides a long series on eugenics by Dr. M. D. Eder the Freudian. And he was planning a series on the foundations of socialist policy by S. G. Hobson.

Beatrice was nosing her way steadily into the paper under a variety of aliases after launching her journalistic career with a review of Orage's own little book on Nietzsche. She was the author of the rather overwrought 'Oriole Notes'—a kind of pastoral column which Clifford Sharp hoped H. G. Wells liked (the reply is not recorded). More seriously, she started her long intervention in 'the woman question' by taking on, in the character of 'Beatrice Tina', two seasoned radicals who could not bring themselves to accept the suffragette claim. One was C. H. Norman and the other H. Oldfield Bax. If the Vote were added to the advantages women already possessed, they argued, they would be better off than men. 'Maternity!' stormed 'Beatrice Tina': 'maternity more than offsets all the advantages women at present have in society, and there is still a large score to be settled.' At about the same time, if her own memoir of Orage is to be trusted, she was consigning to the dustbin the noisome trash about magic which one of Orage's new friends Aleister Crowley had left with him; and it is true that Crowley's one contribution to the *New Age* occurs in 1908—a curious, rather Kiplingesque poem. With Orage she entertained Shaw,[1] whom she bearded with the exclamation, 'But Shaw, you lack emotional understanding!' Shaw was shocked into defensiveness, and she followed up by saying, 'Orage has it, but you haven't.' When Shaw had left Beatrice coined an epigram: 'Poor old Shaw. He was a bit hurt. His trouble is his brains have gone to his head.'

By autumn Orage found himself master of a magazine which was widely read and very highly praised. He was selling a lot of copies. Circulation had risen from less than 4,000 a week to more than 20,000. Twice during the Chesterbelloc controversy he had been

---

[1] C. S. Nott, *Teachings of Gurdjieff*, p. 30. Orage does not name Beatrice in telling this anecdote, but period and style are decisive.

able to report an edition sold out on the day of publication and copies changing hands at double the official price. But he was still losing money, at the rate of about twenty pounds a week. The original £1,000 was nearly gone, and no more was to be got from Shaw. 'Orage', wrote Shaw to Norman in September 1908, 'abuses me because, having given the *New Age* £500 to keep it going for six months, and contributed a thousand pounds worth of copy to it for nothing, I am not prepared to repeat the effort. . . . What the dickens do we lend you young men a hand for at all except to shift our surplus work on to you and your generation?'

Faced with this, Orage took two decisions, one of which was obvious and the other extraordinary. He transferred the paper, together with the associated publishing firm called the New Age Press, which had been launched by Jackson and was doing quite well under Frank Palmer,[1] to a limited company, and appealed to his readers to buy shares. It was a near thing. Out of the 8,500 shares he took 3,000 himself in return for his proprietorship of the paper, and Palmer took a salary of £200 a year plus two and a half per cent of the profits. The other 5,500 shares were marketed to the readers, who may never have got a dividend, but were getting value for their money if they went on taking the paper. Even in the last month or two before floating the company Orage had printed the first poem ever to be published by James Elroy Flecker and an important article by Upton Sinclair.

The other step was more dangerous, and some thought it was prompted as much by personal ambition as by a desire to save the paper. Orage had never been a Fabian at heart, and as long ago as the summer of 1907 he had written privately to Wells saying he thought the work of the Fabians was done. The question now was whether the Fabian Society 'has not become so dogmatic as to make its future as an intelligent organ of discussion and enquiry very doubtful. . . . The *New Age* will steadily work for the Socialist *Movement*, and not for a socialist party, be it Fabian or any other.' But in the same letter he had agreed with Wells that 'after consider-able doubts' he had come to the conclusion that the idea of a

---

[1] A Fleet Street advertising agent who had become business manager of the *New Age* soon after Orage and Jackson took over the editorship. He later published under his own name.

doctrinaire socialist political party should be rejected. Now, he changed his mind. The *New Age* espoused such a party.

Several of his political friends, such as Cecil Chesterton and G. R. S. Taylor, had long been inclined to the idea, but its chief apostle in the *New Age* circle was S. G. Hobson, later to be the leading proponent of Guild Socialism. Hobson was an unusual man and a life-long socialist, bred a Quaker in Newry, one of the most Catholic towns in Ulster. He had been one of the earliest Fabians and had served on the executive committee of the Fabian Society since 1900, so that he was Orage's senior in socialist politics. His beard caused him sometimes to be mistaken for Bernard Shaw, but unlike Shaw he genuinely liked and trusted Orage, and he admired his gifts as an editor. He was, moreover, tireless, and had some independent means.

The exact influences which dictated Orage's step to the left are difficult to assess because the results were so bad and none of those who played a part were afterwards anxious to admit it. Orage, as Hobson said later, was omnivorous, even gullible in his acquisition of talent for the paper. In a sense he could afford to be, since he rarely paid the contributors and his open-mindedness, while it admitted a proportion of failures, picked up a startling number of successes. On this basis credulity can yield dividends. At any rate, in October 1908 Orage announced that Victor Grayson was joining the *New Age*. 'I hope', he wrote to Wells, 'you will appreciate the significance of that.'

One wonders whether Orage himself fully appreciated its significance. Grayson was a young working-class socialist who in the previous year had been carried into Parliament on a tide of popular passion at a by-election for the Colne Valley in north-east Lancashire. The watchword of the election had been the state of the unemployed (there was still no unemployment insurance) and it was as their champion that Grayson entered the House of Commons. Though born to the working class in Liverpool Grayson had been well educated and he had a handsome presence. On the platform he was the equal of any contemporary orator except Lloyd George. His socialism was fervent and unintellectual, the very opposite of Fabianism: and so was his character. Nothing could be further from Grayson than the austerity of Mrs. Sidney Webb or the abstemiousness of Shaw. In the end he was destroyed by self-indulgence, and literally vanished from the scene.[1] But in 1908 it looked as if he might capture the leadership of the Labour Party, and among those who believed this was Orage.

His arrival on the *New Age* was carefully contrived. Only six days before the announcement that he was to become joint editor Grayson was suspended from the House of Commons for making a demonstration. He had demanded that the business of the day should be interrupted to discuss the unemployment problem, refused to sit down, and after being 'named' by the Speaker, had left shouting that the Commons were 'a House of murderers'. The next number of the *New Age* gave maximum prominence to the proceedings.

For several months afterwards the *New Age* was the Grayson paper, devoted to the cause of socialising the Labour Party and advancing Grayson to its leadership. Socialist Representation Committees (on the model of the old Labour Representation Committees) were promoted in the constituencies, and the personality of the champion was projected in every number. Alone among the older Fabians 'E. Nesbit' was a devoted Graysonite and wrote poems in his praise: but most of them were alienated from Orage once for all, and the breach was mutual. Early in January 1909 Hobson, despite the reservations he claimed afterwards about 'Grayson's metal not being heavy enough', moved unsuccessfully that the Fabian Society should disaffiliate from the Labour Party in order to found a truly Socialist party. Orage declared in his report of that meeting that it was no longer a body of informed socialists . . . Mr. Shaw, Mr. Webb, and their *claqueurs* had run their course. The circulation of the paper kept up wonderfully and Beatrice gained the impression that Orage himself would soon be at Grayson's right hand leading a socialist Labour Party. She took the idea with a grain of salt, but 'life was picnics every day so long as Orage hoped something from his hospitality'.

What had started so passionately ended in a practical joke. That January of 1909 Grayson was to move a formidable motion at the Labour Party Conference at Portsmouth. The *New Age* exerted

---

[1] In 1920 he left his mother's house in Liverpool saying he had to address a public meeting in Hull. There is no satisfactory account of his movements thereafter, or of his ultimate fate.

itself to the utmost and the labour leadership of MacDonald, Snowden, and Clynes was said to be seriously worried. On the morning of 30 January, the day he was to move his motion, Grayson was approached by two men professing to be admirers who kindly, but firmly, propelled him into a car and drove him to Petersfield where, in the words of one of the kidnappers 'we had a jolly good lunch . . . smoked and drank liqueurs, and talked about the problems of the day. After that we took him for a ride in the country, and there we had a breakdown.' One of these hospitable men was a certain Captain 'Matabele' Wilson V.C., a hero of the South African War and a strong opponent of socialism; and the other was a naval friend of his. The platform at Portsmouth waited with growing relief as the item on which Grayson was to move his motion approached, and was passed, without his putting in an appearance. In February 1909 Grayson ceased to be joint editor of the *New Age*.[1]

This episode had a twofold importance in the career of Orage. It induced, or perhaps confirmed a distrust of party politics and a preference for broad movements of opinion as the basis for his paper; and it permanently separated him from the forces which had created and sustained him as an editor. From now on the *New Age* circle bears Orage's personal stamp. The established socialists, except for S. G. Hobson, begin to fade from his pages. Nietzsche and the Nietzscheans—Oscar Levy and J. M. Kennedy—take up more and more space.

John McFarland Kennedy won Beatrice's particular admiration. He earned his bread working for the *Daily Telegraph*, and had established himself as an exponent of Nietzsche to popular audiences. He was widely read, and knew several languages, including, it was rumoured, Sanskrit. His particular field was foreign affairs, but he could turn his hand to almost anything, and did not need to be paid. He positively enjoyed writing in another *persona*.

But for the time being the principal contributor to the *New Age* on foreign affairs was C. H. Norman, under the alias of 'Stanhope of Chester', and that summer of 1909 he decided to run a major campaign about Spain. In the previous month a minor colonial war

---

[1] The episode of Grayson's kidnapping is described by G. D. K. McCormick, *Murder by Perfection* (1970).

in Morocco had touched off a syndicalist rising in Barcelona. It had been quickly suppressed, but, warned 'Stanhope of Chester':

> Everybody realises, we hope, by this time, that the Spanish people have been, and are being, shamefully and horribly betrayed by their own rulers.

'Their own rulers' being King Alfonso XIII, and his ultra-conservative Prime Minister, Maura.

On the last day of August, soon after this article appeared, a Spanish radical named Francisco Ferrer was arrested as the alleged leader of the Barcelona rising. He was a fiftyish, rather pedantic, even priggish rationalist, who for several years had devoted himself to establishing secular schools in Spain. An earlier brush with authority, resulting in a trial at which he had been acquitted, had made Ferrer something of a European figure, and Anatole France was chairman of an international committee supporting his work; but he was very far from being a picture-book revolutionary. He had spent the spring and earlier part of the summer of 1909 in London and appeared not to be taking part in any noticeable activity, though it is not unlikely that he came into contact with C. H. Norman and other radicals. Much of his time seems to have been occupied with arranging for suitable textbooks to be translated into Spanish for his schools, and while he no doubt sympathised with the Barcelona revolutionaries, there is no reliable evidence whatever to suggest he was their leader, and a good deal to suggest he was not. 'The Spanish Dreyfus' (as Ferrer's supporters christened him) was to have a shorter agony than his French counterpart, but a more tragic end.

The campaign in the *New Age* reached its climax in an article published on 23 September under the heading 'Shall Ferrer Die'. So far there had been no trial, and the article, with little to go on, consisted mainly of a passionate denunciation of Catholicism and lurid atrocity stories of Jesuits beating Protestant women on their breasts 'with light stinging canes', virgins raped by gaolers 'especially syphilitic gaolers', and Madrid in danger of a 'second St. Bartholomew'. All this was accompanied by furious jingoism, calling on 'Tommy Atkins to break down the gates of Montjuich'. 'What is the use of our Navy if we cannot blow the Spanish Catholic hierarchy into a premature Hell?' 'English property, and English ideals, have been trampled on by the Spanish government of black-coated priests.' 'The Nonconformists know the dangers England is running by the toleration of the Catholics.' Someone should move in the House of Commons for a war credit of ten million pounds for the purpose of undertaking operations against Spain.

And what, the *New Age* furiously demanded, was the policy of the Foreign Secretary, Sir Edward Grey? He took refuge in the doctrine of non-intervention in the internal affairs of another state. He was attacked in the House by a number of Labour members, one of whom was Grayson, but he refused to budge. The *New Age* sent him a public telegram demanding he should intercede for Ferrer. Letters filled the correspondence column. Public meetings were organised. There was an article every week. By now the *New Age* was only one voice among many throughout Western Europe. Even the Pope intervened privately with Alfonso XIII. Ferrer was tried on 9 October and shot four days later. Grayson, supported by Arthur Henderson, tried to move the adjournment of the House. The Foreign Secretary received a telegram: 'The *New Age* to Sir Edward Grey. *New Age* holds you responsible as accessory to Ferrer's murder.'

A story which cannot be verified is associated with this passionate campaign.[1] It is asserted that some of the *New Age* group concocted a plan to kidnap the Spanish ambassador in London and hold him hostage for the reprieve of Ferrer; what is more, that a secret negotiation took place between Orage and a cabinet minister (un-named but almost certainly John Burns, then President of the Local Government Board) in which a promise was given that there would be a private but effectual intervention on Ferrer's behalf by the British government. The promise prevented the kidnapping plot from being put into operation, but no intervention ever took place.

The tragic scandal of Ferrer had roused liberals everywhere. There had been riots in Paris and meetings of protest all over Europe. It was one of the earliest examples of an international

---

[1] *See* Mairet, p. 56. Mr. Mairet told me that the information given in his book, which relates to a period before his own association with the *New Age*, came direct from Orage as he records it. He could not add to it. Research at the Public Record Office has produced no evidence for the allegations.

agitation of this type. It also marked an important turning-point in the history of Spain. Within a few weeks of Ferrer's execution at Montjuich the Prime Minister, Maura, was discarded by King Alfonso after violent debates in the Cortes; and was to maintain, for the rest of his career, that the decision not to grant a reprieve was the gravest political mistake he had ever made. The period of instability that followed led via the dictatorship of Primo de Rivera to the downfall of the Bourbon monarchy and the bitter ideological and political rivalries that fuelled the Spanish Civil War.

Chesterton and Belloc were permanently alienated by Norman's wild anti-Catholicism, and Belloc, at least, tried positively to defend the Spanish government's behaviour. If kidnapping had been discussed in Cursitor Street or the basement of the Chancery Lane A.B.C., it is unlikely to have been a serious project. The conversation with John Burns is a shade more probable, since Orage's political importance was beginning to be recognised. One is on surer ground in saying that the episode brought about a change in the *New Age* itself. Not long after the Ferrer campaign, and as a result (it is said) of pressure exercised by the Foreign Office on Orage's financial backers, C. H. Norman was replaced by J. M. Kennedy, over the signature 'S. Verdad' (the Spanish implication being *es verdad*—'it is true').

'S. Verdad' was better informed, more sober, and much duller, than 'Stanhope of Chester'. Orage put it about that his new contributor had a direct line to Foreign Office thinking, and one may suppose that Kennedy suited the Foreign Office a good deal better. 'S. Verdad' was strongly anti-German where his predecessor had been anti-Russian—a change of front that was not without importance. Readers of the *New Age* were growing used to the inevitability of a war with Germany by the time it broke out in 1914.

By 1909 the paper had taken on the shape it was to have for a number of years. It began with 'Notes of the Week', a political commentary most of which Orage wrote himself. This was followed by one or more political or campaigning articles and a 'lead' book review. Then came a cartoon or a lithograph, which more or less separated the political half of the paper from the literary and artistic section. These pictures, which did a great deal to lighten the paper, were among its most successful features. For some time Orage used a talented Polish cartoonist called Roscisewski, who signed himself 'Tom Tit' and produced a series of excellent caricatures. But by 1910 the *New Age* was printing a series of Sickert lithographs, and later still produced work by Epstein and Gaudier-Brzeska. Ultimately a New Zealander, Will Dyson, succeeded to the cartoonist's post and became one of Orage's most trusted lieutenants.[1]

After a middle section which was increasingly taken up with articles on Nietzsche, psychoanalysis and theosophy, came the literary commentary itself, marshalled under the heading 'Books and Persons' and signed 'Jacob Tonson'. It was by Arnold Bennett, and the best literary column in London. Perhaps the greatest of all Orage's successes was to persuade Bennett to write it, week by week, for three years, and for nothing. He did it by giving 'Tonson' a completely free hand—to denounce Smith's and Wyman's and the circulating libraries, to needle the publishing trade, and to introduce his fancies. When Bennett gave up, the heading was changed to 'Present-day Criticism', which was usually written by Beatrice; and then to 'Readers and Writers', which Orage wrote himself. But even 'Readers and Writers', good as it was, did not quite come up to 'Books and Persons'.

Through Bennett in the *New Age* a large public was introduced to Tchekov and Dostoevsky, who were then only just beginning to make their way in English translation. Tolstoy and Turgenev had become well-established in England by the end of the nineteenth century, but Dostoevsky had not become an English literary classic, Tchekov had not been built into the repertory of the English stage till Bennett, Murry, and in her way Katherine Mansfield made it so. In general 'Jacob Tonson' propounded a cosmopolitanism the English reader had never known before. It was not only the Russians he praised: he created a taste for Claudel, Valéry, Stendhal, Romain Rolland, and Gide. The rift with the insular taste of the preceding age was as remarkable as it has been lasting. Till the turn of the century the taste of the English general reader had been for English authors, whether giants of Victorianism or recommended English

[1] Just as Kennedy was employed (and paid) by the *Daily Telegraph*, Dyson earned his living as cartoonist for the *Daily Herald*. It was part of the science of the *New Age* to give professional journalists a chance to escape from Fleet Street discipline.

writers of earlier centuries. Bennett's recommendations had a notably enlarging effect.

On the tail of 'Books and Persons' came the lesser reviews and squibs—an area where malice and irresponsibility were allowed free play; and somewhere towards the end came the column headed 'Pastiche', which was used for all sorts of purposes, but above all for the apprentice work of Orage's latest nurslings. Last of all came the letters, often made up to quota by members of the staff writing under their own or assumed names to keep controversies on the boil. Sometimes there would be a 'Literary Supplement' of eight or more pages carrying extra reviews of books which had accumulated. But even without this the reader got forty or more pages written by some of the ablest political and literary journalists alive, for a penny.

Of course it could not possibly make money, even on the 'No Pay' principle which was now Orage's open boast. Backers were still needed, and there was probably never a time in the whole history of the *New Age* under Orage when the paper could do without them. Beatrice was unfair, as so often, when she wrote that 'There never was a paper more thoroughly kept': the backers did little to influence either staffing or editorial policy. But the Wallace subsidy continued at the rate of £100 a month throughout the pre-war years, and in 1914 the ever-loyal Pudsey coal merchant died leaving Orage £1,500. Beatrice had the decency to admit he gave her £400 of it, either in recognition of her services or repayment of money she herself had provided from her allowance. But the rest must for the most part have gone in printer's bills.

It is possible, even in the absence of any surviving accounts, to reconstruct the *New Age*'s budget in the years of its glory, if one makes a few reasonable assumptions. On an average sale of 10,000 copies a week the revenue (allowing for the usual discounts) would be rather less than £1,400 a year. Advertisements, for which the rate was an absurdly cheap shilling for sixteen words, might possibly have brought in enough to raise the total income to £2,000. The printer's bill must have been rather more than this—say £2,500—and even if the office was supplied by the printers for nothing, as it almost certainly was, and the copy was free, there must have been some expenses that brought the outgoings to not far short of £3,000 a year.

Wallace's subsidy just about balanced the books, leaving little or nothing for the editor to live on.

There was, of course, the share capital raised in 1908, on which it is most unlikely a dividend was ever paid. And there were other backers, though it cannot be said with certainty when they appeared. Paul Selver, a school teacher who came into Orage's orbit in 1911,[1] met Wallace and describes him with 'white silky hair, a drooping moustache to match, a rosy face and a general air of self-depreciation, no matter who he was talking to'. No such description survives of another prosperous backer, P. T. Kenway, on whom Orage exercised his charm during a game of golf, extracting, together with some money, a reminder that the donor was a Scot. The response from the editor was an unkind, but irresistible—'Scots wha hae wi' Wallace bled'; and it is the case that Wallace's personal fortune was much reduced by his benefactions.

[1] His first poems—translations from the Czech—were accepted in a letter which is characteristic of Orage's style and methods: 'I should be very happy to publish them in the *New Age* if you cannot have them published and paid for elsewhere. You must have gathered that the New Age is written for love ...' (Selver, *Orage and the* New Age *Circle*, pp. 12–13).

❧ 4 ❧

The Marmozet

So far, as between politics and literature, Orage had been more successful in setting up established literary and controversial men as politicians than in promoting literature for its own sake. But early in 1910 Cursitor Street received a visit from a man named George Charles Bowden and his wife with the offer of some stories which Mrs. Bowden had written under the name of Katherine Mansfield. George Bowden, a professional tenor who lived on the edge of literary life, stayed outside on the landing while his wife conducted the interview. It is possible, even probable, that Beatrice was also present in the tiny office. At any rate 'The Child Who was Tired', one of the stories which later appeared in Katherine's first collection, *In a German Pension*, was printed in the *New Age* for 24 February 1910. The story bore, as a matter of fact, a fairly close resemblance to a Tchekov story, 'Spat Khochetsia'.

'Katherine Mansfield', like 'Beatrice Hastings', with whom she rapidly developed a close friendship, had come from a colonial background to seek her fortune in literature. Like Beatrice, too, she had adopted a new name, having been born Kathleen Beauchamp, the daughter of a wealthy New Zealand banker. When Beatrice, following up this new contributor, went down to visit her where she was living above a grocer's shop in Rottingdean, and looked through her writings, they began to find how much they had in common: above all a desperate desire to excel in the art of words and grow famous by it. Long afterwards Beatrice said that what she found at Rottingdean was 'mostly rubbish', but between February and August 1910 the *New Age* published nine pieces by Katherine.

Katherine's life is far better recorded than Beatrice's. She had been born in New Zealand on 14 October 1888. 'Her childhood had been lonely—the dream face her only confidant . . . she had lived in a world of her own—created her own people—read anything and everything which came to hand—was possessed with a violent temper, and completely lacked placidity.' So Katherine imagined her own youth in the adolescent novel *Juliet* which she began composing at school. At fifteen she had been brought with her sister to England and placed at the studious but forward-looking Queen's College, Harley Street, where she met and permanently attached to herself a fellow pupil named Ida Baker, the daughter of a retired colonel in the Indian Medical Service. For the rest of Katherine's life Ida was to be at her beck and call, always ready to support and provide, often brutally rejected, and as necessary in the one role as in the other.

As with Hastings, so almost certainly it was with Mansfield. Queen's College looks out over Mansfield Mews and thence, recalling her maternal grandmother's maiden name (Margaret Isabella Mansfield), Kathleen Beauchamp conjured her new surname. At the same time she christened Ida Baker 'Lesley Moore' or L.M., as she ever afterwards remained. And the protean habit, as with Beatrice, persisted: Katherine was at different times 'Katie', 'Kathie', 'Yekaterina', 'Katya' and 'Katinka'; 'Katherina', 'Tig' and 'Wig'. It is a multiplication in search of an identity.

Her three years at Queen's from April 1903 to July 1906, when she was nearly eighteen, were in some ways cloistered, but they were decisive in the formation of her career. She read omnivorously and at high speed: according to her notes for the summer of 1904 she read Tom Moore's three-volume life of Byron at the rate of a volume a day, and in June of that year read a total of seventeen books. She wrote not only for the school magazine but for herself in a journal (now mostly lost) and began a novel. She learned German under the strong influence of Walter Rippmann, who also kindled for her the last embers of the fashion for aestheticism and art for art's sake.[1] She fell in love with a young cellist, Arnold Trowell, whom she had met as a child in New Zealand and now saw again as the young star of a musical family in St. John's Wood.

[1] Walter Rippmann (later Ripman), who was then in his thirties, had an extraordinary career, ending as Chief Inspector—an office now abolished—to the University of London. He took no fewer than four parts of the Tripos at Cambridge (twice as many as required for a degree) and two separate M.A.s at London. The list of his language textbooks is almost endless. His wide range of interest extended also to fairy tales. Katherine never forgot him.

Above all, she came to have an almost desperate faith in her own powers of observation as possessing greater validity (if she could capture the skill to record them) than those of other people. 'The views out of the windows, all the pattern that was—weaving. Nobody saw it, I felt, as I did. My mind was just like a squirrel.' It was not the pressure of genius for self-expression that drove her to write, but the passion to imprison and preserve, in precise descriptive words, the intense experience of observation, so making a spar to which her elusive identity could cling. That identity had to be the life of an independent artist, and this, at Queen's, she resolved to be. When she went back to New Zealand with her parents in the summer of 1906 it was with a determination to come back to Europe. 'When I get to New Zealand', she told her room-mate at Queen's, 'I'll make myself so objectionable that they'll *have* to send me away.'

She did not exactly do that, but her stay in New Zealand lasted less than two years. It was a time of continued reading and composition on her side—stories, journals, letters to her friends in England (chiefly L.M.) and unposted romantic outpourings to 'Caesar' as she had designated Arnold Trowell. She read Henry James and Shaw, Ibsen and Heine, Maeterlinck and Nietzsche, and above all the infant prodigy Marie Bashkirtseff, who had died so young. From her parents' side came well-meant but unsuccessful efforts to reintegrate her with the conventional life of Wellington. The elder Beauchamps were not wholly unimaginative. Her father sent her on a long safari in the almost trackless North Island, and even contrived to have some of her pieces published in an Australian paper. But the self-conscious thrust in the direction of a life devoted to art, and therefore towards Europe, was far too strong. It even survived the news from L.M. that Arnold Trowell's affections had moved elsewhere. By May 1908 she had screwed herself up to her most determined, self-dramatising mood:

9 P.M. SUNDAY NIGHT MAY 17 FULL MOON
Now to plan it.
O, Kathleen, do not weave any more of these fearful meshes—for you have been so loathesomely unwise. . . . 'You'd better go and see the doctor tomorrow about your heart—and then try to

solve all the silly drivelling problems. Go anywhere. Don't stay here—accept work—fight against people. . . . It is really extra-ordinary that I should feel so confident of dying of heart failure—and entirely my mother's fault.

This preoccupation with her heart was never to leave her: even when she was coughing her lungs away ten years later it was 'her heart' that she felt was diseased, despite all medical assurances to the contrary. A month or so later her father agreed that she should go once more to London. She should have an allowance of £100 a year, which does not sound much but was more than Orage had lived on as an elementary school teacher, and learn the cello. Other-wise no proposition about the future seems to have been laid down. She arrived at the end of August 1908, shortly before her twentieth birthday, with what must have been a considerable accumulation of notebooks and half-finished literary work.

That she had been made to study music, and even now was officially a music student, is not unimportant. As one of her bio-graphers has pointed out, it gave her a habit of practice which she carried into her literary work. She literally fiddled with words, working a theme over and over again in an effort to produce what she regarded as an adequate performance. Not only was precision a virtue, but the notion went to her own idea of herself as a per-former. The sight of Arnold Trowell on the concert platform at Brussels was readily transferred to her view of herself as a perform-ing literary artist. On arriving in London she settled in a hostel for music students not far from the Trowells in St. John's Wood. It was called, appropriately enough, Beauchamp Lodge.[1]

Arnold Trowell, the former 'Caesar', she now treated as no more than a friend; but a love affair quickly developed between her and his younger brother Garnet Trowell, who was a violinist. In October she was taken briefly, and for the first time, to Paris by a fellow student at Beauchamp Lodge, Margaret Wishart. Then, in Novem-ber, she paid a visit to Hull, where Garnet Trowell was playing in the orchestra of the Moody Manners Opera Company. With him she lost her virginity; and became pregnant.

[1] It stands just beside the canal in what is now called Little Venice, and today houses the Beauchamp Lodge Settlement. At one time, before Katherine Mansfield's sojourn there, it was owned by the French Embassy and Napoleon III had spent a short time there after his overthrow in 1871.

The outcome of this adventure was a mixture of farce and tragedy which led, quite incidentally, to Orage's office in Cursitor Street, by way of the singing master, George Bowden, whom she had met earlier that autumn at the house of a certain Dr. Caleb Saleeby[1] in Hamilton Terrace. It was not to be the last time Katherine encountered a future husband in that handsome street. She was demure and inconspicuous, but she interested Bowden, who lived in some style not far away in Gloucester Place; and when he next met her as a result of inviting her to a party there, the demure but witty girl had changed into a stately celebrity. 'Motionless after a step or so into the room, it was she who "received" rather than we who hastened to receive her.'

From then on Katherine was bombarded with ever more enthusiastic letters from Bowden until, round about Christmas, he had to go into hospital to have his tonsils out—a serious matter for a tenor. When he was better she collected him in a taxi, and they became engaged—it must have been about January. The engagement ran its decorous course, with tea at Rumpelmayer's, concerts, and talk in which Katherine's oblique references to 'a casual roadside campfire rather than the open road' were treated by Bowden as no more than literary embroidery. For she showed him her literary work as well as introducing him to her grand relations de Monk Beauchamp and the Countess von Arnim, authoress of *Elizabeth and her German Garden*. He even dared, once, to criticise her punctuation and gave her the chance to deliver one of the most crushing of her snubs: 'As I looked up I saw her head and neck rise as she slowly turned and said over her shoulder very distinctly indeed, "You can't tell me anything about commas." '

In March 1909 they were married at Paddington Registry Office. She was dressed, according to some accounts, entirely in black. The faithful L.M., who was heartbroken by the whole business and may or may not have known that the bride thought herself pregnant by another man, tucked into Katherine's dressing-case a note saying the two words 'Bear Up'.

But with all her power to pose, bear up in such circumstances was

[1] Saleeby was a progressive young doctor of thirty. He later became a leading exponent of eugenics and the medical value of sunshine, about which he wrote a best-seller. The seaside industry owes much to him. He was also a temperance campaigner.

what Katherine could not quite manage. The bridal night in a London hotel was a disastrous episode of repulsion and disappointment, in the course of which L.M.'s well-meant note was discovered by the frustrated Bowden. Next morning Katherine fled to a small room above a hairdresser's shop in Paddington, sent for L.M., and refused to have anything more to do with her husband. Very soon afterwards she fled still further, to Liverpool, where the Moody Manners Opera Company was now performing, and rejoined Garnet Trowell. Her stay with him cannot have lasted long, though it gave her brief experience as a recruit to the back row of the chorus of *Maritana*, and by the beginning of April she was back in London, telling L.M. she could no longer bear the way Garnet ate his eggs. By Easter, travelling under the name of Mrs. K. Bendall, she rushed off to Brussels, where she stayed until the end of April.[1]

In the meantime Mrs. Beauchamp, in New Zealand, had been alerted to her daughter's impending marriage and had set off for England to regulate matters properly. On 27 May she arrived. Within a fortnight she had interviewed all the principal characters, swept her daughter off to Bavaria, placed her in a convent, and sailed again for New Zealand. In July farce ended in tragedy, and the pregnancy ended. English structures stick out of the stilted, inelegant German with which Katherine tried to rally her confidence.

[1] This is where the published evidence leads us. On p. 38 of Katherine's *Journal* Murry gives the November date for her stay with Trowell in Hull when she became pregnant. His only authority, though he does not quote one, must have been Katherine herself. If so, the pregnancy had advanced four months when she married Bowden, and six when her mother arrived in England. But could it then have been concealed from her mother, and would her mother, in such circumstances, have sent her married daughter off to Germany, and then sailed away to New Zealand? It seems very improbable, especially when one adds that a still birth would certainly have been recorded in a quiet German village, and there is no such record. One is left with two other explanations, both of which seem more probable. The first is that her meeting with Trowell in the latter part of March, and not the meeting in November, led to the pregnancy. In that case it was after her marriage to Bowden, though if it was revealed to her mother in May it could have been attributed to him. If not, her mother's decision to pack her off to Germany could be explained merely by a desire to get her out of bad company. The end of the pregnancy would have been an unrecorded miscarriage. The other possibility is a 'phantom' pregnancy, which would fit with the extremely vague and conflicting accounts of how the pregnancy ended.

Ich muss streiten um vergessen zu können; ich muss bekämpfen, um mich selbst wieder achten zu können. . . . Ich *will* arbeiten, ich will *mit* dem Glück, um die Zufriedenheit kämpfen.

Wir mussen jeder allein sein—allein arbeiten, allein kämpfen, um unsere Kraft, unsere Opferwilligkeit zu beweisen.[1]

She did indeed work during the next six months. She moved from the convent to the mountain health resort of Woerishofen, where she lodged with the postmistress and ate at a neighbouring pension— whence also she drew inspiration for stories. And at the pension she discovered congenial company in the shape of two young literary Poles named Yelski and Floryan Sobieniowski, the second of whom offered an elopement which, after getting as far as Munich, she declined. For a few weeks a small cockney boy named Walter appeared at Woerishofen: he had been found by L.M. in Paddington and sent out as a kind of consolation. Christmas was spent at the pension, and in January 1910 Katherine returned to London to try, as she put it 'to straighten out the tangled web I have made of my life'.

She decided to return to Bowden, who was then on tour, and sent him a series of letters and telegrams from the Strand Palace Hotel (where L.M. had booked her a room) signed imperiously YOUR WIFE. Rather reluctantly he agreed to resume, or rather commence, married life, and although the experiment lasted only a few weeks it brought Katherine and her stories to the *New Age*, Orage, and Beatrice. Soon after the visit to Cursitor Street L.M. was sent to tell Bowden that the marriage was finally over.

The new friendship with the editor of the *New Age* and Beatrice was extraordinarily congenial for Katherine, and decisive for her future. Orage's charm, knowledge, and personal magnetism; Beatrice's apparent strength and literary commitment; the fact that they were in a position to print her work; and above all, perhaps, their literary and sexual partnership with one another, made them almost unbeatable in Katherine's eyes. They knew more about

[1] I must try to be able to forget; I must struggle to respect myself again. . . . I *will* work, I will *with* luck, struggle for tranquillity. We must each be alone— work alone, struggle alone, to prove our own strength and our own willingness to sacrifice (*Journal*, p. 43).

commas than she did. 'The friendship', wrote Middleton Murry, 'which now developed between [Katherine] and Orage and Beatrice Hastings was the one period in her life between 1908 and 1911 upon which she constantly looked back with delight. She stayed with them frequently in a cottage in Sussex, and had the joy of being among her own kind.' She endorsed the photograph of herself taken at Rottingdean in 1910 as 'the first picture showing some character'.

In fact Katherine even looked a bit like Beatrice, and L.M. has said that a photograph often printed as Katherine is in fact a picture of Beatrice Hastings. In Beatrice she found another woman, ten years older than herself, of similar background, who was well advanced in the same literary pilgrimage as she herself had begun. What was more, Beatrice, like Katherine, had reflected the peripheral Englishness in which they had both been reared. Murry indeed notes that Katherine's 'resentment against New Zealand was as it were the symbol of her resentment against life itself'. The same words could be written about Beatrice and South Africa.

Murry exaggerated in one respect. Orage and Beatrice, that spring of 1910, spent only three weeks in the cottage they hired at Seaford. But three weeks was enough. Orage took immense trouble with his new story-writer, and there is no knowing how much those first stories owe to his tutelage. Perhaps Katherine would not even have cared if she had known the nickname he had coined for her behind her back—'the Marmozet'.

For the first six months of 1910 there was hardly a number of the *New Age* without something by Katherine. 'Bavarian Babies' (later renamed 'The Child Who was Tired') in February was followed by three stories in March, one in May, and two in July, quite apart from poems and briefer contributions. She was initiated not only to the cottage that Orage and Beatrice had taken at Seaford, but to the copy-clearing circle in the Chancery Lane A.B.C.

In that first half of 1910 the *New Age* was also virtually a duet of Beatrice and Katherine, Beatrice of course soaring far higher than her pupil. She was crusading, as ever, about capital punishment, but her main concern, as the suffragette agitation rose to its crescendo of militancy, was with the 'woman question'. She had already written a pamphlet about it, 'Woman's Worst Enemy—

Woman',[1] and now she was savagely attacking the Woman's Suffrage Union for its hypocrisy. Two of her aliases, 'Beatrice Tina' and 'D. Triformis', were mobilised to denounce one another. On 12 May 'D. Triformis' was made to write, in comment on some remarks by 'Beatrice Tina':

> It seems positively dear to some women to think of themselves as the revolting slaves of men. That parrot phrase, proper enough for a slave, is improper for a woman . . . if we set our minds on becoming free from within, we shall see that such epigrams ('the militant suffragettes have saved us from the last ignominy of the slave') are untrue.

A week later 'Beatrice Tina' was apologising for her 'unlucky epigram' and agreeing with 'D. Triformis', 'from whom I have learned a good deal':

> but some things I have *not* to learn. I have long since protested against several of the undesirable features of the suffrage movement. . . . The real question of women's suffrage is whether it will lead to progressive or reactionary legislation. . . . It is also a distinction to be the only woman in England who does not want a family. . . . I resent the lies about marriage which I was allowed to grow up believing, and my ignorant and unwilling maternity I regard as an outrage. For saying these things I was cast out by advanced women.

The remarkable congruence of their two careers and their twin ambitions gave Beatrice, with her ten-year advantage and established position, a considerable ascendancy over Katherine. The story 'At Lehmann's', published that summer in the *New Age*, sharply shows Beatrice's influence. Later they even collaborated in a series of wicked skits on Chesterton, Bennett, and other leading names. Long after Katherine was well known and Beatrice's star had begun to fade, the younger woman referred to the older as 'Biggy B.'.

She had not been well at Rottingdean, and at one point had had

[1] I have been unable to trace a copy. It was published by the New Age Press and cannot have been much more than a pamphlet, since the price was only 1s. But it was of course enthusiastically reviewed in the *New Age* (22 July 1909).

to go into a nursing home, watched over always by L.M. and at a further remove by the manager of the Bank of New Zealand, whose duty it was to pay her allowance and send reports to her father (who was by now Chairman of the Bank of New Zealand). In the early autumn, just in time for her twenty-first birthday, she moved back to London, occupying a studio flat at 131 Cheyne Walk which belonged to a printer who had gone abroad. Orage was the intermediary. L.M. virtually moved in, a happy protectress and doormat, doing everything she was told, even to paying instalments on the grand piano neither of them could play.

Katherine had arrived in her Bohemia, and perhaps she was never to be quite so happy again as in that autumn, the autumn of the Post-Impressionist Exhibition:[1]

Wasn't that Van Gogh, [she wrote to Dorothy Brett ten years later] yellow flowers brimming with sun, in a pot? I wonder if it is the same. The picture seemed to reveal something that I hadn't realised before I saw it. It lived with me afterwards. It still does. That, and another of a sea-captain in a flat cap. They taught me something about writing, which was queer, a kind of freedom— or rather, a shaking free.

She wrote for Vivian Locke-Ellis's genteelly earnest little miscellany *The Open Window*, and took a lover, a young schoolmaster and contributor to the *New Age* called William Orton, with whom she adopted the style of 'Katherina', and played tennis in Hampstead. As the train paused for a moment at Chalk Farm she asked him archly, 'Do you believe in Pan?'[2] Orton describes her room, or rather studio, in which everything except the grand piano, glistening in the dim candlelight, was at floor level, 'with herself accurately in the centre . . . the one cluster of primary brightness in the room'.

From Cheyne Walk her gipsy existence carried her to a flat in a grim block called Clovelly Mansions, in the Gray's Inn Road. It had been found, of course, by L.M., who adorned it with a stone Buddha her father the colonel had brought home from Burma which

---

[1] Noticed, with great effect, in the *New Age* by Arnold Bennett.
[2] A remark which may be compared with her sudden cry to Hugh Kingsmill in the Gray's Inn Road, suggesting how wonderful it would be to be running on the beach with the sand between one's toes. Kingsmill's hearty reply, *'Rather'* was not considered acceptable.

eventually found its last recorded resting place in the garden of a cottage in Sussex. For a second time Katherine was pregnant, not by Orton, but by a charming young man she had met shortly before Christmas. His name is not known, and the only record of his existence is the miniature Russian village he brought Katherine as a Christmas present. He seems never to have been told that he had fathered a child when he tried to break off the relationship: both Katherine, who wrote to him, and L.M., who was sent as her ambassador, were too proud to mention it.

In April 1911 L.M. went on a prolonged visit to her father in Rhodesia, leaving sixty pounds in the bank for Katherine, and the lonely Katherine turned to Beatrice. They had been out of touch for a few months, but now Katherine's work began to appear again in the *New Age*. The Bavarian portfolio had obviously been exhausted, and New Zealand was the background of her writing. Undoubtedly, too, Beatrice contrived an abortion, and in May the two were together at Ditchling putting together squibs for the paper. She even, under Beatrice's sway, provided the paper with a skit on the coronation of King George V. Then, just two years after her first flying visit, Katherine's mother arrived in London, accompanied, this time, by most of the Beauchamp family.

As in so many other respects the 'two female women' Beatrice and Katherine were alike in this—they both had adored brothers. Beatrice had bored Orage and the readers of the paper almost to death with Richmond Haigh's *Ethiopian Saga*, and now came Leslie, or 'Chummie', Katherine's younger brother and advocate in the family. The older Beauchamps might disapprove, but Leslie Beauchamp (it was not for nothing that Katherine had given his name to L.M.) was one with L.M. in his heroine-worship. 'She is exuberant, Idie', he wrote to the absent L.M., 'her work is conquering London. Don't you see the triumph in sight?' The whole family were to stay to see that triumph, later in the year.

But it was not Katherine who was publishing a book now: it was Beatrice. Early in 1911 a publisher using the imprint 'Stephen Swift'[1] brought out her novel, *The Maid's Comedy* which had already appeared in the paper as a serial. A. E. Randall, one of the

[1] 'Stephen Swift' was a publisher whose real name was Edward Granville. As will be seen, he chose an apposite alias.

regular contributors, duly reviewed it in the *New Age* in February: 'The test of Nietzsche, applied to this story, approves it as a work of art. It is impossible to read it without being refreshed.' Oddly, for someone so avid for recognition, Beatrice never put her name to it, and a copy of her 'Chivalric Romance' was not even deposited in the British Museum.

It is a very strange book, narrating in self-conscious ninetyish language the adventures of a female Quixote ('Dorothea') and her black female Sancho Panza in the uplands of Beatrice's youth, above Port Elizabeth. Dorothea's father, crazed by reading Cervantes, drives the heroine out of the house on the argument that the world needs damsels in distress. 'We must become', she exclaims to her follower, 'instead of damsels in distress, damsels errant!' The thing is absurd with its high style borrowed from Malory, its reminiscences of the speech of Boer ostrich-farmers, and its glimpses of Beatrice's personal outlook:

> They drank to the golden age.... Law was not yet left to the interpretation of the judges. Maidens and modesty went about without fear of danger; and if they were undone it was entirely owing to their own natural inclination.

All through there is the figure of the father: 'I was afraid of only one ill chance—lest my daughter, assisted by some sage, might gain entrance and seek to overcome my heart'; and, in a distorted way, by the 'woman question'. 'The new and enthusiastic craftsmen', declares one character, 'should emigrate before their enthusiasm is beaten down by the greed of women debauched by cheapness and by nature content with shoddy goods.' It is full of utterances and crockets. At one moment the heroine is declaring, 'Not by the aid of swords may we become Damsels Errant, since swords are never the affair of damsels'; and at the next her devoted follower is describing (in words that must have been taken from the life) how she read the Bible night and morning to an ox that had rinderpest. It is a feminine declaration darkened by mannerism, a world of devotion and obscurity brightened, in one of Beatrice's best phrases, by 'splinters of light'.

'Stephen Swift' had also, by this time, agreed to publish Katherine's German Pension stories as a collection. It must have given her a sense of the success she dreamed of. She knew nothing about publishers and journalists: she knew only that the help of Beatrice and 'Stephen Swift' was not by way of an allowance from her parents but credit to her own labours. Certainly, in the year 1911 Katherine owed much to Beatrice.

There was a reason for the acceptance of her stories for publication which was perhaps not altogether creditable. Their deft, detached observation, as it happened, put Germans in a bad light. From Katherine's point of view this was the merest of accidents, but just the same, such stories as 'Germans at Meat', with its horrid emphasis on gluttony and philistinism; or 'The Baron', stressing absurd and abject snobbery, were apt to catch the public mood, particularly the mood which 'S. Verdad' was inducing week by week in the political part of the paper. The war was still some years away, but the undercurrent of dislike and fear was already running strongly:

> 'I suppose you are frightened of an invasion too, eh? Oh that's good. I've been reading all about your English play in a newspaper. Did you see it?'
>
> 'Yes.' I sat upright. 'I assure you we are not afraid.'
>
> 'Well then, you ought to be,' said the Herr Rat. 'You have got no army at all—a few little boys with their veins full of nicotine poisoning.'
>
> 'Don't be afraid,' Herr Hoffman said, 'we don't want England. If we did we would have had her long ago. We really do not want you.'
>
> He waved his spoon airily, looking across at me as though I were a little child whom he would keep or dismiss as he pleased.
>
> 'We certainly do not want Germany,' I said.

Katherine could hardly have sensed it, but a change was stealing over the paper. Fabianism had long since ceased to have any influence at Cursitor Street and instead the *New Age* was responding to forces which were at the same time more disturbing and more in tune with the questing nature of the editor. The year had seen two unsettling and external cultural events in London: the Post-Impressionist Exhibition and the Russian Ballet. *The Cherry Orchard*, too, was performed for the first time in England. A. E.

Randall, as one of the group of Nietzscheans on the paper who had hailed *The Maid's Comedy*, was beginning to take an interest in psychoanalysis. The picture is no longer one of socialist agitation and the attainment of sweetness and light by organising common sense. It is darker, and more uncertain:

> If it is felt [wrote Orage on the death of Edward VII] that the era of Victoria is indeed at last over, who is so bold as to dare forecast the nature of the epoch that is now opening?

He was not unfair. The old causes of reform were still allowed their space, and the Sidney Street anarchists were duly defended by Beatrice at the top of her form in denouncing one of her greatest enemies, Winston Churchill. But the attacks extended also, and from the pen of the editor himself, to Lloyd George's Health Insurance proposals; and Belloc's doctrines of the Servile State were prominently displayed. So was the menace of Germany.

❦ 5 ❦

The Two Tigers

Shortly before Christmas 1911, and a few months after the successful publication of *In a German Pension*, the novelist W. L. George gave a dinner-party at his house in Hamilton Terrace, St. John's Wood, to which he invited Katherine Mansfield. This was contrived by George, who was a contributor to the *New Age*, to bring about an introduction to a young man he knew who was just starting in literary life with a magazine called *Rhythm*, named John Middleton Murry. A literary introduction between Katherine Mansfield and Murry had in fact already taken place in that Murry had come across a copy of *In a German Pension* in Dan Rider's bookshop and had read it with enthusiasm; and two Mansfield stories had been sent to *Rhythm*, one of which, 'The Woman at the Store', had been accepted.[1]

Murry has left more than one account of that first meeting with Katherine in her dove-grey, filmy dress, managing to talk about the Russian Artzibashev who had not yet been translated into English, and scoring off her host and hostess. He does not record if there was anyone else there except the Georges.

Murry was twenty-two, and at this stage of his life a striking figure: robust, rather above the ordinary height, and with a mop of dark, crinkly hair. His mouth was large and his jaw strongly marked. His greenish eyes were deeply set under long, heavy eyebrows, and his ears were somewhat prominent. 'Fine eyes', wrote Kingsmill of him at this time, 'and regular features . . . but he looked defeated. Standing or sitting, his posture was crumpled. He seemed

---

[1] Alpers (p. 153) suggests that George arranged for Katherine to send her stories to *Rhythm*, but on what evidence is not clear. Murry's account (Mantz and Murry, p. 333) speaks of direct application by Murry to Katherine through her publisher Edward Granville ('Stephen Swift'). George was also responsible for introducing Gordon Campbell to Katherine Mansfield, and so inadvertently to Murry.

to be bending over himself as though he were his own mother.' His nose was slightly crooked, having been broken in childhood as a result of his being struck by lightning. Few men can have changed so much in appearance between youth and middle age, for although, in later life, Murry's face remained smooth and his hair, while it thinned, hardly grew grey, his features and indeed his whole body, shrank, and his hairline receded so as to exaggerate a smoothness which was only broken by faint, self-deprecating smile-marks. In youth there was a seeming valiance as well as intellectuality in Murry's appearance, which was well suited to a man who was now bringing the Promethean fire of Paris to the London literary world.[1]

His origins and editorial qualifications were at all points different from Orage's. Orage had reacted against the rural squirearchy: Murry against the values of the urban lower middle class. He had been born on 6 August 1889, in Ethnard Street, Camberwell, just off the Old Kent Road, the eldest son of a hardworking minor civil servant in the Board of Inland Revenue. His first schools had been the Rolls Road Board School, just across the Old Kent Road from his home, which he first attended when he was two and a half; and the Bellendon Road Higher Grade Board School. He was an unusually good pupil, being able to read by the time he was three, while at the age of seven (he tells us) he had mastered quadratic equations, had learned a good deal of chemistry and geology, and was reading history 'that included a delving into the history of the *curia regis*'. He also obtained full marks for an essay on Gothic architecture. His father, whom he detested, already glimpsed that his son might graduate into the scarcely imaginable glories of the upper division of the Civil Service. A colleague of the elder Murry's at the office suggested Christ's Hospital, and there Murry had obtained a place in 1901 on the strength, as he himself describes the examination, of having read Sterne's *Sentimental Journey*. It was an appropriate enough passport for the journey that lay before him.

[1] The middle-aged Murry gave an impression of swarthiness as well as smoothness. Such, at any rate is my own recollection of him on the occasions I saw him, one of which, when he was seated on a sofa in our house at Keats Grove, is especially distinct. Physical and mental pressure had produced a curious hatching of lines on his forehead.

Murry therefore received a rigorous classical education which was prolonged by entry, in 1908, to Brasenose College, Oxford. It is interesting that although he got a first class in Moderations, and was expected to get a first in Greats (actually he got a second in rather special circumstances) his teachers did not see him as a scholar. 'Whatever you are', said his sixth-form master, 'you are not a classical scholar'; and the tutors of Brasenose thought the same. One clue can be found in the theme of the prize essay he wrote just before leaving school, which was 'Literature and Journalism'. But far more important was a growing sense of alienation. In his later years at school 'I began to be ashamed even of my home and my own parents'. His holidays, almost all of which were spent at home, were a torture to him, and the brightest spots in his whole school life were a summer trip to Jersey with his family and, later, a bicycle tour on his own in Brittany. Anything that was not Camberwell, anything to which his father's influence did not extend, was eagerly mopped up and processed with a highly conscious emotional intensity. 'I left school', he recorded later, 'part snob, part coward, part sentimentalist.' His father's plan that he should go into the Civil Service filled him with horror.

This plan, of course, depended on his success at the University, and therefore spoilt Oxford for him. He made no close friends there, and it was on an Easter vacation, in 1910, which he spent at a farm in the Cotswolds, that he encountered someone surrounded by the mist of admiration which was later to become so familiar. This happened to be a young French naval officer called Maurice Larrouy. The experience was enough to cause Murry to heap together all his resources, including those derived from a tutoring job in the summer vacation, to embark on a prolonged trip to Paris. It took place in the winter of 1910, and was the decisive turn of his life.

It is difficult now to imagine what a single-handed sojourn in Paris meant in 1910 for a young man of Murry's background. Hundreds of thousands have followed him, adventuring impecuniously in the small hotels and cafés of the Left Bank and drenching themselves in the liberating waters of sheer difference from Camberwell and Oxford. But he was among the earliest, and he penetrated well below the surface during the few weeks he stayed. He talked away the night at the Deux Magots and the café d'Harcourt, and acquired a grisette mistress. And he fell under the influence of one of the most interesting artists then working in Paris, the Scottish Fauviste J. D. Fergusson. It was Fergusson, with his watchword 'Rhythm' who supplied the rather inappropriate title for the magazine Murry was soon to found.

Francis Carco, by Bécan

But, to generalise, Murry had discovered a world which was refreshing because it was free, yet regulated in two separate and exciting ways: by its being foreign and therefore setting new bounds to an islander who had to watch his step; and by the Napoleonic apparatus which, by a kind of pattern that was quickly absorbed, restrained the dangers of chaos which English tradition taught as the inevitable consequence of giving free way to the lusts of the flesh. Among others whom Murry met on this first journey was the very embodiment of Parisian Bohemia, and later its gifted chronicler, Francis Carco, then a young man of twenty. Carco, originally Francesco Carcopino, had himself only just discovered and fallen in love with the Montmartre he was to describe so vividly as a respected member of the Académie Goncourt, and was soaking himself in its argot, strange society, and squalid charm:

The Two Tigers

Si transformé que soit ce quartier [Montmartre], il retrouve néanmoins son caractère dès que les premières lumières s'allument et que, des petites rues debouchant sur le boulevard, surgissent des individus de toute sorte.[1]

They met in the café d'Harcourt on the strength of a quotation from Rimbaud in a proof Carco was correcting:

C'était un adolescent de teint clair, aux yeux pétillants d'intelligence et d'ironie, qui cachait mal, sous ses allures décidées, une grande pudeur.

He had his arm round Marguéritte to whom, as Carco was quick to see, 'sa timidité l'empêchait de refuser quoi que ce fût' and he wore shoes with crêpe soles. Carco gained the impression that Murry worked for *The Times*, and quickly taught him the ways of Paris, including the fact that if a girl was paid for the evening it was unnecessary to spend money on sending her flowers the next morning; and indeed that by so young a man, no expenditure at all was really essential.

Murry made a number of discoveries about himself in Paris. One was the importance of every penny. Throughout his life he was haunted by a Camberwell itch for financial security, and this prevented him from ever being a true Bohemian. It would be a great mistake to think that the literary people of that time placed no value on money, and Murry, as his correspondence shows, thought more about it than most of them. He noted very quickly that in Paris one could get a book of tickets entitling one to ten per cent discount if one stuck to one café.

Another discovery was his power to attract women, and this was to have a dominating influence on his life. In many respects Murry distrusted himself, and was tortured with doubts in every step he took. But of his affair with the grisette Marguéritte, to use his own words:

[1] Francis Carco, *Montmartre à Vingt Ans*, p. 16. Carco describes his first encounter with Murry in *Bohème d'Artiste*, pp. 245–8. Katherine and Murry have both left unflattering portraits of Carco—his in *Between Two Worlds* (pp. 148–50) as R— D—; and hers in 'Je ne Parle pas Français' as Raoul Duquette.

I have always been taken by surprise when I have discovered that a woman has a liking for me. My instinctive presupposition has always been that if I like a woman, the woman will not like me. It is just the same today, even though I have to confess that my uniform experience has been that whenever I have liked a woman, it has always turned out that she liked me.

This passage, written in 1935, in the autobiography which he dedicated to his third wife, Betty (who liked him initially but came to dislike him intensely), takes one far into Murry's character, for it illustrates not only his initial attractiveness, of which he was aware, but the curious ambiguity with which he regarded himself. On the one hand is confidence, almost complacency, about his powers, whether intellectual or sexual, which made him ready to confront, singlehanded, the most challenging ideas and adventures: a man, indeed, who actually sought such challenges as a necessity of his existence; and on the other the elevation of diffidence into a virtue and close approach to a denial that his powers have any virtue or, indeed, that they exist at all.[1]

Along with this, in the same paradoxical way, went an infinite suggestibility and a noteworthy amount of canniness. Of himself as a young man he later observed that he was 'something infinitely plastic and suggestible, with no determined character'. The last few words of this diagnosis are not quite accurate. Suggestible he certainly was, but part of his character was an instinctive sense of personal advantage. His importance in literary history, perhaps, arises from the imposition of this intellectual suggestibility (combined with marked literary skill) on the deeply imprinted philosophy of self-preservation that he had acquired in Camberwell.

Murry did not return in spirit to Oxford after his stay in Paris, and his parting from Marguéritte, for which he had sentimental regrets for many years afterwards. He went back instead to the London of Dan Rider's bookshop in the Charing Cross Road and the epoch-making Post-Impressionist Exhibition of that spring. It

---

[1] 'He takes such passionate pleasure', wrote Eddie Marsh, 'in self-condemnation and self-torment that in order to satisfy his craving for molehills that he can make into Golgothas, he is always bringing about situations in which he can do the wrong thing in the wrong way' (E. Marsh, *A Number of People*, p. 225).

was as if his own intense experience of a few months before had suddenly become the cultural fashion of London. But in physical fact Oxford was where he finished up, and there he managed to interest one or two people in an idea for a magazine based on Bergson and Post-Impressionism. It was also to stand for Symbolism, Fantaisisme, Debussy and Mahler, as well as for 'guts and bloodiness'. He added to the manifesto a statement that he himself was 'a yellow syndicalist'. There would be no Shavianism or false aestheticism, and the magazine would be distributed all over the world by subscription. There was something heroic about it and much that was absurd; and a little that was important.

He visited Paris again that Easter of 1911, and with the help of Fergusson assembled what today reads as an impressive list of contributors, though the names were then almost unknown outside Montparnasse. They included Dérain, Van Dongen, Picasso, and Tristan Dérème; and he renewed his friendship with Carco. In June 1911 the first number of *Rhythm* appeared, and it was as good as its word in bringing Montparnasse to London. The cover was a gentle grey with a tasteful sketch of a nude. The paper was good and the typography, which still had a hint of the *Yellow Book* about it in spite of the editorial rejection of aestheticism, was the best the Garden City of Letchworth Press could provide. It cost a shilling, and was excellent value for money. Nina Hamnett, the art student daughter of an army officer, later a heroine and recorder of Bohemia, was a typical subscriber to *Rhythm*. It not only caught a moment but has had many descendants.

It was a considerable achievement for someone who was still an undergraduate, and he stayed sporadically in Oxford even to the point of taking his degree in the summer of 1912. But all that, along with his father's dream of a Civil Service career, was behind him now. He was committed to literary life. Marguéritte, with infinite regret, was finally written off that autumn, and a sordid experience in the company of Hugh Kingsmill at a brothel near Oxford (as a result of which Murry had an attack of gonorrhoea) during the Michaelmas term was succeeded in the vacation by a retreat (for lack of anywhere else to go) to his parents' home in Wandsworth. There could hardly be a greater contrast between the potentialities and pretensions of *Rhythm* and its totally unprovided editor than at the moment he set out for the dinner-party in Hamilton Terrace in December 1911.

In the street after the dinner-party Katherine invited him to tea, but the meeting was deferred to enable Katherine to visit Geneva for the second time in a few months—a passion for sudden travel was one of her most constant characteristics. By the time she returned and confirmed her invitation towards the end of January, Murry had to make his way to the Gray's Inn Road from Oxford. The rush matting, the low furniture, the tea served from bowls on the floor, he has several times described. She had acquired the style from Beatrice, whose seat was at this time always on the floor. It all ended with his being invited to take a room there, and her being invited to become a collaborator in *Rhythm*. Shyness and a native caution on his part prevented their becoming lovers until a few months later.

In this history, which has been related in great detail by Murry, there is one very notable feature. Although, at that time, Katherine was surrounded by other intense relationships, Murry never mentions any of them. Her success in placing herself alone in the centre of his picture was complete. Her parents were still in England. 'Chummie' was a constant visitor. She was not entirely free of Bowden, or of Orton. She was still seeing a great deal of Beatrice and the *New Age* troupers, and contributing to their weekly output. Most pervasive of all, perhaps, was poor devoted L.M., who had been looking forward to spending with Katherine the week-end that was appointed for Murry to move in. 'Alas on my arrival I had to help Katherine fill his cupboard with good things to eat—hiding a £5 note among the provisions, since we knew he was penniless. Then, forlornly, I returned to Luxborough House. Katherine came with me part of the way. . . .' Murry never took in any of this, nor, afterwards, would he ever accept an implication that Katherine was not his and his alone, alive or after her death. It was a strange, distorting persistence in error for which she herself was at first responsible.

But things were not quite what they had been between Katherine and Cursitor Street. The *New Age* people had been rather condescending about *In a German Pension* and they had played monkey tricks with two of her contributions to the paper in the autumn of

1911. In January 1912 they printed a long poem by Beatrice called 'Echo' and it cannot have been difficult for Katherine to spot, in the way the classical nymph was treated, an attack not only on her but on her whole approach to writing.[1] Perhaps it was about this time that the young Ruth Pitter called on Beatrice and Orage to find the floor scattered with beads, and was told Katherine and Beatrice had come to blows with their necklaces. Katherine's last contribution to the *New Age* (for the time being) was in March 1912—a satirical piece called 'A Marriage of Passion'—and by that time Murry was installed at Clovelly Mansions and Katherine had become joint editor of *Rhythm*, whose spring number was just about to appear.

Cursitor Street had been cool about *Rhythm* from the start, and no doubt they felt proprietorial about both Murry and Katherine, whose work they had been the first to print in both cases.[2] But the fury of the *New Age* about the spring number of *Rhythm* cannot be explained purely in terms of journalistic jealousy. At the end of March, under the rubric 'Present Day Criticism' which often meant Orage but on this occasion has strong touches of Beatrice, came two solid columns of savagery. Katherine's contribution (a poem) was reserved for particular attack:

> Miss Mansfield abandons her salt furrow and in two stanzas lies flapping and wappering.... We take it that these frenzies, syncopes and collapses, are really arranged to carry out the editor's notion of rhythm.

For good measure Murry was denounced for plagiarism in printing the preliminary sketch of a Segonzac for which the *New Age* had already reproduced the finished drawing. He was allowed a brief expostulation in the correspondence column, but no respite. Beatrice (the style is unmistakable) fired another volley in April:

> Mediocrity is not a product to treat with indifference, but to destroy wherever possible ... persons who are not living the life of art, but are running after sensationalism; dancing with seals in delirium, dreaming of murdering hags and degenerate children (a hit at 'The Woman at the Store'), playing with sadism

[1] 'My estimate of Katherine as a writer was expressed in "The Changeling", also she served me for "Echo"' (*Straight Thinker Bulletin*, June 1932).
[2] They printed a piece of his about Hegel in 1911.

and devil-worship, gazing at drunken tramps and daffodils until
themselves lost all sense of decency, studying the nude until any
gross figure seemed aesthetic so it were stark naked. . . . They are
the things that ruin the mind. . . .

At this stage in the *New Age*'s history Beatrice had what seems
an absolutely free run of the paper. In 1912 one can count at least
thirty-three contributions under her various aliases—Beatrice Tina,
Beatrice Hastings, Robert à Field, D. Triformis etc.—on every kind
of subject: poetry, reviews, stories, attacks on the legal system,
attacks on Picasso ('I really hate that sort of thing—as well show me
an abortion or a decayed corpse'), and successive instalments of her
autobiographical 'Pages from an Unpublished Novel'. But of her
many preoccupations her feud with Katherine and Murry (though
later to be briefly laid aside) was the one that lasted. Twenty years
afterwards, in bitterness and failure, she wrote of Katherine as a
member of the *New Age* café meetings in 1911–12:

He [Orage] named her the *marmozet*, thought her vulgar and
enterprising and couldn't understand my putting up with her.
She used to sit among us, silent and furtive, beady, obsequious,
or suddenly pompous, picking up everything everyone said and
did, grist for the sketch-mill, as A.R.O. called her memory.

The Murry who moved into Clovelly Mansions was more prosperous than three months earlier. With the help of his tutor, whose
contact with Fleet Street was as setter of classical brain-teasers for
the *Westminster Gazette*, he had been introduced to the editor of that
paper, J. A. Spender. As a result he had been taken on to write as
many literary 'paragraphs' as the paper would accept, at 7s 6d each,
and given an advance of £5, representing a good week's takings.
With Katherine's income from her father they would have something like £6 a week apart from what *Rhythm* might bring in and
what was left of the £15 which had been 'Stephen Swift's' down-
payment for her book (he paid no royalties). It really looked quite
comfortable, for it was twice the income of a teacher, and four times
that of a clerk. It was also considerably more than poor discarded
L.M. was making as a hairdresser and manicurist—ten shillings a
week.

That May, for the first of many times, Katherine and Murry crossed the Channel together and stayed briefly in Paris gathering promises of copy. This visit is important in that they were met at the Gare Saint-Lazare by Francis Carco, whom Katherine now met for the first time: she recorded it in unsympathetic retrospect in 'Je ne Parle pas Français' much later on. But she was already beginning to detect Murry's weaknesses: weaknesses above all, she felt, of taste.

Among the foreign correspondents recorded for the August issue of *Rhythm* were Carco, Anne Estelle Rice, and Katherine's old friend from Bavaria, Floryan Sobieniowksi. And there was a new business basis. Granville's firm had taken over responsibility for publication (the first number bearing the imprint 'Stephen Swift' is that for June) and had agreed to pay the 'Two Tigers' as the editors liked to be called, ten pounds a month, bringing their prospective income to over £400 a year. They left Clovelly Mansions and set up as Mr. and Mrs. Murry in a cottage not far from Chichester. Bowden refused a divorce, the old Murrys strongly disapproved, but they were launched. The colour of the cover of *Rhythm* was changed from grey to blue, and for the first time Murry's name appeared on it as editor 'assisted by Katherine Mansfield'.

During that summer a passage occurred in Murry's life which he never forgot, and which tells us much about him.

Henri Gaudier, known to history as Gaudier-Brzeska, was a genius with impossible ideals living in impossible circumstances. At the age of twenty-one he was coupled permanently in a platonic relationship with an exceptionally plain and neurotic Polish woman of nearly forty named Sophie Brzeska. Their lives were miserably poor, Gaudier being employed as a clerk in a City shipping office at six pounds a month, while Sophie was engaged in writing an endless trilogy with which even her devoted 'Pipuk' sometimes lost patience. She contributed nothing, even out of the little money she herself possessed, to their joint expenses; and she had lesbian tendencies. Amid these incredible restraints Gaudier managed to pursue the life of an artist, creating statues and drawings of astonishing power and originality. His behaviour was barbarous— by turns affectionate and aggressive—and his views challenged all possible conventions. He had the utter confidence of genius: 'I understand beauty', he declared, 'in a way that was better than the Greeks, and history and observation convince me that I am right.'

By the winter of 1912 Gaudier's talents were beginning to be known to a few people, and someone introduced him to the water-hole of Dan Rider's bookshop, where he met Murry. In due course one of his drawings appeared in *Rhythm* and in the spring, just when Murry had been initiated into true lovemaking by Katherine, Gaudier and Sophie arrived in their lives to form an intense emotional quartet. However, it was not quite harmonious from the first since Katherine did not care for the attention Sophie seemed to pay her.

The situation and its denouement were wholly characteristic of those Murry seemed born to produce, and it was lived out during its brief span, almost like a fable or 'argument' of his future existence. That May Murry and Katherine, in their new-found prosperity, conceived the idea of inviting Gaudier and Sophie to share the cottage at Runcton. The notion was originally Murry's: his sensitive feelers had detected Gaudier's 'superman' qualities, with attendant vibrations in Murry's own 'slave morality' (to use the Nietzschean terminology that was then fashionable). Katherine, who in her own way aimed at achievement of the *übermensch*, was not so sure, and Murry's account that Gaudier overheard their conversation while hidden under a windowsill in the garden, has inconsistencies. But it is certain that what had been intense love between the pairs suddenly turned to hatred, and Gaudier's fury was directed especially against Murry, to whom he wrote in November 1912:

My dear Murry,

. . . I was confirmed into my thought of the wickedness of Katherine Mansfield by a conversation I overheard when at Runcton. It was about my poor Zosik [Sophie] . . . I loved you innerly and still sympathise with you as a poor boy, chased by the Furies, but I must reproach you your lack of courage, discrimination and honour . . . you have no word whatever and I cannot trust you in the least. . . . Before putting the seal on our short but unhappy acquaintance I wish to point out to you, as a friendly counsel, that the less KM writes for you the better it will be . . . for it is not sincere but pure affectation. No art.

There were terrible scenes in which Gaudier demanded payment for his contribution to *Rhythm* (Murry never paid contributors, and Gaudier habitually gave his work away) and then Gaudier and Sophie ceremonially destroyed Murry. It was Sophie's idea. Gaudier, at the time of the quarrel, had almost completed a plaster bust of Murry, and it was decided to pelt it with bricks, Sophie taking first shot, then Gaudier, and then their friend Horace Brodzky, whose fate it was to score the decisive hit. 'Sophie', wrote Brodzky, 'gave a shrill but triumphant "ha, ha, ha, ha". Henri approached the mess, and with a sideward movement of his foot scattered the crumpled clay.' Murry's own characteristic verdict on the affair must be recorded, since the tone and final insinuation are peculiarly his:

> I confess I am out of my depth in this matter. But I have since come to believe that in both Gaudier and Lawrence there may have been some kind of sexual ambivalence, and that this may have been intimately connected with the quite peculiar impression of natural genius which both made on me. (I should make it perfectly clear that I am not at all attributing to them what is generally understood by the word homosexuality.)

It is not at all clear why 'sexual ambivalence' rather than work produced—which in both cases was persuasive—should have had anything to do with persuading a critic or even a friend about the possession of natural genius. Only two and a half years later the crazy, chivalrous, talented Gaudier perished in France as a volunteer in the army he had refused on principle to join as a conscript, and the statuettes he whittled out of the stocks of rifles abandoned in the trenches have perished with him.

During the ructions at Runcton, Orage and Beatrice had also moved to Sussex and settled for a time at Pease Pottage near Crawley, where no doubt some of the sneers from the *New Age* which greeted every number of *Rhythm* were actually written. They had a new protégé, Carl Bechhofer Roberts, who came, highly flattered, to stay with them for a few days, which long afterwards, no longer naïve, he put into a novel. It is an odd picture of flattery, pretentiousness and spiritualistic talk. He was terrified of Beatrice at first, especially when he found out the scale of her contribution to the *New Age*. She was short and dark, 'with her hair done in old-fashioned plaits, gold rings in her ears and a curious dress, rather like a little girl's, and turkish leather shoes with turned-up toes': 'If you're good', she said on greeting him, 'I'll read you my new poem.' And she did too, 'placing the manuscript so close to a plate of bread and butter that "Whitworth" [Orage] kept moving one or the other to safety'. Roberts was especially struck by her ideas on reincarnation. All her previous existences, she explained, after declaring that no woman could be a poet, had been as a man. Indeed she went further. Orage, she insisted, had no ear for music— 'women never have'. 'Dont you remember' (turning to Orage) 'during the French Revolution how frightened you were in your little midinette dress and bonnet, burying your face in my uniform?'[1]

That twelvemonth from the summer of 1912 to the summer of 1913 was probably the high tide of the affair between Orage and Beatrice. They spent almost every week-end together in Sussex, and had many guests. Besides Roberts and Hobson, Ruth Pitter, who Orage maintained was 'very like Mrs. Beatrice Hastings— might be her younger sister', spent a heavily chaperoned day at Pease Pottage, but was not allowed by her parents to stay longer. The Pitters might be progressive but open living in sin was not acceptable. The sixteen-year-old Ruth was shocked but excited by Beatrice in her flowing oriental dress from Liberty's, and her preference for sitting on the floor, smoking, and making free use of the word 'damn'. She also confided in the budding poet that she never wore drawers. As for Orage—no other man entered Ruth's mind for several years afterwards.

No doubt Beatrice's challenging behaviour was mostly for show, but it was of a piece with her evolution on the Woman Question. From being a straightforward champion of the claim to equal rights and the Vote she had evolved into a furious opponent of Mrs. Pankhurst and the W.S.P.U. She denounced the suffragettes as

---

[1] S. G. Hobson was also a guest at this week-end, as he records in *Pilgrim to the Left*, p. 141, where he mentions that it was Roberts's eighteenth birthday, thus fixing the date at 21 November 1912. Roberts's response to birthday congratulations was a sighed 'so little done, so much to do'.

middle-class exploiters of their own sex and no better than the men whose equals they claimed to be. They neither understood nor sympathised with the real problems women had to face, or the real claims they had in society. There were no bounds to her indignation when Mrs. Pankhurst said she would willingly serve a term in prison, but would feel herself demeaned by serving it along with common female criminals in Holloway.

Beatrice's position of ferociously feminine anti-feminism was ultimately set out in an article[1] aimed a few years later at the twin targets of feminism and Fabianism. Anything to do with the *New Statesman* could always expect hostility from the *New Age*, but with this article Beatrice rose above vituperation to put arguments which still have life. After touching gloves with 'the romantic spinsters, married and single, known as the Fabian Women's Group', she pitched into the phrase 'domestic serfdom':

> The ordinary home life of women is referred to as 'domestic serfdom,' every woman is told that she is 'exploited to get nothing but her keep,' and she is jeered on to demand maternity benefit so that she may imitate the 'professional woman' who employs nurses and servants. God knows who, exactly, are to be the nurses and servants, but they would evidently be the imbecile scum of femininity.

In a paragraph which is very nearly worthy of D. H. Lawrence she rams home the point:

> 'In the interest of national health, we want the feminine half of the population driven out of doors—engaged once more to work on the soil or at least obliged to go out to workshop or office.' But who is to cook, sew, wash and mind the baby? It may be true that the Royal Commission declared agriculture to be a healthy life, but someone must do the cooking and the mending and the minding. No matter what you call the Person—someone must perform these unhealthy and degrading tasks of a domestic serf! Whether our soups be cooked in communal vats, our stockings darned by some wholesale process yet undiscovered,

[1] The *New Statesman* Supplement on Women in Industry, *New Age*, 26 February 1914.

our babies minded in batches like so many foundlings—at the bottom of everything stands Some Female. Who is she to be, this type of a chandal to do the unspeakable office of house-wifery? I very much fear it will be some depraved wretch like myself, who sneaks into the kitchen, fiddling about with salt and pepper, and scraping a pot absolutely clean just to see it shine.

Most accounts of Orage as an editor dwell on his gift for attracting and training unknown talent, his patience with inexperienced contributors, his willingness to give unlikely people a chance. Certainly many fell under his magic, the secret of which was in making the humble feel important. But Beatrice makes the strident claim that she did the work, and one can accept her earnest statement that 'I cared for nothing but the paper, that was my life'. And she cared for Orage as well; even in the bitter pamphlet she wrote about it all long afterwards, with the picture of a devoted Beatrice attending on a sick Orage and rushing up to Cursitor Street to look after the paper, the thing comes through. In the end 'he got up as if nothing had happened and returned, serene and Oragic, to Chancery Lane'. She bullied him at the time, and came to hate him afterwards, but her devotion was not wholly centred on the *New Age*.

The greatest name she claims to have brought into the paper is that of Ezra Pound, who first began to write for the *New Age* in 1912. Unlike most contributors he was actually paid something— two guineas a week. He earned it. From September 1912 onwards for several years there are very few numbers of the *New Age* without contributions from Pound, either in his own name or under the pseudonyms of 'B. H. Dias' (art critic) and 'William Atheling' (music critic). For no paper has more shamelessly multiplied its actual staff for presentational purposes.

The recruitment of Pound opened up a new dimension for the literary end of the paper, and at the same time denied the 'Imagists' to *Rhythm*, against whom hostilities continued throughout the spring and summer of 1913, when suddenly Katherine and Murry were torpedoed by the collapse of the firm of 'Stephen Swift'. Granville absconded with his secretary (for 'marrying' whom he was later gaoled as a bigamist) leaving a shower of unpaid bills behind him. Among these was a debt to the Letchworth Press for printing

Rhythm, which the supposedly salaried editors found they were liable to pay. Such, at any rate, is Murry's account. Instead of ten pounds a month plus Katherine's allowance of £100 a year plus Murry's free-lance earnings, Katherine's income was almost all they had.

Still, *Rhythm* had carried the two high out of Dan Rider's into the company of the well-off and fashionable Eddie Marsh, then Private Secretary to Winston Churchill at the Admiralty and dispenser by way of literary patronage of what he called the 'murder money', being the annuity he had inherited as compensation for the assassination of his ancestor Spencer Perceval. *Rhythm* had already been a beneficiary of this fund and Marsh, with his friend Rupert Brooke, had been a visitor at the cottage near Chichester. What more natural than that Murry, after the defection of 'Stephen Swift', should have applied to Marsh for help?

The transaction that followed was a small one, but it was significant and as was so often to be the case with Murry's transactions the two men give different versions. Marsh said he undertook to guarantee an overdraft which Murry was to pay off at £10 a month; Murry claims that Marsh made him a princely gift of £100 which enabled the magazine to struggle on for a few more months. Marsh's version seems the more likely to be true, especially when he describes how he had unexpectedly to find £150, and on taxing Murry with it, received a letter explaining that he couldn't face the shame of admitting he had been unable to keep up the instalments. The affair left a permanently bitter taste. In July 1913 *Rhythm*, now rechristened the *Blue Review*, issued its last number, and Murry was faced with bankruptcy. The cottage at Runcton was given up, and Katherine and Murry were reduced more or less to camping in the two rooms in Chancery Lane which had served as *Rhythm*'s office— only a stone's throw from their exultant enemies of Cursitor Street; and to spending the later summer with their friends the Campbells at Howth.

✥ 6 ✥

Sentimental Journeys

Orage and Murry had a good deal in common, in spite of their different approaches and their early journalistic antagonism. They both came from a narrow background which they had defied and escaped from, with lasting prejudices. Each had enormous facility on paper; and a strong sexuality together with a selfconscious power of attraction to women. 'Women fell into his arms', Philip Mairet said of Orage; Dr. Eder, the Freudian, gave graphic warnings about him to his advanced young women friends. As for Murry, even in later life he found celibacy hard to endure for more than a few weeks. 'I entangled myself with women', he wrote, 'not in the ordinary sense of that phrase, but as it were touching them with my feelers.' But even 'in the ordinary sense of that phrase' the list was a long one.

Both men felt the necessity to ally themselves with causes, or rather with a succession of causes. Orage resisted partisanship for a time, and boasted of being 'an individualist who hated societies'. But from the Grayson episode onwards he was subject in his editorial work, and to some extent in his personal life, to a succession of dominations. The Guild Socialism of S. G. Hobson began to mark the *New Age* as early as 1911 and by 1913 it was the leading political theme of the paper. Other enthusiasms were to follow, each accompanied by heroic and unsuccessful efforts to reconcile the new guru with his predecessors. Murry was more subject to doctrines than to the personal magnetism of prophets, and in his long career embraced Fauvism, Pacifism, Communism, and Anglicanism; but he too could fall under the spell of a strong personality, and within a few weeks of his breach with Gaudier-Brzeska he encountered the man with whom his name will always be linked, D. H. Lawrence.

In the summer of 1913 Lawrence was beginning to be well known.

83

The White Peacock had come out in 1911 and the following year he had eloped with Frieda Weekley, the wife of a professor. *Sons and Lovers*, his greatest novel, was published in June 1913 when *Rhythm* was tottering towards its last number under the new name of the *Blue Review*. Murry and Katherine had sent him a copy in Italy soliciting a contribution, perhaps as early as the winter of 1912. Some of his poems duly appeared in the number for March 1913, and a story was promised. Lawrence liked the sound of the editors, though he thought they ran 'a daft paper'. They finally met—Lawrence, Frieda, Murry and Katherine—in June 1913 in the back-stairs office in Chancery Lane, where the ruined editors of the *Blue Review* had just produced their last number.

The meeting was friendly, but not decisive, and by August the Lawrences were back again on the Continent. There had been an idea that the Murrys should come to Broadstairs where the Lawrences had been staying in July under the aegis of Eddie Marsh, but Murry made excuses. Marsh, who had now taken up the Lawrences and introduced them to the son of the Prime Minister, Herbert Asquith, and his wife Lady Cynthia, was in no mood at that moment to be kind to Murry; and hinted he probably could not afford the fare, whereupon Lawrence, who had at first regarded the Murrys as prosperous, offered to lend them five pounds. There are hints—no more—of the style Lawrence was to adopt with so many of his friends in this incident. 'You *must* save your soul', said the letter offering the loan of the fare to Broadstairs, 'and Mrs. Murry's soul from any further hurts, for the present, or any disappointments, or any dreary stretches of misery.' There were one or two more meetings at most before the Lawrences went abroad again, but by autumn the die was cast. Murry wrote to Lawrence pouring out the problems of his life—his future, his relations with Katherine, his anxieties about money. In return he received the first of many admonitions. It is hard to believe Lawrence did not enjoy knocking Murry about. 'You've tried to satisfy Katherine with what you could earn for her . . . and she will only be satisfied with what you *are*. And you don't know what you are. You've never come to it. You've always been dodging round, getting Rhythms and flats and doing criticism for money.' It was a fair summary. But Lawrence was constructive as well in his advice. 'Stick to criticism', he urged, 'don't try a novel—try essays—like Walter Pater or somebody of that style . . . something concerning literature rather than life.'

Such a letter offers its recipient a choice: accept the advice; reject it and break off the acquaintance; or cling, and Murry clung. It would be wrong to say he could not see himself as Lawrence saw him, for no man was more capable of self-condemnation. It would be wrong too to say Lawrence did not perceive talent in Murry, or was not flattered by his continued attachment. Murry personified the university-educated middle class which Lawrence considered it was his mission to excoriate and reform. In Lawrence Murry perceived a man of genius whose moment had come. His editorial flair—even though for the moment he had nothing to edit—was not at fault. The mistake in the relationship was on Lawrence's side. He did not grasp, until much later, Murry's remarkable staying power or his capacity to attribute the highest motives to actions taken entirely in his own interest.

But for the moment Murry had discovered a new venture. Abandoning Spender and the *Westminster Gazette* he obtained a roving commission from *The Times Literary Supplement* to write some articles from Paris, and in December 1913 he and Katherine were once more greeted, *ivre de bonheur*, at the Gare Saint-Lazare by their old acquaintance, Francis Carco. They settled in lodgings in the rue de Tournon, near the Luxembourg, which Katherine describes in detail in 'Je ne Parle pas Français'. Murry struggled with his work. Katherine explored Paris with Carco:

> Nous avions beau sortir, le soir, en camarades, hanter les bals-musette de la Montagne-Saint-Geneviève ou les petits cafés-concert de la place d'Italie et rentrer quelquefois à l'aube, après de longues promenades boulevard de la Chapelle, je ne me doutais pas qu'un jour notre amitié se resserrerait si étroitement.

Katherine was deeply struck by Carco, and Carco was impressed by her—by her strangely expanding pupils, her 'anxieté du soir', her desperate wish to retain detail, her humble obstinacy in authorship. What was to happen is foreshadowed in the words Carco used about his meeting with the couple at the Gare Saint-Lazare. Murry's 'deference, attentiveness, gratitude, towards Katherine almost touched me'. There is a world in the 'almost'.

The intensity of Katherine's self-consciousness as an artist was by now developed to its full, alarming extent. 'I feel as fastidious as though I wrote with acid.' Her writings were not merely the outcome of a desire to represent life accurately by etching its details, but a psychological justification of herself. She sought insight, not inspiration; precision, not suggestion; completeness rather than universality. Gaudier had been brief and cutting in the last sentence of his letter to Murry. Later on Carco, by then her ex-lover, put almost the same thing into his portrait of her in *Les Innocents*: 'Elle n'aimait pas le Milord [the apache hero of the novel] mais se sentait amoureuse, pour son livre . . . elle vivait ce qu'elle écrivait et, peut-être, était-elle de ce qui détachait le Milord de sa malsaine curiosité.'

The stay in the rue de Tournon lasted about two months, and was not a success from Murry's point of view. Katherine spent most of her time with Carco while Murry wrote articles which, in the event, *The Times Literary Supplement* did not print. Martin Secker, who had published the last *Blue Review* had offered £30 for a book on Dostoevsky in a series of critical studies, but when Murry sat down to that he found no inspiration. Much of his time was spent struggling to write a novel, with the unpromising title of *Still Life*, which was to fall dead-born from the press when it was at last published in 1916. In January 1914, leaving Katherine behind in Paris, he returned to London to file his petition in bankruptcy and find some work. Spender, despite Murry's earlier desertion, was willing to have him back on the *Westminster*, this time as art critic. As he admitted in the *Journal* he began to keep about this time, he was 'an art critic knowing nothing about art', but he faced up to the situation bravely enough, acquired a pair of pepper-and-salt trousers and studied Ruskin's *Modern Painters*, which he found hard going, managing only forty pages in four days. He could have written as many in the time. Murry was one of those who read slowly, but write with phenomenal speed.

In February he went over and fetched Katherine back from the unfortunate Parisian expedition, and after a series of other lodgings they holed up in a Chelsea flat borrowed from a friend. They had never been so hard up against it. Katherine took work as a film extra—it would be interesting to know in what film—and was trying to get work on the stage: 'a damnably sordid business without influence', wrote Murry in a letter to Eddie Marsh which Marsh did not answer. This was probably the point in her career at which she picked up an occasional fee masquerading as a guest at a party to deliver an apparently impromptu sketch to the cue of 'Oh, Miss Mansfield you *are* so clever. . . .' As for Murry himself, 'apart from the labours of reviewing and art criticism, I have constantly to attend the bankruptcy court.'

Yet in some ways he remained jaunty, even complacent about the future. He had high hopes of his novel, and he knew, though on such brief acquaintance, that in Lawrence he had discovered a genius. 'All those save Lawrence are dead,' he confided in his journal after reciting the names of other leading literary figures, 'without imagination or feeling. Lawrence has feeling but no imagination, I have imagination and no feeling.' It was rather too neat, but there was some insight in this first of his journals. Most of the 'Monster Notebook' in which it is written contains speculation about aesthetics which clearly bears on his current work as an art critic; but some is introspective, foreshadowing the style of the journals he was later to keep at much greater length.

Sitting at his desk he found 'that which struggles and that which is struggled against, are both me'. The trouble was 'the impenetrable other', the difficulty of personal relationships and opposing interests. Take matters of business for instance. Why could such transactions not be solved by love? Why, in fact, did Murry have to fight to get his way, why could he not persuade the Official Receiver, the printer, and all the rest of them, that he ought to be forgiven? Proceeding with this train of thought he discovered a clue:

> I have noticed in myself a never-ending desire to be a child. I want to lose myself in another, to resign my personality, to be protected (all these words seem too definite) and almost physically to be mothered like a child. And I have noticed that this instinct is strongest and most imperative in me, when I have had to fight against the material world.

He often said unkind things about himself, usually taking them back again in the next sentence, but here he came very near the truth. He had hardly had a childhood of his own. 'He was never a *real* boy', his aunt said later, 'just a little old man.' His narrow-minded, brutal father, who had struggled from obscurity to a junior clerkship, had used him in an attempt to fulfil a dream, and had been disappointed. So, as a grown-up, Murry lived out his childhood with a child's reliance on attractiveness and forbearance, and a child's occasional treachery, which was not really treachery because it was only done to grown-ups. At the same time his consciousness of talent drove him again and again into unmeasured risks in his search for applause and support; and from them he came reeling back, a refugee.

Those who turned to Murry for refuge during his long career were not many, though it is fair to say there were some. The role of refuge for the coterie that was gradually forming was to be played by a man who was himself, in the strictest sense of the word, a refugee, Samuel Solomonovich Koteliansky. 'Kot', as he was always called by his friends, had the qualities that Murry so conspicuously lacked.

Koteliansky was a Russian Jew born in 1882 at the largely Jewish village of Ostropol in the Ukraine, not far from Kiev. He had been to university in Russia and obtained a qualification in law, and his views, though not at all extreme, had been progressive enough to attract the attention of the authorities. In 1911 he had settled in London to earn his living in a small office in High Holborn which produced translations and certifications of Russian legal documents. It is possibly through his work at 'the Russian Law Bureau' that Koteliansky came to know Gordon Campbell, a young barrister who was a friend of both Murry and Lawrence: certainly it was through Campbell that Kot came to know them.

There was much of the rabbi in Kot, though he had discarded Jewish orthodoxy. His family claimed descent from a celebrated talmudic scholar of the seventeenth century called Yomtob Lipman Heller, and in moments of exaltation Kot would chant in Hebrew from the Psalms. His hair shot upwards in a crinkly thicket and the features beneath were swarthy and saturnine. His eyes 'looked at, through, and over you with a look of desperate and yet resigned intensity'. His crushing handshake resembled what one might receive on an introduction to Elijah. Leonard Woolf thought him 'not a comfortable man' and David Garnett that his moods of Hebraic gloom made him almost baleful. As a young man in Russia he had taught himself to howl like a dog as a measure of self-protection from wolves on his long walks home; and he was willing to howl on demand. 'Kot, howl like a dog!', someone would cry, and Kot would howl.

Two characteristics earned Kot the special place he was to occupy in English literary life. He was no writer, whether in English or Russian, but he had a wide knowledge of Russian literature and the Russian literary world and he had many contacts in Russia itself. It is said, though the evidence is lacking, that he had a prolonged correspondence with Gorky. At a time when the English literary public was becoming enthusiastic about every aspect of Russian culture, English literary men were woefully ignorant about it. Kot was more than a translator: he was a finder of material and technical expert in Russian matters. With this expertise he combined a strong, honourable and upright character. He could be touchy and quarrelsome, and was given to dark fits of depression, but his sympathy and loyalty to his friends were unquestioned. His shoulder was always there to be leant upon, though his critical opinions were at no man's bidding. When Lawrence returned from Italy in the late spring of 1914, and met Kot for the first time, an immediate mutual respect and friendship developed between them.

Lawrence's return to England also renewed the acquaintance with Murry and Katherine, and to such effect that they were the witnesses of the wedding of Lawrence and Frieda on 13 July 1914. Nobody looking at the wedding photograph taken in the garden of Campbell's house in Selwood Terrace, Kensington, could have guessed that the jaunty figure of Murry represented an introspective, penniless bankrupt. Katherine was disenchanted and despairing about everything—including the Russians. 'I long and long to write, and the words just won't come. Yet, when I read people like Gorky, for instance, I realise how streets ahead of them I be. I simply cannot believe there was a time when I cared about Turgeniev . . . I do not trust Jack.' As for the Lawrences, 'We were envious', wrote Murry, 'but unfeignedly happy.' Envious he might well be, for Lawrence had just been offered £100 for his next novel. With an impulsive but tactless gesture Frieda presented Katherine with the cast-off wedding ring of her first marriage.

The shared household of Beatrice and Orage came to an end almost at the time the Lawrences were married and the Murrys shared the rites. Beatrice was tired of Orage, and perhaps he was weary of her. There were differences of opinion about the paper as well, which spilt over into their personal lives. In 1913 Beatrice, as 'Robert à Field', had slipped in a piece called 'The Non-Committal Man' which (as she said afterwards) was meant to show 'what kind of a wobbly I had as companion'. In March 1914 A. E. Randall—allegedly prompted by Beatrice—had managed to insert a paragraph in the 'Readers and Writers' column insinuating that the editor was suffering from 'an inflamed condition of egotism'. Whatever the reasons, in April Beatrice was detached to Paris to write a column from there for the *New Age*. The parting was not unfriendly, but it was Wyndham Lewis, not Orage, who saw her off at Victoria. On 21 May the first of her 'Impressions de Paris' duly appeared, beginning with a touch which was truly in the tradition of Sterne, one of Orage's favourite authors: 'When the train had fairly moved, I regretted not to have kissed the dear in spite of the world, which was a fat man, a thin woman, and a middle-sized one.' Yet even as late as a few days before her departure, her partnership in the paper was recognised by Orage. 'I like the Rondeau very much', he was writing to George Pitter about Ruth's latest poem, 'and so does Mrs. Hastings.'

The editor she left behind was now forty, and just passing the peak of his achievement. Between 1910 and 1914 his personal output of both political and literary journalism had been astonishing. In number after number he had supplied the greater part of the political commentary 'Notes of the Week' and of the literary column 'Readers and Writers' over the initials R.H.C. He wrote and wrote well on almost any topic, from National Health Insurance (against which he ran a long campaign) to easy-going bookish causerie— 'Browsing', wrote 'R.H.C.' recovering from a bout of 'flu, 'is a rather more advanced regimen for convalescence than the re-arrangement of books. The latter can be performed without the smallest taste for reading ... but browsing means dipping into the contents here and there. ... In the last few days I must have nibbled in a hundred different pastures, chiefly, I think, in the pastures of books about books. De Quincey, Matthew Arnold, Bagehot,

Macaulay, Johnson, etc.—what meadows, what lush grass, what feed.' This might give too conventional an impression—but it was only one mood. He had recruited T. E. Hulme and Ezra Pound. He had published original work by Sickert, Gaudier, Wyndham Lewis and Epstein, which now curls and cracks on the inferior newsprint he had to use. He ran long controversies about the new, hardly discussable work of Freud. Futurism and Impressionism he might not care for, but they were given their showing: 'To criticism, at least, these three men, Marinetti, Picasso, and Roger Fry, have done incalculable service. They have demonstrated, in four or five years, with the rapidity of a galloping consumption, where lies the blind alley.' Murry, in his pepper-and-salt trousers, would never have ventured such authority. Orage had created an all-round, earnest, and still unfashionable public: he had discovered a hunger to be satisfied with a high standard of cultural journalism.

But perhaps, as Beatrice would have said, it was all too 'Oragic', too much in the model of Addison via the *Culhamite* or, as Orage himself would have liked to fancy, Swift. But if one turns to contemporary politics both of them had moved a long way from the crusading socialism and feminism of their early days together. Beatrice now came dangerously near saying a woman's true place was the home, so determined was she that female salvation did not lie in being a voter. The campaign for the Vote meant abrogating the true rights, the true privileges of women as against men in exchange for a formal juridical equality which in the end would be exploited by men to the disadvantage of women. As for Orage, by 1913 he had so alienated the Webbs that they had started a rival socialist weekly committed to Fabianism, the *New Statesman*, and detached Clifford Sharp from the *New Age* to edit it. Orage was quick to see the threat to his circulation, though he was courageous enough when he encountered Sharp in Chancery Lane soon after the *Statesman* had been launched. 'Have you seen our Blue Book Supplement?' asked Sharp. 'Which', demanded Orage, holding up the latest *Statesman* and the Supplement, one in each hand, '*is* the Blue Book Supplement?' But the axe was laid at the foot of the tree, and very soon the price of the *New Age*, already threepence, had to go up to sixpence.

A rival attraction to Fabianism was necessary, and Orage found it in Guild Socialism, developed in a series of *New Age* articles just before the war by S. G. Hobson. It was conceived as an organic, as contrasted with a bureaucratic path to socialism, and it did indeed represent a tradition which still divides socialists in the search to reconcile freedom with efficiency. It broadened the attack on the economic system by moving the emphasis of criticism from bad conditions and unemployment to the notion of employment itself. A powerful group of advocates was assembled, including Rowland Kenney, later editor of the *Daily Herald*, Maurice Reckitt, a young Christian Socialist of independent means, and, early in 1914, a young Fellow of Magdalen, G. D. H. Cole. 'The next step', Orage was writing in January 1914 to George Pitter, '*before* the penny weekly, is the re-establishment of the *Daily Herald*. I've got a notion to capture or kill it; and I *think* I shall do one or the other.'

Orage, perhaps, was so much of an egotist that it seemed to him the world moved while he remained constant in his search for truth. He was not yet conscious of the distance he had travelled in pursuit of the special knowledge he believed would release the springs of power: theosophy, Nietzsche, Fabianism, Grayson, Guild Socialism—all silted up in his mind as he continued with his quest. True, he did not as yet fully commit his paper to the Guild idea—something of the determination to keep the *New Age* open to all new ideas still persisted. And this was all the more important now that he had the *New Statesman* at his heels.

The possibility of a world war hardly seems to have troubled the *New Age*. Week by week 'S. Verdad' analysed the situation in the Balkans from a viewpoint that was on the whole favourable to Austria–Hungary; and even after the assassination at Sarajevo he was calmly balancing the dubiousness of Austrian legitimacy in Bosnia against the undoubted benefits Austrian rule had brought to the province. The 'Military Notes' commented on 'the present concentration of the Flying Corps on Salisbury Plain' and observed that 'it is not the business of these notes to deny that the influence of aircraft upon war will be a very considerable one.' The writer found it necessary to protest against the 'moral deterioration which has now begun to affect all arms and which can most properly be described as "airfunk".' It was all very detached.

Nor was 'Alice Morning', on her way to Paris, thinking of the approaching storm, though she was delighted with the attentions of a French soldier ('the very tulip of his regiment') on the train. Her arrival had clearly not been improvised, and she had plenty of introductions in both Montmartre and Montparnasse through Max Jacob, who probably had as wide a circle of bohemian acquaintances as any man in Paris. From the very beginning Beatrice wrote about artistic and literary Paris in one of its greatest periods as an insider, not a special correspondent.

Max Jacob, by Picasso

With intervals and changes of name Beatrice's columns from Paris were to last nearly four years, and contained the best things she ever wrote. Like all her writing this Paris journalism suffers from her ineradicable waywardness, but it is none the less remarkable, both intrinsically for what it says, and stylistically. She loved that world. She said afterwards that she had never realised the horrors of Montparnasse; she had been 'Minnie Pinnikin' and thought everyone lived in a fairyland as she did. For the first of her 'Impressions de Paris' she was clearly under the influence of Sterne. The vivid, yet oblique power to convey the significance of small incidents is unmistakable:

> I was being tossed from side to side of the Boulevarde by excited persons all directing me wrongly—at least some of them must have been wrong—when a giant Anglaise rushed up and commanded me in a fashion to make me weep for our high schools: 'There—over there—where that lady in blue is—light blue—it's no use waiting here—they'll only stop at the proper places' . . . I scored, though, over the clerk at the bureau. 'Iss betterr you spik Ingleesh?' he suggested. I wasn't going to stand this. 'Look here', I said, in unmistakable Saxon, 'I prefer the scrunch of my French to the squeak of your English. J'ai l'honneur de vous dire si vous ne pouvez pas me trouver une chambre plus tranquille je. . . .'

In her description of ridding herself of a tedious and lecherous companion the Sternean note is even stronger:

> 'Last week I was drunk only three times. On but one occasion did any slight violence occur. A knife and a broken glass found their billets, but, I assure you, on my salvation, only skin deep! believe me, monsieur, the world made this four times drunk and the total loss of an ear. I am not a violent woman monsieur. I could not have done it even in my cups.' I will never believe that the G.B.S. ear was more than pierced. I sank into a glowering reverie over my wrongs.

She was plunging rapidly into the life of Montparnasse by attending an artists' ball, and 'Impressions de Paris III', published on 4 June 1914 reports that 'a peintre is making profane love to me, and it takes me all my time to think up serviceable frigidities'. There was also a sculptor, as yet unidentified:

> The fair and pure English bourgeoise came with a bodyguard to see life. She was satisfied when she saw me wake up from a sulk to be very glad with the bad garçon of a sculptor. He has mislaid the last thread of that nutty rig he had recently, and is entirely back in cap, scarf, and courduroy. Rose-bud was quite shook on the pale and ravishing villain.

This 'pale and ravishing villain' was Amadeo Modigliani. His talent had long been recognised in Bohemia, but his way of life was desperate even among bohemians. In Beatrice's words he was 'a bohemian pur sang'. Three years earlier he had been rescued, after being found half-dead in his studio, by Epstein and Augustus John, who had bought some of his pictures and sent him back to his prosperous middle-class home in Italy. When he met Beatrice in 1914 he had been back in Paris for nearly two years, and was barely thirty.

It is possible her knowledge of him came originally from Epstein, and she met him first (shades of Chancery Lane A.B.C.) in a crèmerie, then at the Rotonde. 'He was a pig and a pearl', and at first she claims not to have known who he was—'he looked ugly, ferocious, greedy'. But on the second meeting at Rotonde he was shaved and charming: 'raised his cap with a pretty gesture, blushed to the eyes, and asked me to come and see his work'. She noticed, like many of his friends, that he always carried the same book in his pocket—Lautréamont's *Mogador*. He despised all the artists in Paris except Picasso and Max Jacob; and never, according to Beatrice, did any good work under the influence of the hashish he took so often.

Their friendship ripened very quickly in, of all places, a cinema. ' "You mustn't go to sleep on my shoulder", I objected— "all the world knows you." "Not a soul," he said, and waved anew to somebody else. "You mustn't fall in love with me," he said, "it's no use—yes, do!—no, don't!—it's no use!" "Don't be absolutely ridiculous," I said, "you're much more likely!" "Ah, that's all accomplished," he said, "but you look at me responsively, like my first statue." ' By 9 July he was identified for the readers of the *New Age* and shown quarrelling with 'Alice Morning' about le Douanier Rousseau at an exhibition. She found Rousseau 'bourgeois, sentimental, and rusé' and was furious when Modigliani airily replied 'Oui, très joli.' As for Picasso, she was equally cutting. 'One of Modigliani's stone heads was on the table below the painting of Picasso, and the contrast between the true thing and the true-to-life thing nearly split me.'

In July she briefly returned to London, after a triumphant scene at the Gare du Nord, where Modigliani had tried to stop her from going. He was, to use her own words, 'very much so', blocked her taxi as it was leaving for the station, leapt in, pursued her on to the platform, and 'fainted loudly against the side of the carriage, and all the English stared at me. I said, "Modigliani, someone says you've been three years fiddling about with one type of head, and you'll be another three on the new design." He came round. "Crétin!" he glared at me as though I had said it. "Mais, ma-a-a-is, ma petite, he is right! I might have grown asparagus in the time." ' The train left. Beatrice was relieved to find the lady in the opposite seat, whom she took to be a governess, did not mind her smoking, and even accepted a cigarette 'though she will never be much of a hand at it'.

If the visit to London had any idea of reconciliation with Orage in it, that soon evaporated, and she quickly returned to Paris, whence her column splashed merrily away. 'One of Us, Ladies, is explaining to her husband that things are not so amusing as they once were. . . . I'm not such a fool as to want to come back. I wish I had never set foot in your old house. I wish I'd never seen you. You are as boresome as your house, and nearly as flat. It is a stupid house, uninteresting—yes, it's all that. I'd as soon——'.

As the war broke out she was bursting with confidence. She was going to write a novel about the menopause with the title 'I asked for bread and ye gave me a stone'. 'Je m'en fiche du tout of men novelists—they are outside, and that's all about it. I will pray for the grace of God, for this is required. But a female make-up is even more of a help.' As for the Woman Question, she had made up her mind about that too:

> Votes for Women! who are welcome to them. Give me all the other trifling considerations, and room for a crinoline if I choose.

In July 1914, a fortnight after his wedding, D. H. Lawrence left Frieda in London with the Campbells and set out on a walking tour of the Lake District. He did not choose Murry as his companion. The other walkers were Koteliansky, whom he had only just met, and two men from the Russian Law Bureau called Farbman and Horne. It seems likely that the trip had been originally planned by Horne and Kot, and it is certain that it was meant to last longer than the four days they actually spent on the fells. They left London on 31 July, and spent the first few days of August trudging the hills and dales of Furness, staying the night at village inns. On the march Kot chanted the thirty-third psalm in Hebrew—'Rejoice ye righteous to the Lord: Ranane Sadhikim Sadhikim bananoi', from which Lawrence caught a sound like 'Rananim' that chimed with his idea for a colony where he and his chosen friends would retreat from the world's corruption.[1]

'We *were* happy—four men', Lawrence wrote later to Lady Cynthia Asquith. He twisted water-lilies round his hat 'and girls who had come out on a spree and who were having tea in the upper room of an inn, shrieked with laughter ... we crouched under the loose wall on the moors, and the rain flew by in streams, and the wind came rushing through the chinks in the wall behind one's head'. On 4 August they came down from the fells to Barrow in Furness and read in the first newspaper they had seen for nearly a week that the whole of Europe was at war.

[1] Professor David Daiches appears to have settled the question of the source of 'Rananim' in his letter to *The Times Literary Supplement* of 6 January 1956.

❦ 7 ❦

Defying the War

The war found most of them not so much unprepared as un-concerned. Later that lack of concern was to turn, for some of them, into fear, hatred and alienation. But at the outset their plans of life continued without interruption. Lawrence stayed for a few days longer in Furness, struck by impressions of 'electric suspense, visionary beauty, and immense pain'. Beatrice went back to Paris and Modigliani. Katherine did not so much as mention the out-break of war in her journal.

The reflections of the *New Age*, though grave and in some ways far-sighted, were still detached. Writing on 6 August 1914 Orage gave his support to the war because 'we believe that England is necessary to Socialism, as Socialism is necessary to the world'; and it was Germany's fault the war had broken out—Germany, in an odd phrase, had become 'the mad Suffragette of Europe'. But it was 'with both eyes open that we must intervene, if intervene we must. One eye must see that we behave honourably to France: the other must see that in disestablishing Germany we do not establish Russia'. The strident patriotism of the Northcliffe Press was denounced, and in a moment of insight Orage went on:

It is not to be supposed that forms of government, already obsolete in theory, should be permitted to continue in practice, when it is seen that they can, by the decision of a few men, submerge a Continent in blood. For it is not now, as formerly it was, the case that any nation in so close a federation as that of Europe can be at war without involving all the rest. . . . We shall see in the retention of autocracies a menace to the world. Costly as the experience necessary to establish popular faith in this may be, perhaps the war now upon us will give us it. In that event,

Germany, Austria, and Russia may look to their peoples for civil revolutions immediately following the war.

But there was no concept of the damage the war would do to Britain. Her superiority and durability were not for a moment in doubt. 'I have no belief', wrote Kennedy in the same number, 'in what journalists love to call a general conflagration lasting for an indefinite period.'

And even if a widespread war resulted, we stand to lose less in consequence of it (barring the United States) than any other Power in the world. . . . Unless we are being governed by lunatics, we hold the balance of world-power in our hands to an extent never before approached.

It is true that Orage, in his more reflective moments, did not share this notion that Britain enjoyed a peculiar immunity and detachment in relation to the war: 'the origins of the war are not to be found in its immediately precedent excuses, but in the diplomatic and general history of the involved Powers during the last decade'. But nobody reading his editorials could doubt that they are under-laid by a sense of belonging to the richest and most powerful country in the world. And as he later told Herbert Read, he for-swore 'the publication of anything realistic about the war'.

Murry, unlike the others, was for a moment caught up in the wave of emotion. Early in August he sought out Hugh Lunn (otherwise 'Hugh Kingsmill'), his crony from Oxford and the world of Dan Rider's bookshop, whose stentorian geniality often attracted those in need of consolation. Under Kingsmill's influence Murry joined a cyclist battalion, and (as with so many of his enthusiasms) at once regretted it. There were no cycles or even uniforms for the recruits, so Murry was sent home, and used the interval to obtain a medical certificate which effectually excused him from service. The endorse-ment of the certificate was 'Pleurisy. ?T.B.', in recording which, Murry hints that it was given more out of sympathy than medical science. But one should not be too sure. In those days doctors had a chilling familiarity with the symptoms of tuberculosis, and the conditions of Murry's life during the last few years could easily have made way for the disease. It is not at all unlikely that Murry was tubercular, and the disease was to play havoc with the lives of those to whom he was closest.

That autumn, the first of the war, Murry and Katherine took up residence in a cottage not far from Chesham; and not far also from where the Lawrences had settled. Rose Tree Cottage, on the Lee, was a beastly little place, well suited to the wretchedness to which the Murrys were now reduced. One must remember the times. Such cottages lacked all the conveniences that are now almost universal. They were lit by lamps or candles, the tap (if there was one) ran only cold, a telephone was unthinkable, and so was the idea of any mechanical transport. It was to be several years yet before Murry would have even a motorbike, to be succeeded in due course by a three-wheel Trojan. To reach the Lawrences or the shops meant a trudge of several miles. But they did not have to do the housework. There was a servant.

The sojourn at Rose Tree Cottage, though one of the longest he ever spent in the neighbourhood of Lawrence, then working on *The Rainbow*, was one of the most miserable of Murry's existence. There was a certain irony in his inheritance of Lawrence's discarded razor, for Lawrence was growing a beard.

The relations between Lawrence and Frieda were under strain, with Frieda pining for her children left with her first husband, and Lawrence resenting it: Murry vividly describes the harangues he delivered (from mixed motives) in his efforts to reconcile them, and his horror at the thought that his interventions might end with Frieda detaching herself to Rose Tree Cottage and making it an anti-Lawrence camp. There was another presence at these quarrels —Kotel-iansky's. One dripping afternoon in an autumn that seems to have been perpetually wet, he sombrely admonished Frieda to stop repining: 'Frieda, you have left your children to marry Lawrence. You must choose either your children or Lawrence, and if you choose Lawrence you must stop complaining about the children.' The effect was to make Frieda quit the house at once and, as Murry had feared, trudge three miles across the fields to take refuge at Rose Tree Cottage. The two men, Lawrence and Kot, were left alone and a few hours passed: then 'Suddenly the door opened and there stood a young woman with her skirts tucked up in wellington boots, soaking wet' who announced that Frieda would not be coming back. Her reply to Lawrence's defiant, 'Tell her I never want to see her again' was to close the door and disappear into the rain.[1]

The quarrel between Lawrence and Frieda was quickly made up, as always happened, but the incident had started something else. The dramatic young woman in wellingtons had been Katherine Mansfield, and that brief moment, framed in the doorway with her skirts tucked up was the first time Kot had set eyes on her. Out of it developed the great, unrequited and often regretted passion of his life. His lasting love made him able to forgive all her faults, though he understood them profoundly. Long afterwards, writing to his friend Waterlow, who had criticised Katherine, Kot was to write:

> I quite understand what you say about Katherine Mansfield. But I have never been 'just' to Katherine the writer. I loved her so much that her writing to me was and remains one of the non-important manifestations of her being. It is her being, what she was, the aroma of her being, that I love. She could do things that I disliked intensely, exaggerate and tell untruths, yet the way she did it was so admirable, unique, that I did not trouble at all about what she spoke it was just lovely. You see, temperamentally, I am not a judge, and tolerance and fairness are somewhat extraneous to me. . . . Hence my attitude to Katherine the writer. I love her too well to judge her fairly and tolerantly.

By February 1915, and constantly thereafter, he was her devoted friend, offering everything from cigarettes (which she loved, but could not afford to buy) to moral support. Her replies, signed with varying Russian diminutives—'Katinka', 'Kissienka'—were grateful and bold. 'Koteliansky', she wrote, 'it is my turn to give. Tell me— what shall I give? One thing if you want it is yours to keep.' Whether this hint or a later one was the occasion, it later had to be withdrawn, for among the Koteliansky papers there is one undated letter which was never copied for the edition Murry later published, and was not even included in the papers he bequeathed to the British Museum. It runs thus:

[1] It was, however, just about this time that Lawrence made his will leaving everything to Frieda. *See* Appendix.

No dear Koteliansky, my letter did not 'mean that'. Let us meet perhaps, quite by chance, tomorrow or months or years hence. That is best. Katherine.

She was under no illusion about her conquest of Kot, but her thoughts were not of him, though she was becoming more and more disenchanted with Murry. 'Jack, Jack', she wrote in her *Journal* for December, 'we are not going to stay together'; and in January, after he had given her a reading from *Still Life* she recorded that he 'must beware of a kind of melodramatic intellectual sentimentality'. Her own intense powers of self-dramatisation were fixed on a Parisian setting and the world inhabited by Francis Carco, and, now, by Beatrice. At the same time Murry was developing an intense (and as Lawrence thought, unhealthy) friendship with Gordon Campbell.[1]

Carco had retained an affection for Katherine ever since the days of the rue de Tournon, when he had been living in a flat on the quai aux Fleurs, looking across to the Île Saint Louis, and had shown her the sights of Paris while Murry was writing for *The Times Literary Supplement*. And she had written to him since coming back to England describing (in rather imperfect French) the fever of war: London was like a 'soupe aux larmes' and full of 'ridicules cocottes de music-halls avec les cocardes belges à leurs chapeaux'. But he had not written to her: he had written to Murry. It would be easy to infer from the entry in Katherine's *Journal* for 16 November recording the arrival of 'a letter from F—' that it was addressed to her. 'I had not expected it and yet, when it arrived it all seemed to me inevitable . . . he and I are so close . . . I want to laugh and run out into the road.' Yet the letter was addressed to Murry.

By the turn of the year Katherine was obsessed by the idea of an adventure with Carco—'had a shake on him' as Beatrice unkindly put it long afterwards. Sleeping with Murry was followed by long agonies of remorse. She went up to London, saw Kot, posted a letter to Carco, and a little later sent him a lock of her hair. On

[1] See the remarkable letter from Murry to Campbell printed in Lady Glenavy's autobiography *Today We Will Only Gossip*, p. 63 and ff. It remained unposted for thirty-seven years when Murry found it and sent it to his now elderly friend. Characteristically, however, he retained a copy.

14 January came an invitation from Carco to stay with him in France—he was not in Paris, however, but serving as a post-corporal with a cavalry regiment stationed at a small place called Gray, near Dijon, well behind the lines but in the War Zone.

She now had to make up her mind, and despite the strength of her feelings, this could not be done without an exhibition of self-consciousness. She had long discussions with Murry, as a result of which 'we gave ourselves our freedom in a strange way'. The Lawrences were told, and she set out for London, where she had more than one interview with Koteliansky who bought her presents and entertained her at the Dieppe Café. 'I rather cling to him', she recorded after this; but also, soon after a meeting with Kot, 'the setting was very good for a short story some time.'

Work—though she actually did none—was her simultaneous obsession. Her New Year resolution had been 'to write, to make money', and a little later, at the end of a day, she was writing, 'Oh God, my God let me work! Wasted! Wasted!' In a kind of way the whole enterprise was the creation of a short story, and a short story in due course it became.

A second summons from Carco arrived on 6 February, just after she had finished *Crime and Punishment*, 'and very bad I thought it too'. On 15 February her brother 'Chummie'—now in England as a soldier—saw her off at Victoria among the crowds of soldiers returning to France and soon to take part in the second battle of Vimy. He had given her the money for the fare. All Katherine's strings were at their tensest—her passion for work, her passion for Carco, and her newly discovered sense of alienation from England. 'I was possessed by hate of England. It is, after him, my one passion —a loathing for England.'

It was the first of many difficult journeys. Gray was not easy to get to at the best of times, and in wartime was almost inaccessible to civilians. The only way was, after Paris, to strike southwestwards as far as Châteaudun, and then by rail across country to the east, encountering the barriers of military officialdom at every stage.

Katherine stayed only a night or two in Paris, at Carco's flat on the quai aux Fleurs, before making her way onwards armed (if we take literally her account in 'An Indiscreet Journey') with a bogus invitation from imaginary relatives in the War Zone and wearing a

Burberry borrowed from a friend in Paris. There can be little doubt that Beatrice was that friend, and Beatrice herself confirms it long afterwards: 'She came to me in Paris on her way to Francis Carco, on whom she had a shake. She meant to write him up of course, but that was Carco's own game.'

Beatrice was installed in a little house at the very top of Montmartre in the tiny rue de Norvins, whose remains, she wrote in her September contribution to the *New Age*, 'are still a dream of town beauty—but all is doomed. A kind of little hilly park with a falling brook was crowded along its paths with bare-headed women, sewing and embroidering, and very interested in my smocked Liberty frock.' She was at the height of her journalistic powers, had lived through the Parisian drama of the Germans on the Marne, and written her copy in the intervals of being sketched by Modigliani. 'He did the Mary portrait of me in a café where I sat thinking what a nuisance he was with his perennial need for more pastels, and wondering if I should get my impressions of Paris written in time for the post.'

During the autumn of 1914 she had been passionate for victory:

> If we should lose this war, equipped as we are to win it, the race of men would fall under powers founded upon injustice—and such powers are not known on this planet. Injustice is well known by men to be without the right or faculty of preservation; it must work from cover while it exists, and is pursued to extinction when it is seen.

She went further:

> I feel as if I would like to be an awful traitor to Mankind and forget all about the war, go and do anything outside a state of siege. But there's nothing possibly to do. You can't fall in love during a war. More likely you would fall out. You can't abide love.

But as the war went on she was feeling acutely for the poverty it was inflicting on Parisian Bohemia. They had always been poor, now they were starving. 'The misery is so quiet that you may sit next to it quite a while before catching that dreadful gesture of the hand to the dizzy head.'

I may seem to be grumbling at Paris [she went on], which is very stubborn and brave, but here a music-teacher giving lessons for her bread is made to feel almost an enemy of the people. And I am grumbling because I hate, almost as much as sensationalism, its complement kill-joy. When I say that the concierges like one woman chase away from the courts starving singers and musicians, many of whom a few weeks ago were employed in the cabarets on the boulevards, I only give a faint hint of the universal and systematic suppression of everything but grief and grocery.

That article, printed on 8 October, ends with her own recourse to the soup kitchen for starving Bohemians started by Marie Wassilieff. In the company she describes, though she gives no names, one can recognise Modigliani, the Japanese artist Foujita and Picasso.

As time went on her commentary on wartime Paris, though still strongly anti-German, dwelt more and more on the life of the streets, the artists and the thoughts that floated through her mind. Sometimes she became almost prophetic:

The generation to come after this astonishing buffet of war upon a mechanical civilisation should produce a youth unlikely to become food for powder—not mad, not melancholy—no timid blustering student youth making a jolly row all night, and, in the morning, a sad poem about his row. . . .

Katherine's idyll with Carco at Gray lasted three days and has been three times described, twice by her, in her *Journal* and in 'An Indiscreet Journey'; and once by him in *Montmartre à Vingt Ans*. His flat in the quai aux Fleurs remained at her disposal, but three days together had been enough for both. Katherine had fled from one man in horror of his excessive intellectuality. As for Carco, he reflected that he had 'less taste for analysis than Katherine Mansfield', and had never suspected that while she was with him at Gray 'she was noting down her impressions to communicate them one day to her husband'. He noted regretfully that long afterwards, when he published a book of verse, she enthusiastically mistranscribed in her journal an extract from what he regarded as one of the feeblest poems in the collection.

She spent a few days in Paris (perhaps returning Beatrice's Burberry) and then, though not repentantly, crossed once more to England. But it was not to be for long, and not, yet, for taking up life again with Murry, though she duly went back to Rose Tree Cottage and they 'wearily forgave one another'. The inducement to return was her brother, and she was in England for barely three weeks. By 19 March she was back in the flat on the quai aux Fleurs.

The main feature of those three weeks had been a renewed confidence in her ability to write, and the flirtatious correspondence with Koteliansky, who denounced her 'wickedness' and sent her presents of cigarettes and whisky. They are curiously little-girlish letters, but appealing desperately for sympathy. The last, written just before setting out for Paris, urges him to write '*often, often,* for I shall be very lonely I know ... I press your hands *tightly.* Goodbye.'

Between the collapse of the *Blue Review* and the arrival of 'Chummie' in England, she had written almost nothing, in spite of her resolutions. Now, turning back to New Zealand and her childhood for inspiration she was launched on one of her longest and most successful stories, 'Prelude'—projected originally under the title 'The Aloe'. This, and others, were completed during the spring of 1915, mainly in Paris and much in the company of Beatrice, though from her correspondence with Kot one would judge she was entirely alone.

Amadeo Modigliani had now more or less moved into Beatrice's four-roomed cottage in the rue de Norvins which was later to be the love-nest and deathbed of President Paul Deschanel. 'Un petit homme large', wrote Max Jacob some years later, 'à profil vaguement dantesque, mais à nez court. Il était juif. Il riait vite, clair et court. Généralement il était mécontent, indigné, et grondeur. Sa figure était large, belle, très brune. Il avait la tenue d'un gentilhomme en haillons.' This nobleman in rags was famous for his drinking, his furious temper, and his partiality for hashish. He was beginning to be recognised, and his work had been shown in the Salon des Indépendants as long ago as 1910. But thanks largely to his irregular habits he was miserably poor and the war made life even more difficult for him. Much of his work he either gave away or sold for a few francs to patrons of the cafés in the Boulevard

Montparnasse who had probably served unwittingly as models. 'Odd,' said Picasso. 'You may find Utrillo drunk anywhere . . . but Modigliani is always drunk right in front of the Rotonde or the Dome.'

'B.'s flat is really very jolly', wrote Katherine to Murry, 'four rooms and a kitchen, a big hall, a cabinet and conservatory. Two rooms open on to the garden. A big china stove in the salle à manger heats the place. . . . Her own room with a grey self-colour carpet, lamps in bowls and Chinese shades, a piano, two divans, two armchairs, books, flowers, a bright fire, was very unlike Paris, really very charming. But the house I think detestable.'

This letter to Murry is particularly interesting in that it records an air raid which happened just after she had got home to the quai aux Fleurs after dining with Beatrice. 'Dearest of all', it ends, 'I love you entirely, TIG.' How then, did almost the same words describing the air raid get into the mouth of 'Winnie' in Carco's novel *Les Innocents*? Carco explains that he took them from a letter that Katherine wrote him at almost the same time: 'Toutes les impressions de Paris m'étaient alors fournies par Katherine Mansfield qui les transmettaient d'ailleurs à son mari.' The incident—and there are other parallel passages of the same kind—illustrates not only Katherine's economy in her use of material and her methods of dealing with her two lovers (detracting somewhat from the endearments they contained) but leads to the kernel of her literary character. Her carefully cultivated powers of apparently objective description were very much at the service of the scenery against which she acted out her own life. As Louis Gillet says in his introduction to 'Bliss', she 'had this privilege of living in a fairy land, in the middle of a strange little phantasmagoria of which she was at the same time the creator and the dupe.'

She noticed this in herself when she considered her relationship with Beatrice, whom she found 'strange and really beautiful . . . with the fairy air about her and her pretty little head still so fine. There is no doubt of it. I love her, but take an intense, cold interest in noting the signs.' The signs were signs of ruin. Beatrice was becoming an alcoholic. When Katherine came back from Gray the two had got drunk together, and Katherine had vowed she would never get drunk again. Beatrice admitted solitary drinks and even made a scene at a café in Montparnasse begging to be saved from a man who did not exist but adding bravely, 'But of course people here simply love me for it. There hasn't been a woman of real feeling here since the war.'

Katherine's talk of cold detachment was a pose—in fact Beatrice's power over her was still strong. Writing to Murry she spoke with a kind of jesting deference about 'Biggy B.' and her determination 'not to make daisy chains in her meadows'—meaning she would not try impressionistic journalism. Carco, who never met Beatrice, says Katherine always spoke of her 'sur un ton singulier d'effroi, d'admiration'. In his novel *Les Innocents*, with its highly recognisable, if unsympathetic, portrait of Katherine, he had to draw on what he had been told for his account of her companion, even though he called her Beatrice and made her a South African. As a result he created a frightening massive blonde painter who dominates 'Winnie' with a kind of lesbian superiority, and needles the apache hero of the book on his desire to avoid military service. Beatrice was much offended by the picture—the more so no doubt because she saw in it the kind of person Katherine thought she was.

The break between Beatrice and Katherine came at a party in Beatrice's flat on 22 March 1915. Among the guests, Katherine wrote to Murry, was 'a very lovely young woman, married and *curious*—blonde—passionate. We danced together.' Beatrice was unable to bear it and after a furious row the friendship was ended. 'A very decent and pleasant man saw me home.' Bitter things were certainly said, though the spell was never to be finally broken. Naturally her quarrel with Beatrice extended to Orage. 'I think O. wants kicking—just that. Of course what is peculiarly detestable is his habit of lying so charmingly—his "I should be delighted, Katherina" rings in my ears. . . . To tell you the truth, both of them are bitter because they have nearly known love, and broken, and we know love and are happy—Bogey, really and truly how happy we are.' But they both remained in her mind. And she in their minds.

Murry, receiving endearing letters by almost every post, was hard at work fitting up a flat he had found in Elgin Crescent, Maida Vale. The Lawrences had moved to a more comfortable cottage at Greatham, in Sussex, and the melancholy first winter of the war in Buckinghamshire was nearly over. He was, as Katherine put it, 'floating on a sea of blue Ripolin', and getting advice from her in Paris about having loose covers made; but he was horribly short of money. In fact he had spent most of the time of Katherine's absences with the Lawrences at Greatham, where he had taken refuge soon after Katherine's flight to Carco. There Lawrence had lectured him about the excessive intensity of his friendship with Gordon Campbell, enlisted him in the laying of lino, and discussed large, imperfectly formed ideas of a revolution. Lawrence, for a moment, was confident about Murry. 'One of the men of the future—you will see. He is with me for the Revolution. He is just finishing his novel—his first—*very* good. At present he is my partner—the only man who quite simply is with me—One day he'll be ahead of me. Because he'll build the temple if I carve out the way—the place. How big we talk.'

These last words were written to Lawrence's new disciple, Lady Ottoline Morrell, who had brought him into contact with Bertrand Russell and E. M. Forster. These acquaintances were in due course to be more important to the Murrys than they were ever to be to Lawrence who, despite his surging ideas of communities and utopias, shied away from the practical demands of both leadership and subordination when they were presented.

Early in April, after an infuriating exhibition of indecision, and a flirtatious preparatory letter to Kot—'Yes, Koteliansky, you really are one of my people—we can afford to be quite free with each other—I know', Katherine returned for five weeks to the blue Ripolin of Elgin Crescent. Poor Koteliansky. All he had from Katherine on her return was a request to put a letter to Beatrice in the post (it was not to be trusted to Murry) and within a few days he was getting a lecture from Lawrence: 'You *must* do something—anything. Really it is a disgrace to be as inert as you are.' Lawrence promised to send him *The Idiot* to read and asked if he had seen Katherine. By the beginning of May she was back at the quai aux Fleurs bombarding her darling 'Bogey' with affectionate longing.

It was almost her last stay in Paris. She was working hard now at what she intended clearly at this time to be a full-length novel, though it turned out to be the longest and most celebrated of her short stories. Her imagination had undoubtedly been stimulated and turned back to her New Zealand childhood by seeing her brother again in England. It is tempting to see her soldier brother as the true identity of the figure in khaki whom she reported meeting in a dream and identified as Murry—'very handsome and happy'. As she realised a day or two later the thought, with the slaughter only a hundred miles away, was a hideous one, even though Murry could still rely on his suspected T.B. against the growing demands for conscription. In the meantime Katherine realised that it was impossible for her to remain any longer at the quai aux Fleurs unless she was willing to throw in her lot with Carco, who announced that he was coming back on leave. A conversation overheard on the staircase, in which the concierge referred to her as 'la maîtresse de Francis Carco' made her pack her bags.

Katherine's return to London, towards the end of May, brought about what looked like a reconcentration of her life with Murry in a new house, 5 Acacia Road: a handsome early Victorian villa in a quiet, broad street which runs between Finchley Road and Avenue Road on the borders of St. John's Wood. Their belongings were retrieved from the damps of Rose Tree Cottage and the dismal flat in Elgin Crescent. There was a garden back and front and a servant called Mrs. Peach. Katherine's allowance had been increased. Koteliansky made a third and his artist friend Mark Gertler almost a fourth. Just about this time Kot and Murry had entered into a literary partnership with a publisher called Maunsel to produce a series of translations from the Russian at £20 apiece—Kot supplying the English version and Murry polishing it, dividing the fee between them. The agreement was to be the source of much subsequent trouble.

For the time being they were all being carried along in the wake of Lawrence and his mood of furious defiance—defiance not of the war itself but of the social system which he sensed would be fatally damaged by the war. There were to be lectures by Russell on Ethics and by Lawrence on Immortality, under the presidency of Lady Ottoline whose home at Garsington was to be turned into a kind of sanctuary. The Murrys, Lawrence insisted to the hesitant Ottoline, should also be part of it. But Lawrence's vision was far from being Russell's. Where Russell was arguing for liberal democracy, Lawrence conjured up visions of Platonic guardians, Samurai, angels released from the oppressions and sordidities that surrounded him. Russell disliked them all. He was taken to Kot's office at about that time, and the result (in Russell's words) does credit to nobody:

> He [D.H.L.] took me to see a Russian Jew Koteliansky, and Murry and Mrs. Murry—they were all sitting together in a bare office high up next door to the Holborn Restaurant, with the windows shut smoking Russian cigarettes without a moment's intermission, idle and cynical. I thought Murry *beastly* and the whole atmosphere of the three dead and putrefying. Then we went to the zoo. . . .

The outcome of it all was the strange little magazine *Signature*, of which the three numbers appeared in the autumn of 1915. It is important to remember that with all their knowingness, their experience, and their confidence in the life they had chosen (not the same as self-confidence) in the summer of 1915 Katherine and Murry were still only twenty-six. Lawrence led them by four years, and was barely thirty. They were not famous. They were detached from the main currents of war fever. They had no access to the popular press, and they had no money. Their strength, though it was the strength of a rebound, came from the same source, ultimately, as the general sense that the war would be won: a sense based on the fact, which at the same time they repudiated, that the open British society, mounted on worldwide power, could not fail.

The *Signature*, poorly produced by an East End printer found by Kot, who acted as business manager, lasted from Martinmas to St. Giles' and was almost entirely written by Lawrence, Murry, and Katherine (under a new alias 'Matilda Berry'). Brief though its span was—two issues in October and one in November—it bridged a decisive event in Katherine's life. The war insisted on its quota; on 7 October 1915 Lieutenant Leslie Heron Beauchamp was killed by a hand-grenade near 'Plug-Street Wood' in Flanders. The news reached Katherine four days later at Acacia Road and Murry, who was with her at the time, made a note in an exercise book[1] he had laid aside some months previously:

> Three minutes ago Tig had a telegram to say her brother is dead . . . I cannot believe it yet; and she cannot. That is the most

[1] The notebook in question is among the Koteliansky papers. How it got there is a matter for speculation. Perhaps it was just left behind at Acacia Road.

terrible of all. She did not cry. She was white and said: 'I don't believe it; he was not the kind to die.' And now she has gone off to Kay for news. When she was going she drank some wine to hold herself together. She opened her bag to look for the tele-gram: 'That will give me luck' she said. She wanted to know what day was the 7th. It was the day before she got his letter saying that he felt like a child of seven—the day she bought the badge of his regiment to wear. I don't know what will come to be now. I feel terrified of the future: he was so much to her; and that last letter——

The handwriting is neat and clear. What words of consolation he may have uttered are unrecorded, but there follows this confession:

How cool I am and cold. These things stupefy me? or do they not touch me in themselves?

'You know', Katherine wrote in her *Journal*, after hearing of 'Chummie's' death, 'I can never be Jack's lover again.'

Leslie Beauchamp had occupied a peculiarly sensitive place in Katherine's complicated affections. It was not an accident that she had given him the same pet name 'Bogey' as she bestowed on Murry just as she had given his first Christian name to L.M. and his second to her idealised home 'The Heron'. After his death she sent a poem about him to L.M., built round an image of poisoned berries—Berry was the name of a contemporary executioner, and the name, also, that Katherine had adopted for her articles in *Signature*. With the poison and the horror of her brother's death she was to be pushed further and further into reminiscences of childhood for inspiration:

> *By the remembered stream my brother stands*
> *Waiting for me with berries in his hands . . .*

❧ 8 ❧

Impressions of Bandol, Paris and Garsington

The death of 'Chummie' made Acacia Road unbearable to Katherine, and at almost the same moment the prosecution of *The Rainbow*, on which Lawrence had built such high hopes, drove him into plans for leaving London. The little group that had huddled for a moment round *Signature* was shattered. Acacia Road was let furnished to Kot's friend Farbman for the substantial rent of £7 10s a week, Kot himself retaining a room in the house he was now to inhabit for the rest of his life.[1] Very soon afterwards Katherine and Murry were on their way across the Channel— Katherine's seventh crossing that year. There was no stopping in Paris now. It was haunted by the presence of Beatrice and the recollection of Carco. They headed south through the bitter winter, and on 19 November Katherine was sitting in a café at Marseilles reporting her impressions to Kot. Her powers of observation, she found, were heightened, as always, by being abroad—not perceiving perhaps, that the heightening effect is due to thousands of tiny differences in the daily scene, rather than one's own capacities. On the mantelpiece of her hotel room she had placed a photograph of 'Chummie'.

Marseilles, packed with soldiers and appallingly cold, was no place to stay, and they pushed on along the coast to Cassis, finally establishing themselves in the Hôtel Beau Rivage, Bandol, which was as yet untouched by any sense of war. On the journey, wrote Katherine furiously, 'everybody cheated Murry *at sight*'. Her grief for her brother made her an impossible companion, and after only three weeks Murry gave up and made for England in response to an invitation to spend Christmas at Garsington with the Morrells.

---

[1] The tenancy agreement, in Katherine's hand and signed 'Katherine Murry' is among the Koteliansky papers. It is dated 11 November 1915.

From Lady Ottoline's description the last year or two had told on him:

> He was an odd remarkable-looking man, with a rather cavernous face, large unseeing vague dark eyes, and a lithe figure.

This is hardly the jaunty Murry of Lawrence's wedding photograph, taken less than two years previously.

He talked to Lady Ottoline about the beauty of his relationship with Katherine, who recalled him to Bandol by telegram a few days after Christmas. Lady Ottoline lent him five pounds for the fare, and soon afterwards received enthusiastic letters of thanks from them both—Murry assuring her that 'the moment that I knew you I felt that I had found a friend—well I must use our magic word again—*for toujours.*'

In his own account of this short stay in England, to which he devotes nine pages of his autobiography, Murry hardly mentions his stay at Garsington, and does not refer to Lady Ottoline at all. He chronicles in detail his contacts with Lawrence, who was packing up for a retreat to Cornwall, and with Koteliansky. Above all he was pondering his relationship with Katherine, and it is possible to infer from these pages that the possibility of a permanent break was in his mind. Looking back afterwards he decided that these were the weeks in which he and Katherine finally surrendered to each other and perhaps, from the copious letters they exchanged at that time, one can extract two fragments of realism on which they were able to build the happiness of the next few months together: his 'surely I might live on a tiny bit of your money'; and hers 'I hope you don't kiss anybody at Garsington'. As Murry observed, there had always till then 'been, in each, something that did not yield, something that claimed its freedom, and refused to say *toujours*'. And it was not said quite yet.

So followed the productive months at the Villa Pauline, Bandol. Katherine renewed her work on 'The Aloe', the longest piece she had ever attempted. Murry worked on improving Kot's versions of Shestov and Dostoevsky's letters and embarked on the book about Dostoevsky which Secker had commissioned long ago. They wrote, said Murry, on either side of the kitchen table, in sublime happiness.

Impressions of Bandol, Paris and Garsington

> *We might be fifty, we might be five,*
> *So snug, so compact, so wise are we.*
> *Under the kitchen table-leg*
> *My knee is pressing against his knee.*

So wrote Katherine. In March 1916 Sir Harold Beauchamp raised his daughter's allowance from £120 a year to £156; and the rent of Acacia Road was regularly remitted by Kot.

It is odd to think of them so close to each other physically, while she etches so painfully for the slightest detail, and he boldly strikes out into the most tremendous generalisations about the significance of Dostoevsky for the western world. His book is a *tour de force*. It runs to 55,000 words and was written in exactly five weeks.[1] It is true that it contains a good deal of quotation, and one must allow for the fact that the works he had by him for consultation were few: the novels themselves, in Constance Garnett's translation; *Letters from the Underworld* (Everyman Library); *The Journal of an Author* (in a French translation); and an English translation of a German translation of Dostoevsky's letters. Such was the equipment of an ambitious literary critic only sixty years ago.

Fyodor Dostoevsky, A Critical Study made Murry's reputation and perfectly exemplifies his methods. The assertions are bold, the utterances far-reaching. 'Dostoevsky is to be thought of more truly as an idea than as a man'; 'we cannot discern the new logic, but a sure instinct tells us that it exists to be discovered'; 'they are in time: those others have their being in a world beyond time'. The phrases drip onto the kitchen table like salad oil into a mayonnaise. Well might Hugh Kingsmill comment that Murry was like an auctioneer who would leave you, as the result of an unconsidered gesture, with a fragment of Blake or Keats or Dostoevsky that you did not really know what to do with. In *Fyodor Dostoevsky* Murry himself is rarely absent from the scene: 'There are times, when thinking about the spirits which he has conjured up—I use the word deliberately—I am seized with suprasensual terror. For one awful moment I seem to see things with the eyes of eternity, and have a vision of suns grown cold, and hear the echo of voices calling *without sound* across the waste and frozen universe.'

[1] Two postcards to Kot record its beginning and its conclusion.

J. W. N. Sullivan, who was then living in Montparnasse, and a little later came to know Murry well as the result of a common interest in Dostoevsky, makes it clear that the style of *Fyodor Dostoevsky* was also the man, Murry:

> [He] attracted and repelled me in about equal measure. On the whole I thoroughly distrusted and disliked him, and yet he could, at times, touch me more intimately than anybody else. He professed a great affection for me, meaning, I think, that I amused him, that my attitude to him flattered him, and that he also found me somehow pathetic. He made it almost a point of honour to be sentimental over anything he regarded as pathetic. He immensely valued his sentimentality; it made him feel more alive; and in order to awaken it he would sometimes use the vivisector's art with great subtlety and complete ruthlessness. . . . He had quite unusual and perfectly genuine insight which was often so singular and unexpected that one never felt quite safe in supposing that he was talking nonsense. He was perfectly aware of this insecurity in his hearer and it amused him to bully one into a pretended agreement with his most 'transcèndental' remarks. We had wonderful conversations, especially on Dostoevsky and the 'higher' consciousness. They would last for hours, and during them he would mount, as it were, from one transcendental height to another, the ascent culminating with some such remark as 'the inhuman is the highest form of the human', and in the ensuing silence he would gaze vaguely at a corner of the ceiling with a faint, wondering smile.[1]

The strength of the Dostoevsky book is not (in a phrase Murry himself would have been happy with) as a critical work, or, still less, as a literary biography. It is a candle for intense conversations, an encouragement to talk at large. Despite the author's apparent boldness ('Dostoevsky's novels are not novels at all') his only qualification is his having read Dostoevsky. The assertiveness has none of the voice of scholarly authority. He claims only that if his reader had as sensitive a soul as he had, he and the reader could soar in

[1] Murry reproduces this (without giving its source) in *Between Two Worlds* (p. 437). It is from Sullivan's autobiographical novel *But for the Grace of God*, pp. 152–3.

company. That, combined with a remarkable fluency and a solid grounding in the classics, is the secret of his success as a literary man. Creative literature was beyond him. He had failed in fiction, and in poetry. His contribution was criticism in the stirring manner.

Murry, in retrospect, considered the months at Bandol as the happiest of his life. Certainly they were months of effective achievement and a warm relationship with Katherine. But the letters he wrote back to Kot hardly reflect serenity. Kot, Murry clearly felt, was fussing unnecessarily about Maunsel's financial reliability. No, Murry would not write to Maunsel asking for an interim royalty statement on the last two translations; Kot did not understand the conventions of publishing. This assumption of authoritativeness about the commercial side of literature is characteristic of Murry, though his determination to have faith in the system sits curiously with his own experience over 'Stephen Swift' as a result of which he was still an undischarged bankrupt. Deep down in Murry there was an absence of scepticism, a willingness to accept situations rather than confront them, a dislike of making a fuss. Koteliansky, on the other hand, was never better than in confrontation, and the same was true of Katherine.

In Paris, Beatrice was living out her life among the artists, but was very far from having severed her connection with the *New Age*. The Impressions of Paris had continued almost throughout 1915 with characteristic verve and incisiveness.[1] That of 12 August, describing a tour through the villages to the south of Paris was among her very best. But that autumn, the autumn of Chummie's death, the autumn of Loos and the Dardanelles, she suddenly began to strike out too strongly against the tide for her reputation as a journalist. The subject she chose for her column of 18 November was the execution of Nurse Cavell, and the wave of emotion that had followed it. Even Bernard Shaw had shared in the wave, by suggesting Parliament should concede votes for women as a recognition of Nurse Cavell's sacrifice.

Beatrice was still, at this point, a vigorous supporter of the war

[1] 'Unparalleled in outspokenness', said the *Athenaeum* in June 1915. It added correctly, that 'Alice Morning wastes much of her superfluous—not to say essential—energy in various *New Age* bypaths'. Beatrice commented loyally that she could not 'admit anything wasted which is really *New Age*. I'm afraid I am all bypaths' (*New Age*, 22 July 1915).

and she had always been a passionate campaigner against capital punishment; but over Nurse Cavell she chose, with deliberation, to differ from almost everyone else:

> It is a difficult business [she began] to find words in which to express one's dissent from the plaudits of half the world. I am thinking of the case of Miss Cavell, and not only of the applause which has, for the moment, heroised her action, but of the action itself. This action seems to my mind to have been plainly wrong, and, perhaps, amidst so much hypocrisy and hysteria, the plainest expression will seem the least offensive.

The British and French, she pointed out, were perfectly prepared to shoot people—men or women—who had done what Edith Cavell had done. Nor was this wrong. No army at war could tolerate the activities of someone who systematically helped disabled enemies to escape and fight again. Her especial bile was reserved for Shaw: 'that man always turns me into a fishwife':

> If this person were a whole man, he would not always be inciting us to make men of ourselves.

Orage printed it, but it made him uncomfortable, and he wrote Beatrice what she later called a 'dignified letter', and after one further brief appearance the Impressions of Paris came to an end. But it was far from being the end of Beatrice in the *New Age*. Before very long she was writing a series of fantasticated fables. She was, as she put it, 'a person who must write or pine away', and for the moment she would write 'what diverts me'.

Her life with Modigliani was of course known to Orage, but from his side also, during the first part of 1916, came something which can hardly have pleased Beatrice. The *New Age* began to publish instalments of a kind of novel under the signature 'R. H. Congreve', which was one of Orage's best-known pen-names, normally contracted for his literary articles to 'R.H.C.'. It was called 'A Seventh Tale for Men Only' and dealt with the relationship of three serious-minded men, one of whom, 'Doran', is unquestionably Orage himself: 'brought up in an out-of-the-way village in Cambridgeshire', personally educated by the vicar and the eldest son of the squire who 'combined to distinguish him not only from the boys of the village but from boys of any normal type' so that 'at twenty-one, without boasting he felt himself to be at once outside and above the rest of human kind'. He was 'habitually absorbed in a kind of inarticulate meditation' and paid no attention to the ordinary life of the world. Doran was 'not unsociable . . . he mixed with other people; but all these things he did vegetatively rather than with self-conscious appetite. The normal world, in fact, passed as a dream in which he himself was a figure.' London, when he arrived there, was a revelation, 'like coming out of an egg', and he formed three resolutions: 'to understand human life at all costs to his feelings, his tastes and his predilections; to avoid no society and to seek none; to accept the first guide that offered itself.'

Doran has a mistress, a girl 'who looked as if she had been brought up in moonlight' whom he met by chance in an art gallery and accompanied home in accordance with his third principle. His two friends begin to notice her interest in other men, but the passive Doran, though he no longer cares for her, cannot bring himself to break with her. This curious struggle against escape, in which his two friends, rather like the comforters of Job, play an important part, is the central issue of the novel. The final crisis looks as if it owes something to the reality of the parting with Beatrice. The moon-girl grows more and more outrageous, and at last packs her suitcase and declares she is leaving—but will come back whenever she chooses. Doran is stung into saying that if she goes he will not have her back, and reflects the next moment that 'it is not what a woman says to a man that convinces him that all is over; but it is what he finally says to her'. The moon-girl leaves, saying as she goes, 'There are the makings of a man in you after all: but not for me.'

No doubt it hit Beatrice as hard as *Les Innocents* hit Katherine, to see her life with Orage, and perhaps her very words, thinly disguised as copy for her beloved *New Age*. Yet in the first half of 1916, some of the very numbers which carried 'A Seventh Tale for Men Only' printed no fewer than ten of her fantastic pieces[1] in

---

[1] 'Feminine Fables' (6 January 1916), 'The Style of the Peri' (13 January 1916), 'The Seat of Virtue' (20 January 1916), 'In Between Whiles' (27 January 1916), 'A Likely Lie' (3 February 1916), 'Conquering the Passions' (2 March 1916), 'Victoria' (9 March 1916), 'As It Fell Out' (16 March 1916), 'While the World Wags' (30 March 1916), 'Interlude' (4 May 1916).

which her ideas about women, men, society, and literary style were woven into the form of fables. Although she and the editor were estranged they were still, between them, providing as many columns of the *New Age* as ever, and while 'Feminine Fables' sometimes recall *The Maid's Comedy* their style also owes a good deal to Orage.

The central figure in these tales of the rue de Norvins is supernatural and flamboyant, and always female. If there are any male characters (in some stories there are none) they are vapid and contemptible. Her Peri is the invariable mistress of the situation, sometimes triumphing over the feeble males, sometimes successfully defying the world and its works, sometimes just chatting in the curiously arch style Beatrice had developed in *The Maid's Comedy*. 'I was becoming disconsolate at the decay of the short story, this decay being largely due to that great blot of a realist full-stop, Coherence. I meant to have a fling at Coherence; not, of course, that Coherence at which life works for generations and which the great dramatists re-create from cause to result, nor either that mad, merry Coherence which Mr. Wells made in his mad, merry days, but the kind which is manufactured a thousand times a week in as many magazines the world over, and which is nothing more necessary and profound than ten thousand writers' piling up of accident.' Her aim was the reverse of Katherine's passion to hold and etch some internally consistent scrap of perceived reality. To Beatrice experience had to be carried through the imagination before it could be expressed. At their best her Peri stories are vivid and effective: in one the glorious supernatural being twenty feet high, with jewelled claws insists on being transformed into an ordinary fashionable young lady—'Miss Perry'—and in another she is late getting back to paradise and decides to settle for an earthbound existence rather than pay the statutory penalty of a day spent looking at herself in a distorting mirror. Paradise is boring anyway—'the same dances and dulcimers, and sackbuts and sherbet. The same jealous conceited houris. The same old veils and earrings. The same old fallen angels boasting about their past glory.'

Like everything else Beatrice wrote, the Peri stories are wildly uneven: some are pure pastiche, some are so full of curlicues as to be difficult to follow—yet sometimes she rises to notable insights:

'Everything shows' [she makes her Peri say] 'that your mortals are wearied out of their dull existence and will have it changed, or perish here or hereafter. I think they will perish, however. . . . Poets, orators, clerks, and journalists—these are the equals of Kings, Courtiers, Bishops, and Judges.'

During 1916 her involvement with Modigliani still persisted. The painter did not actually share her little house in the rue de Norvins (he had a shed near by, where he painted) but when he was drunk he was known to batter down the shutters to get in. She maintained a kind of balance by cultivating another near neighbour, the homosexual poet Max Jacob, who was making it his duty to maintain, by correspondence, some kind of liaison between the Bohemians scattered by the war.[1] When Katherine Mansfield had noted 'the faithful M.' doing Beatrice's shopping, this was almost certainly Max Jacob and not Modigliani, who in any case was referred to as Dédo by Beatrice and her friends.

It was a most productive period for both Beatrice and Dédo: she with her almost weekly contributions to the *New Age* and he (for she kept him away from drugs, of which she had a horror) producing some of his finest paintings—many of them portraits of Beatrice herself.[2] But it was far from being the kind of idyll that was going forward at Bandol. Katherine had noted the brandy, Max Jacob commented on the whisky, which Beatrice was taking in increasing quantities. 'If I happened to be drunk too,' she wrote afterwards, 'there was a great scene. . . . Once we had a royal battle, ten times up and down the house, he armed with a pot and me with

---

[1] Max Jacob had many of the qualities of a saint. Of Jewish origin he became a devout Roman Catholic and perished at the hands of the Nazis towards the end of the Second World War. His charm, talent and gifts of friendship earned him not only friends but respect in Bohemia. Beatrice got him to write for the *New Age*. 'Max's anti-woman side was, and long remained, a secret from me,' Beatrice wrote later. 'He went to Mass at six every morning, worked every day in his famous den in the rue Gabriel, and came in between ten and eleven with all the news. . . . I think no one, not even the most obscene of fat-heads, ever thought sinfully of us two. We were taken for granted. A literary ménage' (*Madame Six II. Straight Thinker*, 6 February 1932). In some ways Max Jacob played the same part in the Bohemia of Paris as Kot played in the literary world of London.

[2] Four are listed by Franco Russoli in *Modigliani Drawings*. In addition there is an oil painting in the Ritter Foundation Collection (*see* Alfred Werner *Amadeo Modigliani*, Plate 93). Most are dated 1915.

a long straw brush. . . . How happy I was, up in that cot on the Butte.' Max Jacob spoke of 'scènes avec revolvers' but that came later.

Beatrice, Max Jacob, and Ilya Ehrenburg were among the readers of their own work at the celebration given to welcome the wounded Guillaume Apollinaire back from the front in July 1916. She read from a novel in progress (but now lost) entitled 'Minnie Pinnikin', and she read in French, which she now spoke exceptionally well— far better than Katherine. After more than two years of Paris she was committed to the adventure. She leaned on nobody, and could only fail herself. It was lucky for her that towards the end of 1916 she inherited—presumably on the death of her father—a small income.

Orage, the recipient of her strange contributions from Paris, including for a time an extraordinary series on French phonetics which he loyally published, no longer held court in the Chancery Lane A.B.C. but in the Domino Room at the Café Royal. The *New Age* was still a forum for almost any sort of unconventional view, and it still reflected the editor's willingness to back a name that had never been heard of or an idea that had never been ventured. But it was changing.

Orage was still a brilliant recruiting sergeant, even though he offered his recruits nothing but a little glory and a certain amount of training: the 'no pay' principle was still in force. Among them were some considerable names of the next generation of English literature and journalism: Edwin Muir, recruited first in 1913, when working as a wretchedly paid clerk in a Glasgow beer-bottling plant; Ivor Brown; Herbert Read; Ruth Pitter; C. E. M. Joad; Hugh Kingsmill; C. M. Grieve. But they were not the pith and marrow of the *New Age* in the early years of the war. This was provided, on the literary side of the magazine, by a very different group, who would never have fitted with Fabian socialism.

Pound continued to write thousands of words for the paper. Beatrice, signing herself 'Ninon de Longclothes' had a dig at him in 1915:

> *The apparition of Ezra at the party*
> *To his right the curling sandwiches*

> *And the fruits that are somehow watching—*
> *The apparition of Ezra*
> *Under the tree-branches triangularly waving . . .*
> *Ezra at the party, half friz, half nibble*
> *Ezra talking Art.*

Alongside Pound came T. E. Hulme whose 'Notebooks', written in the trenches but reflecting a modern and trenchant traditionalism, appeared regularly until his death in 1917; so close was Hulme's connection with Orage that when his unpublished manuscripts came to light in Frith Street in 1920 they were turned over to Orage. The third, and most influential of Orage's leading lights in 1916 and 1917 was the Spanish syndicalist, Ramiro de Maeztu, already an idealist in politics, and in the end to perish in the Spanish Civil War as a supporter of Franco.

In fact it can be seen in retrospect that the *New Age* was evolving away from Socialism as it is generally understood today. But this is to leave aside Guild Socialism, which was still the dominant theme of the political pages and the correspondence columns. Orage's old ally, A. J. Penty, had returned from America to strengthen the cause and was the paper's chief writer on the subject. The absence of any institutional mark left by the movement must not be allowed to conceal its importance as the counterpart, in socialist thought, to bureaucratic Fabianism. In the Fabian tradition control was conferred on the planner and the intellectual who, according to Beatrice Webb, would claim no privilege and no superiority except that arising from experience and intelligence. Guild Socialism proposed instead that control should rest with the incorporated workers and the Trade Unions, and the idea was in due course hammered out into a programme by G. D. H. Cole and others at a meeting in a Sussex inn, whence it is known as 'The Storrington Document'.

But although Guild Socialism (in the form of the National Guilds League) became a vigorous and organised movement during the last years of the war, its basic inspiration was capable of producing many different strains—and not all of them proved to be socialist. Penty's craft-based, romantic approach to the guild idea led him, and the paper, away from the stream of popular shop-floor agitation which was generated by the movement in the country, and to some extent Orage leaned to Penty's side. 'Why democratise it?' he asked Cole, 'the right thing is to give people a genuine idea and they will realise it in their own way.' Cole urged him to make the paper the official organ of the Guild Movement but Orage shied away.

Orage still reacted instinctively against making his paper the servant of any programme, and although he saw a great deal of the Guildsmen until the movement was finally destroyed by the effects of the Russian Revolution, with one fragment floating into the Communist Party and another towards notions of a 'corporate state', he allowed the paper to look at the notion of workers' control from all angles, and the contradiction between Syndicalism and Fabianism remains even now unsolved at the heart of Socialism. The heterodoxy of the *New Age* worried even Edwin Muir, who on Orage's instructions (and with startling consequences for his whole development) had conned and annotated the whole of Oscar Levy's edition of Nietzsche; but Muir was also the editor of the local Glasgow *Guildsman* and found it necessary 'to mitigate in it the exclusive note struck by the *New Age*'.

For Orage, Guild Socialism was, above all, rejection of the collectivism against which he had campaigned even in the days of Lloyd George's National Health Insurance. On that basis he was prepared to open his columns to craft enthusiasts such as Penty, Christian socialists such as Maurice Reckitt, romantic syndicalists such as de Maeztu, socialist theoreticians like Tawney and Cole, and Glasgow shop stewards who eventually became Communists. It was too wide a spread, and the *New Statesman*, not the *New Age*, was going to capture the next generation of radical young people; but the *New Age*, despite its socialist contradictions (against a ground base of T. E. Hulme's traditionalism) was undoubtedly the more lively of the two papers.

In April 1916 Orage received and printed a very curious piece from 'Alice Morning' headed 'Interlude'. It rambled cryptically and incoherently about life and letters. The only clear message was that the Peri had been discarded as a lunatic lay figure who would only do the things Beatrice made her do. But the title 'Interlude' was significant. What followed was a series of six articles, the first headed

'The Enemy in the House', and the remainder 'Peace Notes', which Orage courageously printed between 15 June and 10 August.

They are very far from incoherent, and constitute a determined, comprehensive, and vitriolic attack on the war and all it stood for. More than this, taken as a whole, they show Beatrice as having assembled a general attitude which was uncommon in her own time (especially at the height of the war) but became almost endemic some fifty years later: an alienation from traditional political authority and corporate English national consciousness; a revulsion from war; a distrust of national symbols of all sorts and of history; a conviction that the forces of the existing order cannot prevail against a true radical challenge; and what she called, in a striking phrase, the need for 'the endowment of women, whose existence is necessary though unmarketable' and 'the freedom of children from examiners, labour-masters, and magistrates'. The antagonist she selected was from the columns of the *New Age* itself—T. E. Hulme.

She plainly admits the original reasons for her support of the war: 'It used to be a stand-by that *they* began it ... our men who did not begin it were dead too; also the masculine delight in the adventure of war influenced us—this was something which we did not understand, but we accepted the fact; also we had no notion of modern war. ... Well there is no more stand-by in all that. The German youth now being thrown away at Verdun did not "begin it". ...' And from that point she passes on to a denunciation of the war which is remarkable for its eloquence and absence of cliché. She extends the hand of friendship to Shaw ('my old pet aversion') and roundly denounces Hulme and de Maeztu. 'But who has brought us to this position? The clique of politicians, financiers, certain militarists, and certain of the press, including most of the comic papers.'

The British, in particular, are to blame for it all. The French see through the British, with their sexual hypocrisy, their repressive policy in Ireland (Easter 1916 had clearly had a great influence on her) and their snobbery. 'Our virtues are deep', she observes in summing up what the French think of us, 'but what is the use of having virtues so deep that they only shine after years of acquaintance?' The French, she had become convinced, placed a higher value on the liberty of the individual: 'This *spirit* of civilisation and liberty is what one stays in France for.'

She is shrewdest when she looks forward to the consequences of victory. 'If Germany is badly beaten she will find more tolerance than we shall as victors.' And again, 'There is no possibility of occupying, even if you were a conqueror. The conquered are too cunningly modern. In ten years they absorb you, recapture their parliament, make you seem a boor and a bully, and laugh at your exasperated efforts to make a graceful exit.' As for women, 'Women should have no employment in war. In striking at men who do not wish to shed blood, the master madmen of the world are striking at civilisation, but in menacing women on this matter they are striking at Nature. It is in Nature that a woman turned from pity is worse than a man. Women should have nothing to do with war but to speak against it.'

It does Orage great credit that he had the courage to print not just one, but five of these unpalatable articles which flew in the face of the general public mood and denounced the views and even the good faith of two of his most valued contributors. The articles were within the guide-lines of the law[1] but they must surely have lost him readers and attracted the unfavourable notice of the authorities. Clearly from the garbled account she has left, he expostulated with Beatrice; and the 'Peace Notes' for 10 August 1916 were the last of her contributions to the *New Age* for some time.

Though life for the Murrys at Bandol had been happy and productive, it had also been hard. Apart from Katherine's allowance and the rent of Acacia Road they had nothing but intermittent shillings for Murry's reviews in the *Daily News* and the *Westminster*—which were rare because Murry could no longer visit the galleries or pick over the new books arriving at the newspaper offices.[2] It

[1] The guide-line (announced formally in 1917 but the general rule came some time earlier) was that 'the expression of the view that the war could have been avoided by better statesmanship, or that it should be ended straightway by negotiation' was to be tolerated. But would even this extend to some of Beatrice's wilder passages? 'The nation is led away to slaughter and be slaughtered, having, of course, been educated to consider man-slaughter in war as something worthy of a medal and death in battle as the greatest service a man can render to civilisation, not to mention his wife and children.'
[2] The invariable custom of the humbler free-lance reviewer right down to the thirties.

meant not much more than a pound a week for housekeeping, and a reason for going back to England. There were other reasons as well. *Still Life* was going the rounds of the publishers,[1] and the Dostoevsky book had to be seen through the press; and Lawrence was developing plans for a communal life in Cornwall.

Murry rather suggests that he obliged Lawrence by falling in with the idea, though as he truthfully says, 'Katherine distrusted the very idea of a community'. Lawrence had discovered a group of cottages seven miles from Penzance on the north coast, called Higher Tregerthen, 'a tiny granite village nestling under high, shaggy moor-hills, and a big sweep of lovely sea beyond'. But until March the invitation can hardly be said to have been pressing, and they had hinted a return in the spring in any case.

'Dont bind yourselves in the *Least* about the house', Lawrence wrote in February at the end of a letter devoted to advice about Dostoevsky, which was not incorporated in Murry's book. 'This I cannot stomach', wrote Lawrence on this point. 'People are not fallen angels, they are merely people. But Dostoevsky used them all as theological or religious units . . . they are bad art, false truth.'

Lawrence's next letter, in March, was certainly more urgent. He was writing *Women in Love*. True, the cottages were more or less derelict (he enclosed a map) but there was a woman who would do the cleaning and there was a tower where Lawrence had already located Katherine's study. One must remember that Lawrence knew Murry a great deal better than he knew Katherine; and they had been both warned as long ago as December 1915 of the perils of communal life with the Lawrences. 'My dear Katherine', Lawrence had written then:

> you know that in this we are your sincere friends, and what we want is to create a new, good, common life, the germ of a new social life together. That is what we want. But we must grow from our deepest underground roots, out of the *unconsciousness* [perhaps Lawrence had been reading the contemporary popularisation of Freud in the *New Age*] not from the conscious concepts which we falsely call ourselves. Murry irritates and falsifies

---

[1] It was published later in the year, yielding a minimum of impact and £8 in royalties.

me, and I must tell him so. He makes *me* false. If that must always be so, then there is no relation between us. But we must try that there is a living relation between us, all of us, because then we shall be happy.

Lawrence could be both wise and inconsistent: inconsistent in asking a man whom he distrusted to share his life; wise in perceiving the literary self-consciousness and ambition that propelled both the Murrys.

This second effort at communal life was unpromising from the start. Katherine had hated leaving Bandol, the journey had been long and exhausting, and when she arrived at the inn at Zennor— the Tinner's Arms—she knew she was going to hate it all. She had been told by Lawrence what to expect as long ago as January:

> The world is gone, extinguished, like the lights of last night's Café Royal—gone for ever. There is a new world with a new thin unsullied air and no people in it but newborn people: moi-même et Frieda.

No Katherine, she must have reflected, and no Murry. Only moi-même.

It was not, and could not have been a success. The roof of her tower leaked. The little maid, known as 'the Cornish Pasty', lacked every grace and Katherine swore she could 'hear her *ankles* clumping about in the kitchen'. The boulder-strewn landscape, which Lawrence had assured Katherine she would love, she found hateful. 'It is not a really nice place', she wrote seeking her usual solace in a letter to Kot. 'It is so full of huge stones, but I do not care . . . it is very temporary. It may all be over next month; in fact it will be.' In fact it was. 'They are too tough for me to enjoy playing with.' Early in June the Murrys departed for a different cottage at Mylor, on the south coast, leaving behind not only the boulders and the leaks but the terrible quarrels between Lawrence and Frieda, which were regularly followed by placidity on both sides; and their images incorporated in *Women in Love*.[1]

[1] Yet even two years later, when Virginia Woolf rented the Higher Tregerthen cottages, Katherine's recollection had been purged: 'Perhaps the house itself is very imperfect in many ways but there is a . . . something . . . which makes one long for it. Immediately you get there you are *free*, free as air . . . I mustn't talk to you about it. It bewitched me.' To Virginia Woolf, 29 April 1919. *KML* 228.

There had been other reasons besides Lawrence's rages and Katherine's sense of being left out, that had made Murry uncomfortable. Even at the tip of Cornwall there was no escaping the war. Conscription had been introduced, and on 18 April a policeman had appeared to arrest Murry for avoiding enlistment. The two-year-old certificate showing 'pleurisy, suspected T.B.' was duly produced, but failed to impress. He had to go to Bodmin, was classified B2, and told to hold himself in readiness for home service. Although he now picked up with his reviewing again (mainly for *The Times Literary Supplement*) it becomes fairly clear that Murry was glancing uneasily towards such influential friends as he possessed, the chief of these being Lady Ottoline Morrell.

The failure at Higher Tregerthen left a lasting poison between Lawrence and the Murrys. It was not just that Lawrence used the opportunity to immortalise Katherine as Gudrun and Murry as Gerald in *Women in Love*; or even his furies, in the course of one of which (according to Murry) he described Murry as 'an obscene bug that was sucking away my life'.[1] The trouble was that the Murrys wanted conventional literary success, and Lawrence, with a schoolmasterish shrewdness, had spotted it. At the same time Murry hoped for some advantage from Lawrence's almost unmanageable creative gift, and Lawrence was quick enough to spot that too. To the end of his life Murry remained fascinated by Lawrence, and disappointed that things could not have been managed better.

Now there was much travelling between Mylor and London, with Murry renewing his literary contacts and casting about for work that would keep him out of the army. As he put it a little later, 'I was not going to meet the war a step nearer than I could help.' Literary work, the work he felt qualified to do, was what he ought to do. Not that he did not feel, as he was careful to note, a reasonable measure of patriotism and national pride; and the war itself was not

---

[1] The authority for this remark as applied to Murry rests entirely on Murry himself (*Between Two Worlds*, p. 416). Whether this does him credit or not is a nice question. But it may be wrongly reported. In a letter to Koteliansky which vividly describes a quarrel between Lawrence and Frieda (11 May 1916) Katherine records Lawrence as using this very phrase against Frieda.

wrong. It was simply irrelevant to his personal situation.[1] This was
the mood in which he and Katherine went to stay with Lady
Ottoline at Garsington in August 1916. The company included
Keynes, Clive Bell, and Lytton Strachey—all intellectual opponents
of the war; and J. T. Sheppard, later Provost of King's, who was
then working for M.I.7, a section of the War Office concerned with
information and propaganda.

The Murrys were a great success at Garsington. Lady Ottoline
had been following their fortunes through her correspondence with
Lawrence, who had assured her Cornwall was too bleak for them.
'They should have a soft valley, with leaves and the ring-dove
cooing. And this is a hillside of rocks and magpies and foxes.'
Katherine reminded Lady Ottoline by turns of an early Renoir and
a Japanese doll; and they captivated everyone by their romantic
accounts of their early literary life together. One would scarcely
recognise the humble cottage at Runcton in 'the large house in the
country' (hired by the adventurous and scampish Murrys) where
they lived for some months, going every Sunday to church, where
Murry would read the lessons, with the villagers touching their
hats to them, enjoying the fun of being Landlord and Landlady,
and then decamping leaving rent and tradesmen and gardeners
unpaid; and another time, 'they had a piano on the three years hire
purchase system . . .'. Lady Ottoline was not wholly taken in. She
wished she had known Katherine 'before the ambition of being an
artist and a great writer, and of using people for that end, had
become such an absorbing game'. 'She speaks', Lady Ottoline went
on, 'as if she and Murry belonged to some sacred order superior and
apart from other people.' Murry, however, she found 'very
sympathetic' though she noticed, as others had done, a 'queer blank
way of looking out as if he saw nothing, as if his eyes were turned
in on himself'. Gertler, Kot's painter friend, who was also at

---

[1] See the passage in which he analyses his feelings on this subject in *Between
Two Worlds*, pp. 426–7. 'I would die if—the case is hardly conceivable—the
battle were being waged against a tyranny which would deny me the right to
do the work I can do. No other battles concern me. Their results do not interest
me. . . . Nor do I pretend that I dont have any patriotic feelings, or national
pride. I have, and I dont crush them, for I dont see why I should. But, though
they are real, they are utterly negligible as compared to the really profound
feelings I have about the work to be done.'

Garsington that August pooh-poohed any possibility of an association between Ottoline and Murry: 'Of course it is *not* true.'

Kot was slowly, and in a series of black depressions, moving
towards the unusual, even unique, position he was to occupy in
literary life. He was still chained to the Law Bureau in High Holborn, which he detested, but with the collaborative translations with
Murry and the growing passion for all things Russian, he was beginning to be recognised not only as a translator but as a finder of new
Russian material. He was also the recipient of demands from
Lawrence that he should not feel guilty—it was the world, not Kot,
that was to blame for his unhappiness—as well as small remittances
to be laid out in cheap editions of *Nana*, *The Last of the Mohicans*,
Herman Melville and Captain Marryat, for dispatch to Higher
Tregerthen. His compliance was followed by a furious denunciation
to Catherine Carswell of all things Russian and an outburst of
Anglo-Saxon literary patriotism:

> It amazes me [wrote Lawrence] that we have bowed down and
> worshipped these foreigners as we have.... They are all—
> Turgenev, Tolstoi, Dostoevsky, Maupassant, Flaubert—so very
> *obvious* and coarse, beside the lovely, mature, and sensitive art of
> Fenimore Cooper and Hardy.

Murry was back in London by September. It seems that he had
impressed J. T. Sheppard with his languages and powers of expression, and something was said to somebody. In September 1916,
with Katherine anxiously following his success, Murry called for
an interview at the War Office and was taken on as a member of
M.I.7 to assist in the compilation of the *Daily Review of the Foreign
Press*, a digest which was circulated every day in Whitehall. The
salary was more than he had ever earned before—five pounds a
week—and his dilemma between serving in the army and doing the
work he was qualified to do was solved.

Lady Ottoline and her friends disdained the war, and indeed were
willing to make sacrifices to defy its encroachment on their lives;
but they did not hate it as Lawrence did. There is a sense in which
Murry's reception into Garsington (which was unaffected by his
work in M.I.7) was a decisive step into established circles and a move
away from the isolated defiance generated among the boulders of

Higher Tregerthen. The two camps were at odds about other matters too. Lady Ottoline, gathering that she was the villainess of *Women in Love*, had dropped Lawrence, and at the same time Bertrand Russell, her received lover, had quarrelled with Lawrence irretrievably. Lawrence's flirtations with the higher reaches of society were over, but Murry remained taken up. The links between the two men remained, but they were watched by both with a measure of distrust.

At Christmas the Murrys came again to Garsington and were very much the centre of attention. Katherine provided a charade called 'The Laurels' in which Murry played a 'Dostoevsky' character. The possibility of a comedy between him and Lady Ottoline was growing closer. So was the possibility of something between Katherine and Ottoline's partner Russell. Katherine had met him again that summer, when she showed him some of her work and assured him of the high value she put in their friendship, and Russell's earlier unfavourable impression seems to have undergone some change. On returning from the Garsington Christmas the letters from Katherine became distinctly more enthusiastic. Quite conceivably it was all put on as a counter-irritant. At any rate the budding affair came to nothing, and Russell was rather surprised when he came across the letters some thirty years later. 'My feelings for her', he commented, 'were ambivalent; I admired her passionately, but was repelled by her dark hatreds.'

There had been another important consequence of the Garsington summer. Katherine had impressed Lytton Strachey. 'Decidedly an interesting creature', he had written condescendingly to Virginia Woolf in July, 'very amusing and mysterious. She spoke with great enthusiasm about *The Voyage Out* and said she wanted to make your acquaintance more than anyone else's. So I said I thought it might be arranged.' The seed thus planted fructified early in 1917 at a dinner-party of the Woolfs at which the Foreign Office man Sidney Waterlow made a fifth to the Woolfs and the Murrys. Another ambivalent relationship was formed. Virginia was both attracted and repelled by Katherine.

In spite of his qualms about the war, Murry was well adapted to the work of M.I.7, and within a few months he had risen to be editor of the *Daily Review* at twice his original salary. It never seems to have occurred to him that in his success he was fulfilling the ambitions of the father he had always resisted. He even began to mingle with politicians, and nearly burned his fingers by becoming involved with a group of M.P.s who were attracted by the idea of a separate peace with Austria–Hungary.

Mylor, of course, had been given up, and in September 1916 the Murrys had moved a step closer to Lady Ottoline and her Bloomsbury friends by taking rooms on the first floor of a house belonging to Keynes in Gower Street which was known as 'The Ark' from the variety of its inhabitants. The upper floors were inhabited by Dorothy Brett and Lytton Strachey's friend Dora Carrington. It was very convenient for Murry's work at Watergate House, Adelphi, the home of M.I.7, where he was finding new friends: 'I don't believe a nicer set of educated Englishmen could have been gathered together.' They included Ronald Knox and Adrian Boult, and in the spring of 1917 Murry recruited the journalist, musician and scientist J. W. N. Sullivan, from the Montparnasse Bohemia. Murry was also able to do a good deal of literary work on his own account, both as a regular reviewer of French books for *The Times Literary Supplement* and for H. J. Massingham's the *Nation*, where he formed a close friendship with H. M. Tomlinson and his brother Philip. Altogether these months, though passed over briefly by Murry in his autobiography, mark further steps in his transition towards respectability. He no longer had to agonise over money, or take any literary job on offer.

But Katherine did not care for 'The Ark', and in particular did not get on with Carrington. In the spring of 1917 the ménage was once more broken up. Murry went to live in rooms in Redcliffe Road, Kensington, and Katherine, with the support of the devoted L.M., who had returned from Rhodesia to work in a munitions factory, established herself in a cavernous, damp studio in Chelsea. L.M., rising at 5.30 each day, set out from her house in Hampstead to her work making aeroplane parts in Chiswick, and returned to Chelsea in the evening to look after Katherine.[1] With Murry so heavily occupied, it was perhaps natural that Katherine should have renewed her old contacts, and notably with Orage.

[1] There was, perhaps, another reason for this particular separation. At last Katherine was managing to obtain a divorce from Bowden, and all could have been ruined, as the law then stood, if the King's Proctor had been able to show that she was living with Murry.

❧ 9 ❧

Katherine and her Destiny

Bohemian life was beginning to tell on Beatrice. A friend who had known her when she was first in Paris and had commented on her good looks and curly hair now said 'she was more haggard than Modigliani'. And she and the painter were beginning to drift apart. He had met the naïve young model, Jeanne Hébuterne whom he was later, disastrously, to marry; and Beatrice had taken up with another Italian artist named Alfredo Pina,[1] and this was followed by an explosion of jealousy. 'Modigliani suspected me; but he never knew distinctly of what until I abandoned him.' The dénouement came at a party given by Marie Wassilieff, one of the patronesses of Parisian Bohemia, to celebrate the return of Braque from the trenches, on leave. Beatrice was invited with her new lover, and a guest records:

> the doors burst open, and there was a whole band of painters and models who had not been invited. Pina, when he saw Modigliani, drew a revolver, and pointed it at him. I seized the gun by mere strength, forced him out of the room, and he rolled down the stairs.

But Beatrice's alliance with Pina does not seem to have lasted long. She was nearly forty, and claimed to have had as many lovers as her years and could bear no more. The charm, the aggressiveness, and the waywardness begin to give way to embitterment and touches

[1] Alfredo Pina was born in Milan in 1883 and studied under Rodin in Paris. From 1911 he exhibited in the salon of the Société de l'Art Français and later in the Salon des Indépendants and the Salon des Tuileries. His work (mainly portrait busts and figurines) may be seen in the Metropolitan Museum, New York and the Galleria d'Arte Moderna in Rome. A more conventional artist than Modigliani, but not contemptible, despite his curious name. The beginning of Beatrice's affair with Pina was noted by Katherine as early as March 1915, when she writes to Murry that 'She has dismissed M and transferred her virgin heart to P.' (26 March 1915).

of paranoia. These last had been reinforced by her removal, at the end of 1916, from the list of those who received free copies of the *New Age*: no doubt it was no more than a measure of economy by an editor who was increasingly beset by rising costs, but Beatrice took it as dismissal. She might no longer love Orage, but she loved the paper to the bitter end.

Her cup would have been full if she had known of Katherine's reappearance in the *New Age* during the first part of 1917 with no fewer than six stories.[1] 'That incredibly vulgar stuff', Beatrice later wrote furiously, 'that I rejected.' In this she was wrong. The stories were the product of the last few years, though they were certainly not among Katherine's best. In her damp Chelsea flat, attended in the evenings by L.M., she was working at turning 'The Aloe', which had been mostly written at Bandol, into 'The Prelude' for Leonard and Virginia Woolf's new publishing venture, the Hogarth Press. It was probably her greatest achievement both in powers of evocation and of technical accomplishment. Her opening paragraph, in which she manages to introduce no fewer than seven of her main characters without any apparent effort or crowding of her canvas is a masterpiece of stage-craft and economy. It was finished by the summer, and she spent the latter part of August with the Woolfs at Askeham, and the friendship with Virginia developed. But there was menace in the bread-and-butter letter Katherine wrote Virginia afterwards. 'It is really very curious and thrilling that we should both, quite apart from each other, be after the same thing. We are, you know. There's no denying it.'

Towards Murry, living not far away in Redcliffe Road, she alternated between dramatic passion and mordant insight. 'I want nobody but you', she was swearing in May, 'for my lover and my friend, and to nobody but you will I be faithful.' The letter is self-consciously amorous: 'Your creamy warm skin, your ears cold like shells are cold.' The next moment she was skewering him with her shrewdness: 'Sometimes when you write you seem to abuse yourself like Dostoevsky did. It's perfectly natural to you, I know, but Oh my God, don't do it. Is it your desire to torture yourself or to

[1] They all appeared in May and June 1917: 'Two Tuppenny Ones Please', 'Late at Night', 'The Black Cap', 'The Common Round', 'A Picnic', 'Mr. Reginald Peacock's Diary'. Beatrice specifically refers to her unawareness of Katherine's reappearance until 1931.

pity yourself, or something far subtler? I only know it's tre-
mendously important because it's your way of damnation . . . when
certain winds blow across your soul they bring the smell from that
dark pit and the uneasy sound from those hollow caverns, and you
long to lean over the dark swinging danger and just not fall in. . . .'
It was too true. Murry could not help tempting providence and
then complaining that he was singled out as a victim.

The decree nisi dissolving her marriage to Bowden with a six
months' delay was pronounced in October 1917, almost at the same
time as the manuscript of 'The Prelude' was delivered to the Woolfs,
whereupon Murry, with the prospect of marriage before him at last,
fell ill with suspected lung trouble and took two months' sick leave
at Garsington Manor. But Katherine's health was worse than his.
Early in August she had been complaining to Virginia about
'rheumatics plus ghastly depression' and by the autumn she was
consulting doctors, one of whom established what had probably
been present for some time—a patch on her right lung. This, she
wrote to Murry at Garsington just before Christmas, 'confirms him
in his opinion that it is absolutely imperative that I go out of this
country and keep out of it all through the future winters'. And that
was what, in spite of the war and the prospect of marriage, she
intended to do.

Murry's stay at Garsington exposed him to important influences
which included the renewed study of Keats and the increasing
interest of Lady Ottoline. 'It was in November 1917, in the drawing-
room at Garsington Manor', he records with an echo of Gibbon[1]
that can scarcely not have been conscious, that he encountered
Sidney Colvin's life of Keats and reread *Hyperion*. Lady Ottoline
adds that she lent him Colvin's book, but whatever were the details,
the idea that the poetry of Keats contained the ultimate truth
'started to his mind' and the plan of his most successful work,
Keats and Shakespeare began to be formed. He was 'thrilled with
the ecstasy of discovery' but he was embarrassed by his hostess,
who has herself described the comedy. Encouraged, late one even-

---

[1] 'It was at Rome, on the 15th of October, 1764, as I sat musing among the
ruins of the Capitol, while the bare-footed friars were singing vespers in the
Temple of Jupiter, that the idea of writing the decline and fall of the city first
started to my mind' (Gibbon, *Memoirs of My Life and Writings*).

ing, by an enquiry from Murry 'whether he might come into her heart' she strolled hopefully with him in the moonlit garden, and was told that he and Katherine believed in her and that they were beginning to be recognised as the most important literary authorities in England. 'If *we* believe in you, it shows you are of value.' This was not at all what Lady Ottoline, the daughter of a duke and the wife of a wealthy M.P., expected or liked to hear, and she found the reference to Katherine especially irritating. She tried to change the conversation to a more personal note, whereupon Murry, now seriously scared, took refuge in his bedroom and left abruptly next morning. The worst of it was when Ottoline learned that he had reported to Katherine the dangers he had escaped. That was unbearable. 'Now you must leave me alone, Katherine and Murry', wrote the mortified Ottoline in her diary, 'I bang the door of my life in your face.'

There were many reasons why the apparent penetration of 'Bloomsbury' intellectual society by Katherine and Murry was never effective, despite its promising beginnings. Russell disliked Murry, and Katherine he distrusted. Virginia shuddered at Katherine's pushing artificiality and was jealous of her direct competition. Murry's absurd arrogance about his own and Katherine's literary prestige did him nothing but harm in the estimation of Keynes, Strachey and Russell—and there was an element of adventurism about them both which might be amusing but implied an absence of cash and possibly of scruple. As a result Murry was always to be on the edge of high intellectual society, never wholly admitted, and never, despite his intense application, able quite to sustain the high place in literature he felt impelled to claim.

At bottom the barrier was social, even moral, as Virginia made clear: 'We could both [she and Leonard] wish that our first impression of KM was not that she stinks like a—well—civet cat that had taken to street walking. I'm a little shocked by her commonness at first sight; lines so hard and cheap.' L.M. came to fetch Katherine from this dinner-party—'another of the females on the border-line of propriety and naturally inhabiting the underworld'. That word 'underworld' nevertheless shows what fascinated Virginia about the Murrys: people who had to make their way by writing, and were marked by it. Yet the relation between the two women, though 'almost entirely founded on quicksands', as Virginia wrote, was to persist.

Rooted in Acacia Road Koteliansky made no such claims and incurred no such criticisms. He was uncreative, a finder of works to be translated and a translator who prepared a first draft for more famous names to polish. He had no loves, except the vision of the girl in gumboots, and he was tortured increasingly by dark moods of depression which brought him to the verge of suicide; but no friend ever doubted him. He did not try to belong, but the correspondence from the Woolfs, the Garnetts, and Katherine, flowed on, not with condolence, but for support. Kot was developing into their conscience and felt a duty, whatever it cost him, to receive and transmit their complex communication with one another. As for the relationship with Murry, however, it had been marred by perpetual bickerings over translation. Murry had brought it to what looked like a final quarrel in June 1917 in a typical letter: 'I shall always have a warm memory of you—but right down at the bottom, I cannot understand you and I'm just as certain you cannot understand me. So it is well that we should go our separate ways for ever. I could have wished—and you too I do not doubt—that the parting had been less sordid.'

Early in January 1918 Murry saw Katherine off once more at Victoria Station, crowded with soldiers on their way back to the never-ending slaughter. Her destination was Bandol of happy memory and the possibility of health. She was to be back in April when the decree nisi would be absolute and she could marry Murry. And she was meditating one of her most celebrated stories, which became 'Je ne Parle pas Français'.

It was intended as a revenge on Carco, for which she had ample justification. In 1916 he had published a novel *Les Innocents* about the half-world between delinquency and bohemianism in Paris. The hero 'Milord' is an apache, and the principal female character is unquestionably Katherine: 'une petite femme menue, gracieuse avec froideur et dont les immenses yeux noirs se posaient partout à la fois'. She embarks on a dangerous, condescending, and in the end unsuccessful affair with the apache, who prefers his shabby, devoted prostitute girl-friend in Nevers. The thinly disguised Katherine with her flat on the quai aux Fleurs (it was Carco's own

flat), and her obtrusive literary professionalism, has a friend whom
he impudently christened 'Beatrice'. The 'Beatrice' of the novel
bears no resemblance to Beatrice Hastings at all. The interest of the
character is that 'Beatrice' is the real Beatrice transmitted through
Katherine. Beatrice herself convincingly makes the point: 'The
monkey talked so incessantly about me that Carco used my beautiful
name for his blonde, fat glutton.'

The portrait of Katherine is shamelessly recognisable: her un-
grammatical French, her obsession with writing, her artificial
amorousness, her sense of drama, are all there, but set against an
instinctual, animal lover whose argot is barely comprehensible, and
whose morality, sometimes touching, has been acquired in street-
gangs and brothels. Worse still, Carco had used Katherine's letters,
and by using them showed she had used more than one touch in
them for other correspondents as well. Carco, as Beatrice later
wrote, 'had a head as well as a pen', and 'regarded her [Katherine]
as belonging to the "floating consciences" [consciences flottantes]
around a rigid ego, and potentially dangerous'. Katherine was not
to meet Carco again for a long time, and then only once.

In 'Je ne Parle pas Français', which she wrote at Bandol that
spring, Katherine tells the story of her first encounter with Carco
during her excursion with Murry in 1913. The first part was completed in only a month, by February, and immediately sent to Murry
for comment. He of course, the man she was soon to marry, was one
of the trio in the story, and he now had to consider a scene in which
he is not only cut out by a corrupt literary tramp, but retreats
ignominiously. Katherine need have had no anxiety about her
request for 'a frank opinion'. The reply came in a magnificently
jumbled telegram:

STHRY RECEIVID MAFNIFIIENT MURLY

The narrator of 'Je ne Parle pas' is a corrupted version of Carco,
so that the whole scene can be viewed through a haze of pretentiousness in strong contrast to the purity and innocence of the child's
vision of Katherine's New Zealand household which she adopted
for 'The Prelude'. The seducer fails with the naïve heroine 'Mouse',
and there are moments when his vulgarity, and his ultimate repen-
tance, become almost stagey. The arrows strike nearer the mark

with Mouse's helpless boy-friend 'Dick' (Murry) whose cowardice and clumsiness culminate in a farewell letter which perfectly captures her fiancé's style:

> Mouse, my little Mouse. It's no good. It's impossible. I can't see it through. Oh I do love you Mouse, but I can't hurt her. . . . Oh God! I can't kill my mother! Not even for you. Not even for us. You do see that—don't you?

That last wheedling phrase, 'You do . . . don't you', or 'You will . . . won't you?' recurs again and again in letters as one of Katherine's own favourites.

Between them, as Katherine herself recognised, 'The Prelude' and 'Je ne Parle pas', written within a few months of one another, bridge the whole of her literary range and personal experience. The first, with its lamplight and lawns, conventional but rounded people with limited ambitions, tiny childish adventures and exact observation, all seen through the eyes of a child, throws the discreditable Bohemia of 'Je ne Parle pas' into sharp relief. One stood for the impregnably secure network of Empire, where everything worked, and the other was the doubtful world in which Katherine was determined to succeed. 'The Prelude' is warm and nostalgic, sympathising even with the faults of its characters; 'Je ne Parle pas' is harsh and unforgiving, and its characters come out of the dark to vanish into it again. 'Dick' is fatuous, 'Raoul' is predatory, 'Mouse' is at a loss. Yet in the end Katherine cannot resist the sentiment of making the predator obsessed with the recollection of his victim: 'Mouse! Mouse! Where are you?' he is made to cry in his dingy café when it is all over, 'Are you near? Is that you leaning from the high window and stretching out your arms for the wings of the shutters? Are you this bundle moving towards me through the feathery snow? Are you this little girl pressing through the swing doors of the restaurant? Is that your dark shadow bending forward in the cab?' Proust was writing of Swann's obsession with Odette at very nearly the same time in similar terms, but avoided the cloying note that obtrudes in Katherine's evocation.

She really seems to have believed—such was her detachment from current events—that she would find Bandol the same welcoming place in January 1918 as in those happy days three years earlier.

The journey, of course, was fearful, and she sent back a long account of it to Murry: Serbian officers, the mistral, officialdom, missed connections, the riot at Marseilles railway station, but one miserable sentence about her final arrival at Bandol stands out: 'Nobody remembered me at all.'

Unawares, on the awful journey south, she had passed someone who would have remembered her very well, travelling on the same railway northwards.[1] Beatrice, for some reason, had been visiting Marseilles and describes a snowbound journey to Lyons in the *New Age* for 17 January 1918. The piece has all, and more than all, the vividness that Katherine managed in her letters to Murry about her journey. And as in Katherine's account everything is there— the mistral, the broken windows, the missed connections, the mixed company.

At last Katherine did find one or two old acquaintances, one of whom greeted her with, 'Ah! Ah! Vous êtes beaucoup changée. Vous avez été *ben* malade n'est ce pas? Vous n'avez plus votre air de petite gosse vous savez!' And ill indeed she was. Sometimes she made light of it in the long sprightly letters she wrote every day to Murry, and sometimes she bluntly said she felt 'bloody ill'. Naturally the news seeped through to others, notably L.M., who immediately decided to leave her job at the aircraft factory, break down all official barriers, and set out for the south of France to succour her friend.

The consequences form the most unattractive episode in Katherine's story. She conceived an almost insane idea that L.M. was planning to alienate her from the intended marriage to Murry. 'What the HELL *does* it mean?' she wrote on hearing L.M. had set out. 'What *can* it mean? She's a revolting hysterical ghoul. She's never content except when she can eat me.' To L.M., 'the decision came from within me, not from common sense', though as events were to show common sense had its claims too. After the same appalling journey as Katherine's she arrived at Bandol on 12 February and was met on the steps of the Hôtel Beau Rivage by a frosty Katherine and the greeting 'What *have* you come for?'

[1] It is just conceivable, though improbable, that Beatrice's journey to Marseilles was connected with Katherine's expedition. That Katherine does not mention it is no proof against it, but in the absence of any evidence to the contrary I have preferred to make it coincidence.

Katherine's behaviour during those three months—for reasons that will shortly be understood—was hardly rational. She was possessed by hyper-activity, by her delusions about L.M., and by dreams which she treated as reality. Altogether in ninety-three days Murry received from her nearly 100 letters and eleven telegrams, and she was in agonies if he missed a post or a letter was delayed even for a day or two. She invented an imaginary child for herself and Murry and christened it 'Rib' or 'Ribni': usually 'Rib' was supposed to be living with Murry, so that his 'mother' could address him in her letters, but sometimes he was with Katherine, and she could enclose a letter from 'Rib' along with one of her own. And she invented a house, 'The Heron' (called after her dead brother's middle name) where she, Murry, and 'Rib' were going to live a life of unimaginable happiness. And along with these imaginings the cascade of elfin prettiness and invalidish petulance bubbles on and on, ringing the changes on 'Tig' and 'Wig' and (once Murry had accepted 'Je ne Parle pas'), 'Mouse', soliciting him to look after his health, praising him endlessly, and levitating them both far above the concern of ordinary mortals. In addition to 'Je ne Parle pas' she completed two other stories, and the letters are not without traces of the old literary ambition. 'We shall always be "little gentlefolk" wherever we live'—what a world of country cottages has been built on that thought!—'Please God we'll get a press . . . my serious stories won't ever bring me anything but my child stories ought to, and my "light" ones.' Then she launches off on a sea of honey dew and milk of paradise. It was a prolonged crisis, from which Katherine emerged as a truly literary woman. The cry of agony over the grease-laden washing-up water at Cholesbury— 'I want lights, music, people!'—was to be answered: but subject to a death sentence.

What she must have feared for some time had now happened, and she found herself face to face with death. On 18 February, just a week after L.M.s arrival, she went for a long walk with her unbearable companion 'to warm up'. Next morning, as she says in her *Journal*:

I woke up early . . . and when I opened the shutters the full round sun had just risen. I began to repeat that verse of Shakespeare's

'Lo, here the gentle lark weary of rest', and bounded back to bed. The bound made me cough—I spat—it tasted strange—it was bright red blood. Since then I've gone on spitting each time I cough a little more. Oh, yes, of course I'm frightened. . . .

'Bogey', she wrote a little later, 'this is *not* serious, does *not* keep me in bed, is absolutely easily curable, but I have been spitting a bit of blood.' A stay until April, she declared, was now indispensable. 'I'd only be a worry. So here I stay and work—and try to bear it.' After all L.M. was there, and that was now important in spite of Katherine's continued detestation of what she felt was L.M.s clumsy fawning, and interference and jealousy of Katherine's love for Murry. 'It's a good thing L.M. came (even though I feel in some mysterious way that *she has done it*. That's because I *loathe* her so. I do). Still I'll use her as a slave.' Of course L.M. got a doctor, who Katherine swore was an abortionist.

Murry, now back at his desk in M.I.7, bowed his head to this extraordinary yoke. He wrote her loving, literary, anxious letters; but even with the pressures of war and against Katherine's wayward-ness, it is difficult to believe that some more effective measures might not have been taken to arrest the tragedy. However, Katherine's will was stronger than his.

✣ 10 ✣

The Decline of the *New Age*

In her ambition to 'get a press' Katherine hardly took account of the precariousness of literary papers. The *New Age*, in the latter years of the war, was struggling for its life, even though it was lighting, week by week, names and causes that would shine in the next twenty years. Ezra Pound remained a stand-by, as did T. E. Hulme until he fell in France in 1917. Flitting across the pages after Ruth Pitter and Hugh Kingsmill are A. S. Neill and C. E. M. Joad—names which at that time had nothing to commend them but Orage's perceptions of originality and talent, let it lead where it would. In 1918 Edwin Muir married Willa, came to London, and became free of Cursitor Street as Orage's assistant editor.

For Muir it was a great adventure. But in fact the circulation was dropping away and Orage had always despised advertisement revenue. 'M.B., Oxon.', silver-haired and rubicund, still provided his subsidy and occasional theosophical articles, but there was no money in Guild Socialist propaganda, and the printers' bills had to be paid. In 1918 newsprint rationing was imposed. In 1914 the paper had offered thirty-two pages for sixpence. By 1917 it was offering twenty, and in 1918 a mere sixteen.[1]

And yet in those years, Orage graduated from the Chancery Lane A.B.C. to the Café Royal where his table was a centre of attention. One of his disciples, Paul Selver, who had made his way on to the *New Age* by offering translations of Czech verse, wrote about the Café Royal at that time:

> *Behold the gay mosaic of the scene;*
> *The poet shares a table with the crook—*

[1] The decline in the *New Age* can be measured as follows: 1914, 1,439 pages; 1915, 1,327 pages; 1916, 1,243 pages; 1917, 1,139 pages; 1918, 891 pages. In

The Decline of the New Age

*The Not-Yet hob-nobs with the Might-Have-Been
And plans a Never-To-Be-Published book.*

Orage's table still included the faithful A. E. Randall, writer under many names, 'lean, hungry-looking and hollow-cheeked, with his burning eyes, consumptive complexion, and his eager, voluble, conversation'; the anti-Marxist Basque syndicalist, Ramiro de Maeztu, who produced a massive series of articles about political theory; and William Henry Dyson, an Australian from Ballarat who was among the first in the great migration of cartoonists from the other side of the world that led the political cartoon in the following twenty years.

Dyson became one of Orage's closest friends. He was some ten years younger than his patron and a lithographer of great talent. His political cartoons in the *New Age*, which for many years regularly carried at least one full-page cut, bear comparison with any of the set pieces of the older weeklies such as *Punch*, to whose tradition Dyson nevertheless still belongs. He first appeared in 1916 and by 1918 he was a weekly feature of the *New Age*; and the number for 14 March 1918 is virtually a portfolio of Dyson, containing no fewer than six lithographs, reviewing the war in a series of bitter commentaries etched from the standpoint of a socialist who saw Prussian militarism as the greatest enemy of progress.

Dyson, Kennedy, de Maeztu, and of course Orage himself, who wrote most of the 'Notes of the Week' and a great deal of the rest of the paper, were the backbone of the *New Age* during the last two years of the war; and there was one other name which appeared with increasing frequency: 'M. M. Cosmoi', a presage of things to come. 'M. M. Cosmoi' was the pseudonym of an attaché at the Serbian Embassy whom Selver introduced to Orage in 1915, and his real name was Dmitri Mitrinović. He combined a wide knowledge of English literature with the gifts of a prophet. His eyes were compelling, his garments sombre, his hair and complexion dark and mysterious. He conducted his acquaintances round the Victoria and Albert Museum, breathing a strange life into the exhibits from the recollections of his extensive reading. He talked of a country, yet

---

1917 the New Age Press, after ten years of life, had to be wound up, and almost carried the paper with it into insolvency.

145

to be born, called 'Yugoslavia', chanted Serbian ballads, and preached a doctrine he called 'Panhumanism', which was very much to Orage's taste.

Among these sages Orage was not without feminine companion-ship. Since parting from Beatrice he was (Philip Mairet tells us) accompanied by 'an elegant young woman', but 'she had no com-parable connection with his working life'. This 'sylph-like beauty was an idealist of complex and elusive character in search of a platonic attachment: and I have reason to believe that for Orage, a man usually so irresistible to women, she presented a new and singular, probably a baffling problem'. With these hints from a man who knew Orage well we must leave this unsatisfactory phase of his private life.

So, in the declining years of the *New Age*, Orage was elevated spiritually, and in some ways socially as well. His circle never inter-sected with the high culture of Garsington or Bloomsbury, as Katherine's, Murry's, and Lawrence's did for a time; and his increasing detestation of Fabianism and all it stood for put him at a distance from those who welcomed the Bolshevik Revolution of 1917 with its unique claim to have established a communist sovereignty in one part of the world: in due course that claim was to shatter the Guild Socialist movement and carry the larger frag-ment of it into the British Communist Party. 'There is nothing left of the Russian steamroller,' he is said to have remarked, 'except the man with the red flag.' His table at the Café Royal was more likely to be joined by Augustus John, Sickert, or Epstein than by a left-wing politician or a fashionable iconoclast.

Yet all this does not quite give the flavour of what was happening to Orage at this time, though the influence of 'Cosmoi' gives a hint of it. He was still obsessed with the search for inner wisdom; 'the understanding of society', and it was an increasing obsession. He had long ago rejected the conventional certainties inculcated at Culham, and much of his achievement during the past ten years had been to wear away Victorian certainties. But for a man apparently so outgoing, he was strangely speculative, even gullible, and part of his success as an editor was due to his willingness to print almost anyone who seemed to him original. As a result Guild Socialism and Mitrinović's 'Panhumanism' jostled with some of the first articles on the theories of Freud and Jung to appear in the British press.

With hindsight, one can trace in the *New Age* lines of thought which lead to almost every operative doctrine of the thirties and forties, including the most horrific. But so far as Orage was concerned all these devastating winds were still safely in their bag, because the British Empire (despite the assaults of C. H. Norman) still seemed so incomparably powerful.

At about this time a new and powerful influence entered Orage's life in the shape of a short, tubby major in the Royal Flying Corps, then on leave in London, named Clifford Hugh Douglas. It seems that they met originally through Orage's old collaborator, Holbrook Jackson, who was then editing a paper called the *Organiser*, but the mediator was soon eliminated, and in a very short time the apostle of 'Panhumanism' and Guild Socialism was bending his mind to a financial solution of the human problem.

Douglas today has no more than a niche in the hall of cranks. He was an engineer by profession, and unlike most engineers of that time had a university degree, from Cambridge. He was almost exactly Orage's contemporary, and much of his life had been spent abroad, first in India as agent for British Westinghouse, later in Canada working for the Canadian Pacific Railway; and on these wanderings he had reflected a great deal about cost accounting, the nature of credit, and the banking system. These studies had convinced him that the economic, social, political, and even the moral troubles of the world were due to an insufficiency in the supply of money and the sluggishness of its circulation. For this defect, which he regarded as easily put right, he blamed the conservative caution and stuffiness of bankers.

The little engineer was in some ways absurd. Though not built for it, he was inordinately fond of dancing, and dancing with him, according to one of his partners, was like taking the floor with a penguin. But there was also a compulsive power about him, and he clothed his simple but exciting doctrine in elaborate calculations and compelling rhetoric. Unfortunately his powers of written expression were not equal to his passion for the truth as he saw it, and his first efforts in the *New Age* (to whose columns Orage recruited him) were well-nigh incomprehensible. Orage took him in hand, and we have it on the authority of Ezra Pound that Douglas was among those whom Orage taught to write.

By a curious coincidence the arrival of Douglas reproduced for a moment the old trio of Jackson, Orage and Penty, who ten years before had come from Leeds to London to launch the Fabian Arts Group. Jackson soon dropped away after introducing Douglas to Orage: but Penty, who after his return from America had begun to work for the Coal Commission, engaged in a long struggle with this new rival, Douglas, to recapture the interest of Orage. For several months the three met in cafés to argue about currency and credit, with Penty trying to persuade his old friend back to the kind of William Morris craft syndicalism to which he had always been loyal, and then to build some kind of bridge between it and the financial theories of Clifford Douglas. But Douglas was not willing to share what he saw was his captivation of Orage, and his influence at last proved the stronger. The hold of Penty over Orage was finally broken, and the architect was left to pursue his ideas apart, ending in the thirties as Pound was to end in the forties, an admirer of Mussolini. 'We discovered', Penty wrote of this episode long after-wards, 'fundamental differences in our attitude towards life and society that could not be bridged.' The very solemnity of the phrase tells something of the seriousness with which intellectual differences were taken in what one can now see were sub-Victorian times.

Douglasism, or 'Social Credit' as it was quickly christened, was a blind alley, at any rate in so far as it offered no social philosophy. Being a purely financial solution it had no comprehensive political force. Yet for the rest of his life it enthused Orage, even when other, more searching doctrines, had become imposed on it in his curiously stratified mind. Within two years of meeting the Major, and in the middle of many other occupations, he was engaged in a study of the reform of the coal industry on Douglasite lines.

Early in March 1918 Katherine's high-pitched stay in Bandol was coming to an end and she was gathering herself for a return to England and marriage to Murry. His position, it must be admitted, was unenviable—commitment to marriage with a woman who now, unmistakably, had a fatal disease. And all the time, by every post, she wrote of 'The Heron', the imaginary house where they were to be so happy and a faithful 'Mrs. Buttercup' would look after them.

'It is the fortress and the hiding-place of our love.' Yet it is not Katherine's hectic insistence on a dream-world that appals. It is Murry's incapacity to take any practical step to deal with their situation—whether cruel, in breaking it off, or effective, in making a serious arrangement for Katherine to enter a sanatorium. He writhed and bemoaned his inadequacy, resembling perhaps nothing so much as a handsome jellyfish: brilliant as it floats with tentacles waving, without direction or purpose, and equipped with a sting.

'And it's March 3 and next month Mrs. Middleton Murry will arrive—which ought to excite you.' It was a shocking pilgrimage. At this point in her life Katherine's hatred of almost anyone she encountered was, in the strictest sense of the word, pathological, and made more ghastly in retrospect by the elaborate endearments of her correspondence with Murry. The voyage had to be undertaken with the help of L.M., and 'she's made me feel again *weak, exhausted* with rage, and so she's happy . . . to hate anyone as I hate this *enemy* of ours. Please, darling love, for my sake don't forget never to give her a loophole. And never, never must she walk into the Heron.' There was no contradiction in writing, a day or two later, that 'I am *extremely* anxious to travel with L.M. as she'd be such a help to me on the journey.'

It is difficult quite to believe in all the obstacles she had to overcome in setting out from Bandol, but one must remember that Ludendorff's offensive was at that moment rolling across northern France in a last great bid for victory that almost succeeded. Even so, Katherine's stratagems to get a travel permit seem exaggerated— what doctor could have hesitated to say she was seriously ill? She became obsessed with the difficulty of complying with formalities, and as a result they became still more intolerable. 'It *all* takes time—*days* and *days.*' By 22 March she and L.M. had got as far as Paris on the strength of the certificate she had charmed out of a doctor who she swore had 'killed some poor girl with a dirty buttonhook'. And at Paris, under the bombardment of Big Bertha, they were again blockaded by officialdom.

The three weeks she spent in Paris straddled the early Easter of that year and produced twenty letters to Murry, apart from several telegrams. She was obsessed by the posts, by the compulsion to write letters and above all the need to receive them. When they were delayed, she moved quickly from pleading to positive indignation: 'Without a sign from you, and when I know that English mails *do* arrive, *are* delivered, my days are intolerable.' Yet Murry was loyally writing every day. The problem of her permit to cross the Channel was finally solved, it seems, by the intervention of the diplomat cousin of Virginia, Sydney Waterlow, whose help Murry had contrived, and on 11 April she arrived in London. 'When I met her at the station', wrote Murry, 'she was barely recognisable. She looked as if she had been for months in some fearful prison.' The photographs bear him out. Three weeks afterwards at Kensington Registry Office in the presence of J. D. Fergusson and the Hon. Dorothy Brett Katherine Bowden at last became Katherine Murry. She remained Katherine Mansfield for all that. L.M. was not present at this wedding, just as she had not been present at the marriage with Bowden. The wedding—on 3 May 1918—was celebrated exactly four days after the decree absolute had released Katherine.

Murry was seriously alarmed about the health of his new wife, and she was alarmed that he should be so. She accused him, whether justly or not, of putting his handkerchief to his mouth and turning away when she coughed. But he had to work. He was now well established at the War Office, and earning £500 a year. After a few weeks together at Redcliffe Road, during which plans were formed for a move to Hampstead, they parted again and he persuaded her to stay at a comfortable hotel in Cornwall under the eye of the poetess Anne Estelle Rice.

Katherine's second stay in Cornwall was very different from her first among the windswept rocks of Higher Tregerthen. She was installed in comfort at the Headland Hotel in Looe, waited upon and plied with kindness. She even came under the care of the local general practitioner and began receiving some treatment for her disease. She watched her weight (only just over seven stone), tried to eat (or at any rate to cheer Murry up by describing enjoyable meals), sometimes wrote joyously, even confidently. She was moved by the old, kind 'Mrs. Honey' at the hotel reciting poetry to her: 'I listened and suddenly I thought of Wordsworth and his "faith" in these people—and again, Bogey, in spite of everything, I believed in England. Not only in England—in Mankind.' But the underlying strain was still there. She pined imperiously for letters, wrought tiny details into occasions for passionate tirades, badgered Murry with teasing arguments about money, and gave freer and freer rein to her gift of fancy to express her mood, whether it was black or, professedly at any rate, cheerful.

One personal relationship had now hardened for ever. In June Murry had written a piece about Gaudier in the *Nation*: 'I, personally', Katherine wrote, 'think your article on Gaudier exceedingly, extremely good—very valuable, too—very well written—*discovered*: that's the word I want. But—*warning*. You have mentioned his poverty and that he did the housework for his sister. She is in London. By all accounts she is a very dangerous horrible woman of the B— type.' There is no doubt that 'B—' is Beatrice.

But others were coming back to better order. Perhaps as a result of Katherine's influence, Murry was reconciled with Kot, Murry holding out the hand in the following manly way:

Dear Koteliansky,

I don't know how you feel about it; but Katherine and I feel we should like to see you again. I think we can safely let the past be the past; it certainly wasn't very important. If you do feel you would like to see us again will you come over one evening to us at 47 Redcliffe Rd. Bus No. 14 from Piccadilly.

Friendly relations had also been restored with Ottoline, and of course had been maintained with Virginia and Leonard Woolf, who were at work printing 'The Prelude'. In July, too, 'Bliss' was published in the *English Review*. 'The Elephant', otherwise 2 Portland Villas N.W.3[1] was nearly ready for occupation, and after a desperate struggle for and against the idea, Katherine had decided L.M. should keep house for them there—L.M. herself obediently giving up her job and her own little house in Hampstead to fall in with Katherine's wishes. The stage was being set for Katherine to emerge in the role she had always longed for—that of an established literary woman, to be taken seriously. All through her marriage with Bowden, her alliance with Murry, her adventure with Carco, the shifting backgrounds of Clovelly Mansions, cottages in the Home

[1] Now 17 East Heath Road. It is almost at the top of Hampstead hill, with a fine prospect over the Heath towards the Vale of Health.

Counties, Garsington, Paris, Bandol, this had been the objective: recognition.

Just after she returned from Looe in July, and before moving to Hampstead, her mother died. There is a slight formality about the letters she wrote to various friends: they strike a note of admiration rather than love, and perhaps that is what was deserved. Of her father they say nothing. The fact never seems to have been mentioned between Katherine and Murry, but it is no detraction from Katherine's love of both her brother and her mother to say that the prospect of Katherine becoming a rich woman was now considerable. The 'Pa-man' was now fifty-eight and chairman of the Bank of New Zealand. His relationship with his erring literary daughter was complicated, and the allowance he granted her was controlled very carefully; but after the summer of 1918 there was to be no son, and no widow.

'The Elephant' was a tall, late-Victorian semi, and Katherine took a great deal of interest in its furnishing and decoration. 'I did not want what the poor middle class want—and I have had grey nearly everywhere. All the doors are to be grey, and the skirting-boards, etc., and shutters, with black stair banisters and black treads. In the kitchen, white distemper with turquoise-blue paint. On the top floor your [L.M.'s] room—lemon yellow with grey cupboards. The bathroom real *canary* yellow—and the "external" paint for the railings, gate, and door—grey again.' It was characteristic that L.M. should simply be told the colour-scheme of the room she was to inhabit. She was to sacrifice more than this choice in the year ahead.

They all moved in towards the end of August 1918—Murry, Katherine, L.M. and two servant-maids. It was a brave venture, full of peril. The war was manifestly drawing to an end, and while peace was one of the miracles Katherine pined for to put all problems at an end, it would also be the end of Murry's well-paid job with M.I.7. He was still an undischarged bankrupt (a consideration which caused Katherine to suggest she, not he, should sign the tenancy agreement). Then, above all, there was the problem of Katherine's health, and her passionate horror of sanatorium treatment which would offer the best hope of a cure. She was now pitifully thin—her rings slid up and down her fingers and her face was pinched and white—and a specialist sent by her father who examined her in

October gave her three years to live unless she would submit to the discipline of a sanatorium. She bludgeoned Murry at once into refusing this advice. 'You do believe it would kill me', Murry records her saying after the consultation. He agreed, and then agreed that of course she would get well by following her own idea of a cure, which was to lead a perfectly ordinary life. 'There was no escape', he notes in his autobiography. 'We were trapped. And I was caught in a web of strange and subtle falsity.' No man has ever been better at exculpating himself by admitting the truth in his own carefully chosen words.

Despite his cowardice and helplessness in the presence of Katherine, Murry worked extremely hard, and never harder than during that autumn and winter at 'The Elephant'. During part of it he was still working full-time at the War Office, but managed to write copiously for the *Nation* and *The Times Literary Supplement* as well. He also set up a printing-press in the basement which he operated with his brother Richard Murry to produce the few publications bearing the imprint of the 'Heron Press'—among them some of his own poems and Katherine's 'Je ne Parle pas Français'.

Near at hand, in Pond Street, lived Dorothy Brett. She had first met the Murrys back in 1915, in the days of *Signature*, and then had shared 'The Ark' with them in Gower Street. She, with Fergusson, had been witness at their wedding: 'a slim straight little figure with a small mouth always just slightly open, and almost totally deaf, even as a girl'. Now she was twenty-seven. She admired Katherine and feared her, as many people did. And she loved Murry. During that autumn and winter an entanglement began which was to last several years.

And not far away, still in Acacia Road, was Kot. He had given up the Law Bureau, and was now established as the cross-roads and point of reference for so many who were or had been friends, or would be friends again. Were the Woolfs thinking of taking a cottage Lawrence knew about in Cornwall? Was Lawrence down to his last penny? Might he be reconciled to Lady Ottoline? These were the elements of Kot's correspondence. He had borrowed a book by Jung from Barbara Low, had lent it on to Lawrence who in turn sent it with a commentary to Katherine, who then got a furious letter from Lawrence demanding its immediate return to the original owner. 'Let her have it by the week-end will you—post it to her direct—10 Brunswick Square W.C.1—and *print* the address, dear Katherine, so that the Jewish magpie shall not settle chattering on my roof. You will understand I can't be chattered at.'

Lawrence reappeared in Katherine's life that November of 1918, just after the armistice, and visited the Murrys in their new-found grandeur of 'The Elephant'. But he did not stay there, and there was no resumption of the intense attraction and repulsion between him and Murry.[1] He suggested they should visit him in Derbyshire, where he was staying, but there could be no question of it. Even Katherine saw that a journey into the Midlands in November would be asking for trouble.

The best and most moving account of life at 'The Elephant' comes from L.M. For her it meant 'living a double life, my own and Katherine's', and that meant sacrificing the first to the second. One day her treasured bundles of letters written, some of them, in the Harley Street days, were produced for Katherine's inspection, which was followed by an immediate order they should be destroyed. It was faithfully carried out. Then two young officers on leave came to call, one of whom had shown himself as a possible husband for L.M. Their reception by Katherine and Murry was such that the potential fiancé vanished. In the relationship between L.M. and Katherine there was a terrible conflict and an equally frightening dependence. On one side a clumsy, self-blaming love; on the other a calculating unresponsiveness which emerged as cruelty and hid a realisation that L.M.'s unsophisticated virtues represented everything Katherine had resolved not to be.

'As soon as she came down she would move around lightly, either touching the flowers, which always responded, or just pushing things a fraction of an inch this way or that, which for K.M. made the room come alive. I once remarked on this habit to her, because I always kept the things exactly as I thought they had been the day before, but somehow it never worked.' And Katherine, now she was established, did not work either that autumn. Her powers of composition seemed to have deserted her. She sat at her yellow table in her grey room with her feet wrapped in a muff, unable to

---

[1] He stayed at Hollybush House, about half a mile away, where I had just been born.

write except in her journal. No stories came, and she could not even correspond with Murry.

They gave a party at Christmas, and with a little imagination one can reconstruct the guests. Not Lawrence, for he was staying with his sister in the Midlands. But Richard Murry, the Campbells, Sullivan, Kot, Gertler, Aldous Huxley, without any doubt, providing, with the host and hostess the main cast of *Point Counter Point*; possibly Walter de la Mare, Robert and Sylvia Lynd, my parents Catherine and Donald, and the thirty-year-old Eliot. 'Murry seemed to wear a paper hat (a large red and yellow butterfly) from Christmas Eve until Boxing Day—we gradually . . . gave a party. . . . Oh I did love it so. . . . I wanted to say to everybody— Let us stay for ever just as we are.' It must be doubtful if Orage was there. He had his own circle now, and it did not seem as if the two would ever again intersect. But Katherine was not unmindful of him, and the intersection was soon to recur.

❧ II ❧

The *Athenaeum*

At that Christmas party Murry already knew—as he put it—the purpose for which the war had spared him. He was sure, as he lay awake in the room next to Katherine, listening to her coughing, that there must have been a purpose. It was to be editor of the *Athenaeum* at the substantial salary of £800 a year.

The *Athenaeum*, traditionally the weekly for dons and consisting mainly of reviews, had recently fallen on hard times under the editorship of Arthur Greenwood, the Labour politician, and had been bought by Arthur Rowntree with the intention of making it a path-breaking literary magazine. How Murry and his proprietor, the Quaker headmaster of Bootham School, came to know one another is not clear, but in January 1919 Murry was appointed and in his turn appointed first J. W. N. Sullivan, and then Aldous Huxley as his lieutenants—the latter having been suggested by Lady Ottoline. Katherine was to review the novels. The first number under the new arrangements was to come out in April. The standards and the brow were to be high to the point of ruthlessness: the young aesthete of *Rhythm* had given way to a seasoned and iconoclastic literary journalist with wide contacts.

Katherine, though she had rejected the advice and verdict of doctors Murry had introduced in the autumn, had now placed herself in the hands of a consultant physician at the near-by Hampstead General Hospital in Pond Street, Dr. Victor Sorapure, a youngish Roman Catholic who had spent much of his career in academic medicine in New York. Altogether he was a much more intellectual doctor than any Katherine had yet seen, and he must have realised that her malady was psychological as well as physical, though as a distinguished diagnostician he could have been in no doubt about her tuberculosis. He successfully treated the mysterious muscular pains from which she had suffered so long, but he was

careful not to press her to enter a sanatorium and it seems possible
that his private prognosis was so grave as to make him think it
best she should come to terms with the inevitable. She wrote herself a little later that he had said it was only her indomitable will
which had kept her alive that year. His consultations tended to grow
into discussions about 'the immensity and wonder of the universe
and the incomprehensibility of space'. Certainly, from this point
onwards Katherine thought more, and more calmly, about the
possibility of death.

The *Athenaeum* under its new editor got off to a distinguished
start. It is true that Ford Madox Ford, writing to Herbert Read
after the paper had been going for six months described it as 'The
Cocoa-Pacifist-Stamp-Collectors' Weekly', but this was a senior—
indeed superannuated—literary editor writing to a new hand: Ford
had edited the *English Review* long before the war, and Read (to
Ford's private fury) had just taken over the literary side of the *New
Age*. In fact the hundred or so numbers of the *Athenaeum* under
Murry were not only distinguished but decisive in forming a new
literary taste. In that time he published seventeen pieces by Virginia
Woolf, a good deal by and about Eliot, and Katherine's regular
reviews as well as several translations from the Russian which she
polished from Koteliansky's strange English. Among other contributors were Clive Bell, Leonard Woolf, Russell, de la Mare,
Julian Huxley, Forster and Lytton Strachey. He brought forward
Proust (not yet translated into English), attacked Sassoon, and
praised Wilfred Owen. Among more senior authors he nailed his
colours to Hardy and Conrad. He would have had Lawrence as well,
but unfortunately after the second number, to which Lawrence
contributed, the two fell out and Lawrentian ill-will towards the
paper and its editor bespattered his letters for the next two years.
For the minor reviews, Orage's discovery Edwin Muir was much
employed, scoring in a good week as much as five guineas in
seven-and-sixpences for notices of books ranging from Wagner to
Christianity, from the Himalayas to Charlie Chaplin. Katherine's
old friend Orton provided one review (for 8s 3d) and Beatrice's
brother's *Ethiopian Saga*, which finally found a publisher in Allen &
Unwin early in 1919, received a curt dismissal from an obscure
reviewer who received 14s for his trouble. The whole tone was high

and exclusive. 'No', wrote Virginia, in May 1919, 'Mr. Hamilton will never be admitted; he and his disciples must toil for ever in the desert sand, and the circle of illumination will, we fear, grow fainter and further upon their horizon. It is curious to find, after writing the above sentence, how little one is ashamed of being, where literature is concerned, an unmitigated snob.' The *Athenaeum* was very much the organ of Garsington and Bloomsbury.

Sorapure had advised that Katherine could not go through another London winter—she weighed less than seven stone—and had managed to persuade her to set out once again for the Mediterranean. A curious but characteristic ambiguity surrounded the terms of her departure. She gave Sorapure (as she told Kot just before leaving) 'a sworn promise not to remain . . . a shorter time than two years'; yet had a private understanding with Murry that she would return to enter on 'The Heron' in eight months. The last days at Portland Villas were confused and distressing—Katherine at her worst. 'It is not being ill that matters', she wrote petulantly to Kot, 'it is having to let people serve you and fighting *every moment* against their desire to "share". Why are human beings so indecent?'

Late in September, supported by Murry and L.M., she set forth. It was another dreadful journey. The first real stop ('terribly hot and swarming with insects and profiteers') was San Remo, where they stayed a fortnight in a hotel and then had to move on because the manager said Katherine's consumptive cough was distressing the other guests. So they established themselves at the Casetta Deerholm, a little villa along the coast to the west, near the town of Ospedaletti, 'built on the slope of a wild hill covered with figs, olives, and tamarisk trees and a thick small shrubbery and herbs like lavender and thyme and rosemary'. There, tottering along the steep paths with the help of her father's walking-stick and the over-solicitous L.M., Katherine was to spend her next six months.

She was comparatively happy, but almost unproductive apart from the reviews for the *Athenaeum* and translations of Tchekov's letters by Kot, which he faithfully paid her for polishing.[1] She often

[1] From payments of about £3 per instalment, as shown in Murry's marked copies of the *Athenaeum*. Katherine received 50 per cent or thirty shillings an instalment.

pictured him there as she and L.M. walked and smoked in the over-grown garden of an evening listening to 'the cicada shaking his tiny tambourine'. He was in fact in a depressed and unsociable mood. 'Your loneliness is precious to you, I know', she wrote to him in December. 'Does it disturb it to know you are dear to me? Do not let it. It is such a quiet feeling. It is like the light opening into a room —moonlight—where you are sitting.' She developed a fellow-feeling for Tchekov as she laboured at his letters: 'If I *do* die perhaps there will be a small private heaven for consumptives only. In that case I shall see Tchekov . . . but the Knipper . . . you know, Koteliansky, I cannot like her.' She had heard from Lawrence, who seemed happy, surrounded by friends; but to her people seemed 'mechanisms' and the memory of people 'like the memory of clothes hanging in a cupboard', a strange presage of what was to overwhelm her. No doubt some news of this rather morbid flirtation got back from the agonised Koteliansky to Lawrence.

Murry had returned to drift, somewhat against his will, into a love affair with Brett, and to score one of the most considerable strokes of criticism of the decade. From the point of view of its consequences the review he wrote of the fourth volume of *Georgian Poetry* was perhaps the most telling thing he ever penned. From the moment it appeared in the *Athenaeum* for December 1919 a whole style of poetry which had held the field for years and was in lineal descent from Wordsworth was swept out of fashion. It did not matter in the least that five thousand copies of the book were sold in the few days after publication, and that the whole enterprise carried the social and literary patronage of Eddie Marsh. Tens of thousands of the next poetry-reading generation, most of whom had never read Murry's article, absorbed its message, and the way was cleared for Eliot.

The weapon used was ridicule, rising with great skill from gentle banter to savage irony and devastating quotation. The Georgian poets, said Murry, were too kind and ordinary to be proper poets. They were too fond of dogs and beer. Their foreheads glistened with benevolent perspiration. It is true that Lawrence was represented in the anthology, and so was Wilfred Owen, whom Murry went out of his way to praise; but the article managed to create a typical 'Georgian' and the movement never really recovered.

Applause came from the Casetta Deerholm, as soon as the paper was read there. 'Your Georgian review is FIRST CHOP. . . . You couldn't have done it better Boge. There's not a chink in your armour either. You have really wiped the floor with them. . . . I had no idea you were going to bathe it in a kind of twinkling, delicate light. . . . Oh with what arrows, to spear those sparrows, to their very marrows! I feel as if we'd been through a naval engagement and now drew away and heaved up and left them—tuned our fiddles, brought out the dishes of gold and the fishes heads of pure jade with lamps for eyes. . . .'

A long literary feud followed between the *Athenaeum* and the *London Mercury*, of which the arch-Georgian J. C. Squire was editor. Murry might be passive and indecisive in many ways, but not with a pen in his hand. With that equipment all the aggression in him came out, and against Squire he won hands down. But he had also to face the private protests of Eddie Marsh, whose friendship was valuable. He had helped the Murrys long ago, Lawrence had had at least one cheque from him when in low water and the rent of Gertler's studio came from the same source. Marsh was a bridge between the establishment and struggling talent, and to alienate him was not only reckless but unreasonable. He was used to having his favours declined by those who could not accept his attitude to the war, which of course had been fervent support, but the reply he got from Murry to his letter of protest was different:

> Now, Eddie, I want you to believe this of me. Nothing in my literary career has given me greater pain than being compelled to fight against you. I want you to believe that I hold you one of the kindest friends I ever had; that it is an agony (no less) to me to be driven to fight one of whom all personal memories are fragrant with generosity and loving-kindness . . . I dont mind how mistaken you think me; but that you should think me base is intolerable. Your devoted friend. Jack Murry.

This letter is typical of Murry's methods of self-justification, with its initial self-righteousness and ingratiation and final snarl. It must have been with some chagrin, very soon afterwards, that Marsh read in the New Year Honours for 1920 that Murry had been created O.B.E. for his services to the war effort. Katherine, a little later,

1a Orage about 1900

b Orage in 1932 by T. C. Dugdale

2 Beatrice by Modigliani, 1915

3a Katherine, 1914

b Katherine, 1918

4 Wedding at Selwood Terrace, 1914. Murry, Frieda and Lawrence

b   Murry in 1935

5a   Murry at Sierre, 1921

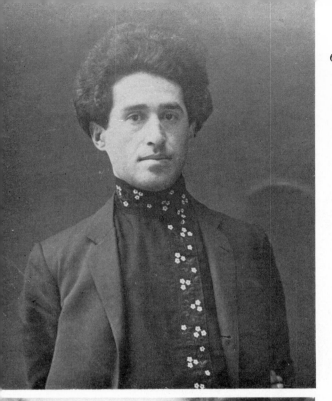

6a Kot as a student in Kiev

b Kot in old age at Acacia Road

7 The Thursdayers: Acacia Road, 1934. Kot in the centre with Sullivan on
the right and Hodgson on the left. Gertler on the left of the back row

8a   Gurdjieff greets New York, 1923

b Ouspensky in later life

light-heartedly urged him to have it entered on his passport. 'These
things are sometimes useful in foreign parts. If we wish to smuggle,
steal, flay alive. . . . If we have no money and only our poor faces for
our fortunes, your O.B.E. may move a "blighter" to some kind of
respeck.'

Of course Katherine was writing to Murry from Ospedaletti
every day, sometimes twice a day, occasionally three times. Fancies
of their impossible future life, their house, their children, their
prosperity, mingle with grim fears of death and emotional blackmail. Yet for all their suffering and intimacy the letters are literary,
and intensely self-conscious. 'These letters [she wrote on 21 Novem-
ber] will one day be published, and people will read something in
them, in their queer finality.' And of course she hungered for post
in return, saying that she lived for letters when she was away from
Murry—*for* them, *on* them, *with* them. When they did not come
quickly across an exhausted, strike-prone Europe she became
petulant, gradually working towards the same high drama of reproach as during her last days at Bandol in 1917. Early in December
(interestingly enough it was not long after a visit from her father
who was touring Europe) she sent Murry a set of verses on the
theme that she was giving up the man who had left her 'ill and cold
in a far country' for a new husband, death.

The pose was theatrical, and perhaps she had not really meant to
cause a crisis. The letters that follow lack none of the enthusiasm,
flattery, and endearment that she habitually lavished on Murry. But
he, fresh from his triumph over the Georgians, was 'shattered', and
decided he must set out at once to see her; though he ruined any
good effect that decision might have had by sending a long, priggish
letter announcing it. The letter was full of agony and ambiguity,
affection and resentment, self-pity and grumbles about money: 'I
mention money because it's important.' The fare would be £14. He
was 'absolutely incapable of work'. The letter ended on a wavering
note: 'I'm coming quickly, darling—then we'll see, we'll see.' Across
the envelope she wrote:

This letter killed the Mouse, made the Worm creep underground,
and banished the Dream Child for ever. Before I had received it
I had learned to live *for* Love and *by* Love. I had given myself

up—and a kind of third creature US was what I lived by. After I
had read it, quite apart from me, my own self returned *and* all
my horror of death vanished. From this date I simply *dont care*
about death! No question of heroics or life not being worth living
or anything like it. I simply feel alone again. Voilà.

Of course she wired repeatedly to him not to come, and of course
he came. He had plenty of grounds for indignation. He was a busy
man, and although his salary was a good one he had debts and was
still technically a bankrupt. He had asked Arthur Rowntree for
another £200 a year. His labours at the *Athenaeum* were designed
to establish him and Katherine as leading literary figures, which
was what she had always demanded of him. Above all it was mad-
dening to be the recipient of so much sweetness and gall. But it
would have been better if he had not tried to explain all this in
writing, and then, as happened, if he had not shied away from direct
explanation when they met. During the fortnight he spent at
Ospedaletti they made a truce. Friendly relations were resumed.
But there was a permanent change in Katherine, and in Murry.
They were beginning to go their separate ways.

The three weeks or so after Murry's departure were registered at
the Casetta as apathy and black despair; and yet she was fast
achieving her ambition. She was becoming well known. 'The
Prelude' had been published by the Woolfs, and was well received;
'Je ne Parle pas Français', printed in the basement at East Heath
Road by Murry and his brother, had gone well. A collection, with
'Bliss' as the title story, was soon to be published in London and
New York and make her famous. Originally offered to Grant
Richards for £20, it had been transferred by Murry to Constable
for £40. She was established as a major reviewer of fiction. Yet her
reports to Murry in her letters and to herself in her journal were
never more miserable; and to make things even worse she had
written another story about Murry, which she sent him early in
January, called 'The Man Without a Temperament'. It was only
too obviously based on their stay together at San Remo in the
autumn. He writhed but arranged for it to be printed, and Katherine
duly received her cheque for it.

The apparent despair and indifference to achievement masked a revolution in Katherine's feelings. She would never be finished with Murry—that was impossible—but he was dispensable. As for L.M., against whom savage hatred had risen almost to the pitch of paranoia during the autumn, the value of her perfect devotion suddenly burst on Katherine in the one way Katherine could truly achieve a personal reaction: by drama. One night early in January the lonely, hillside Casetta was, or was thought to be, attacked by marauders. Anyway from their bedroom the two women heard footsteps outside and the doorbell was rung, though there was no reply to L.M.'s call 'in my best French' of 'Qui va là?'. Someone had lent Katherine a revolver, though as the incident was to prove, she was quite incapable of using it in an emergency; and when the doorbell mysteriously rang again it was L.M. who produced a fusillade of shots into the darkness from the bedroom window, punctuating her fire with cries of 'Qui va là?'. No doubt this adventure only precipitated a change that was already taking place, but the change was actually reported to Murry only a day or two after the skirmish:

> It is not only that the hatred is gone. Something positive is there which is very like love for her. She has convinced me at last, against all my opposition, that she is trying to do all in her power for me, and that she is devoted to the one idea which is (please forgive my egoism) to see me well again. . . . I confess that now I do lean on her. She looks after me; she has become (or I see her now in her true colours) the person who looks after all I cannot attend to. It was only when I refused to acknowledge this—to acknowledge her importance to me—that I hated her. . . .

Help was on the way to complete the transformation. Sir Harold Beauchamp's visit in November had not been without design. Just across the French frontier, at Menton, lived his well-off Catholic cousin Connie Beauchamp and her companion Jinnie Fullerton, and they had been with him when he called at the Casetta. 'Katherine had *so* wanted to impress them', wrote L.M. And naturally a plan had been formed by the Beauchamps to rescue her. In January it was complete. With great difficulty and expense Katherine and L.M. quitted the Casetta and crossed into France. There Connie and Jinnie achieved what had defeated Murry, and got Katherine into a luxurious nursing home called L'Hermitage, while L.M.

established herself in their comfortable villa, the Villa Flora. 'If I don't get well here', wrote Katherine, 'I'll never get well. Here—after the journey—was this room waiting for me—exquisite, large, with four windows, overlooking great gardens and mountains, wonderful flowers—tea with *toast* and honey and butter—a charming maid—and these two dear sweet women to welcome me with papers, books etc.'

The result can be foreseen. From her new security she bombarded the unfortunate Murry with accusations of neglect, indifference, and meanness. She was not, now, too badly off, for her father had raised her allowance, she had an income for her reviewing, and Murry had just got an advance of £40 from Constable for her book of stories—a cheque she insisted on having sent out to France so that she could 'see it with my own eyes and send it with my own hand to the bank'. It was, she admitted, 'orkid' that she had promised the same book of stories to another publisher, Grant Richards, but now the management was in Murry's hands she became extremely fussy. One or another story must be left out or altered. Others, not yet written, should be included. And her husband must support her. When the money she demanded did not arrive by return of post (for which he was made to apologise) she sent back the laggard cheque and said the real reason for her indignation was his indifference. 'It was a question of sympathy, of understanding, of being in the least *interested*, of asking me JUST ONCE how I was.'

She had taken to drawing lines across her letters to mark changes of mood and subject; and between two of these lines in this particular letter mainly devoted to an almost hysterical tirade against Murry's neglectfulness, occurs a report of a letter from Lawrence, then in Capri:

Lawrence sent me a letter today. He spat in my face and threw filth at me and said: 'I loathe you. You revolt me stewing in your consumption. . . . The Italians were quite right to have nothing to do with you.' And a great deal more. Now I do beseech you, if you are my man, to stop defending him after that and never to crack him up in the paper. *Be proud!* In the same letter he said his final opinion of you was that you were 'a dirty little worm'. Well, *be proud*. Dont forgive him for that please.

No original text for the internally quoted words exists, though they are included as Lawrence's in the collected edition of his letters. Murry destroyed it, though exactly when and in what circumstances is not quite clear.[1] Though she uses quotation marks it is difficult to be certain that what Katherine put inside them, given her mood, was not as impressionistic as what she put outside them and the impression as a whole cannot be relied upon; but she certainly received a letter from Lawrence which wounded her. How did this come about? His recent letters appear to have been friendly notes. She had not written to him. The answer almost certainly lies in Lawrence's devotion to Kot, with whom he, like Katherine, was in regular correspondence. If Kot, with his own foible for Katherine, had relayed to Lawrence her recent letter about 'a special heaven for consumptives' an explosion of rage becomes at once explicable. The episode is important, not so much on Katherine's account, because she afterwards forgave Lawrence, but on Murry's—it was this letter that he produced long afterwards in reply to the attacks on him for ingratitude to Lawrence.

Jinnie Fullerton had a good deal of influence in Menton. She got L.M. a job, took Katherine for drives along the coast, smothered her with comforts and (building perhaps on Dr. Sorapure's foundations) sought to convert her to the Roman Catholic Church—a plan which almost succeeded. Katherine told L.M.: 'My dear Jones . . . one day I mean to be received into the Church. I'm going to become a Catholic. . . .' Perhaps she would tell Murry, perhaps she would 'leave him to find out'. At any rate there is no sign of this in her increasingly artificial, though still affectionate letters to him at Portland Villas. 'It is difficult to define so subtle an impression', he wrote afterwards, 'but, having read these letters in their sequence many times, the feeling abides with me, that, taken as a whole, the letters which Katherine wrote while she was at the Villa Flora, Menton, are less spontaneous. . . .'

One such letter concerned Beatrice. Early in March 1920 a letter from her had arrived at the *Athenaeum*'s office in the Adelphi addressed humbly to the editor and beginning 'Dear Sir . . .'. Could

[1] 'Katherine sent it on to me. I burned it instantly' (*Reminiscences of D. H. Lawrence*, p. 165). There is, however, no trace of a letter from K.M. sending it on. 'Murry declared he destroyed the letter after Katherine's death' (H. T. Moore's note in Lawrence's *Collected Letters*, p. 620).

she have work on the paper? Murry, sidelong as ever, referred it to Katherine, hinting, if one reads between the lines, that there might still be affection there. But there was not. 'Darling, your memory is very short-lived. Yes, it is true, I *did* love B.H. but have you utterly forgotten what I told you of her behaviour in Paris—of the last time I saw her and how, because I refused to stay the night with her, she bawled at me and called me a *femme publique* in front of those filthy Frenchmen? She is loathsome and corrupt and I remember very well telling you I had done with her, explaining why and recounting to you how she had insulted and abused me. I should have thought you could not have forgotten these things.'

So Beatrice never found her way on to the *Athenaeum*. There had been three contributions to the *New Age* early in 1918, when she was living with 'Roch Grey', otherwise Hélène, Baroness d'Oettingen in a château to the south of Paris. There was a coronet on the fireplace and out of the window she could see the smoke rise from the hamlet below the hill. An artist called and did a drawing of her and spoke of Pina, for whom she delightedly inserted a plug in her article as 'the only possible successor to Rodin'. But it was in the third of these articles that Beatrice, writing about Paris, did better than Katherine ever managed:

Paris is inside a fairly incorrect circle of fortification walls, lovely, silent, ancient-coloured cliffs, covered with grass and moss above a ditch. Entering, as I usually do, by the Gate of Orleans, which is due south—if I had arms long enough to reach all around the city my left elbow would crook at the race-course of Auteuil, my forearm would be along the Bois de Boulogne, and my fingers would end at Clignancourt, a district of unenviable reputation, where the flea-market is: my right arm would crook at Vincennes —place of donjons—where they recently shot as a spy the dancer Mata Hari, who said the husband, stationed at Vincennes, of the cook of a friend of mine, went in full toilette and defiant to her doom—which doom I disapprove . . . my right forearm would lie along all sorts of horrid places, the Cemetery of Père-Lachaise, hospitals, reservoirs, the slaughter-house of Vilette, a terrible district where, the other night, three people were shot dead in bed. . . .

On the whole she was then still in good heart. She welcomed the Russian Revolution though 'personally, like all the rest of the burjosie [*sic*] I am horrified at the idea of the supremacy of the Fourth Estate. But I am not so foolish as to fight the inevitable, and, besides, my soul rejoices at what momentarily revolts my taste.' As the fire crackled in the coronetted grate she reflected on 'what a pity one ever dies! Though, after all, there may be another life beyond, and whatever may be the rules and regulations of it I am ready to risk the chance of carving it pretty much to my own fashion. A person like me will never come to grief.'

Within a very short time she had to go through the hideous end of the Modigliani story—Dédo's death from drink and starvation and the suicide of her pregnant successor Jeanne Hébuterne a few days afterwards. Paris grew more and more expensive and began to be overwhelmed with cultural tourists. The very last of her appearances in the *New Age* was 11 March 1920 with a notice of the Cocteau review *Le Boeuf sur le Toit*. Perhaps it was the very piece she had hoped to place with the *Athenaeum*: 'Every movement is stained by one or other of the human matters which brew the vices. A tear seems to fall in the witches' pot.' Then, for reasons not known, she had a miscarriage followed by complications and in September 1920 entered a public hospital, the Clinique Tarnier, where she began to keep the journal which she later published as 'Madame Six'.[1]

People came to see her. Ezra Pound, who had just moved from London to Paris, sent her 'a fat packet of books and reviews'. She felt calm—'trees just as I love them, half-stripped and still, against a faint October dawn. . . . Every physical need satisfied. No pain. Head, as always, clear as a bell. . . . A pen full of ink and plenty of paper.' She thought about how she had changed in five years, how she could now accept things which had made her indignant before, about the style of Barbellion and Zinoviev, and about her life with Modigliani. She had been 'a Bacchante with Martha's apron on. Maecenas in a red tie. Messalina coiffed like Mary of Bethlehem.' She doubted if Dédo had ever caught her likeness. 'They cant "do"'

---

[1] It appeared in her sheet the *Straight Thinker* and its successor the *Straight Thinker Bulletin* between January 1932 and December 1933. 'Madame Six' is of course Beatrice herself, each patient in the ward being addressed by the number of her bed.

my face.' They had all—Apollinaire, Max Jacob, Modigliani—suspected her of not being quite what she appeared to be:

Modigliani—always suspicious, always returning to Martha's kitchen, often to find it in the possession of the Bacchante, always expecting his welcome down from the Cross, and sometimes getting the hoof from Messalina, scoffing equally at Maecenas and the Comrade and never quite able to walk around either: inspired every day with something about me—'voilà, encore une' or 'encore un', he would say—I never knew what he meant and was too arrogant to ask. I never posed, just let him 'do' me, as he pleased, going about the house. He did the Mary portrait of me in a café where I sat thinking what a nuisance he was with his perennial need for more pastels, wondering if I should get my 'Impressions of Paris' written in time for the post, hearing, not listening, to his spit as he lowered his eyebrows on the aesthetic canaille who all went to his funeral. . . .

Literary reflections and her own reminiscences are tangled with descriptions of the hospital routine, the meals, the nurses, the cries of 'Couvrez-vous, Madame Onze! La soupe, Mesdames!', the ice-bags and sheet-changing, the 'hissing, whispering, furtive, gossip' after lights-out. Her flawed but considerable gift still flowed in curious little cascades. She tried to define genius: 'perhaps what we call genius, namely, materialised and manifested intellectual emotion, is only a malady, a mania for exposing others and oneself'. Then her egoism drifts back. 'If the police could see what goes on behind this flesh of mine, they would put me in a lunatic asylum.' And so back to literary recollection:

All their grand systems . . . couldn't bring a little crinkling smile to my nose as still may the souvenir of trivial past and lost things—a memory of Apollinaire saying to me after dinner (we and Picasso and Blaise Cendrars were chez Madame E.; the pretty rose-cheeked, blue-eyed, white-haired Chilean), 'Won't the tap run?' It was a question of writing an extempore dedication to Madame; and I couldn't. Also Apollinaire, in the salon of my dear little hovel on the Butte of Montmartre, gazing at a wondrous new petticoat I had of daffodil satin heavily brocaded with the flowers in white: 'Mais, ma chère, c'est solennel!'

Max Jacob came to see her and asked her to contribute to a new review *Action*. She read Browning ('really a novelist') and girded against Eliot's 'Prufrock', which contained 'ten lines of pretty good prose'. 'He criticises too, does Eliot, "Aristotle", says he, "Aristotle, curiously enough, is more purely a poetical critic than Coleridge." There isn't grass enough in the sweet heavens to match the colour of it for judgment. Impayable, that "curiously enough".' One can see that Murry's editorial instincts were not at fault in thinking she might have added spice to the *Athenaeum*. She even wrote to Katherine, but the no doubt arch letter fell on the same stony ground. 'A hateful, sniggering letter', Katherine reported to Murry, '—a hiccup of a thing. People are rather dreadful Boge.'

Orage also entered into her thoughts, in the train of recollecting an Oscar Wilde anniversary dinner where she had sat next to Frank Harris—'a dreadnought of a Bore'. Orage's manners, she reflected, were quite bad. He was an elementary schoolmaster at heart, who 'knows no equal and resents a superior'. She then went on to etch his character in language almost as rich as Aubrey's:

Of saucy and audacious eloquence, the spare words of a bigger man than he could make him wilt. No more ruthless jockeyer ever mounted the jade, Ambition; but he never quite knew where he wanted to go, and more than once found the man he had left behind plodding on in front. With ten men's minds, and not one of his own, he must always be secondary and can never be intellectually good-mannered, for good manners without impunity are not to be thought of.... Orage does the preux chevalier of La Belle Pensée on a pocketful of intellectual change. I wouldn't trust him not to mistake Turveydrop for a Prince... or the prompting of his amour-propre for a Mandate from Parnassus to clear the literary field of the Offender. This will be Greek to certain. 'Tis the stuff of a bygone romaunt about a Moon Girl who came home with the milk.... And her name wasn't Moon, but Sun, Girl. The Man it was who mooned.

The allusion is clearly to 'The Seventh Tale for Men Only'. Very soon she was to be launched on the last of her great affairs—with the eighteen-year-old Raymond Radiguet.

Orage was certainly showing his chameleon-like nature in 1920, though it is unlikely that his latest work, in collaboration with Douglas, actually reached Beatrice in the ward of the Clinique Tarnier. This was *Credit Power and Democracy. With a Draft Scheme for the Mining Industry*, by C. H. Douglas, Major, R.A.F. (Reserve) M.I.Mech.E. *With a Commentary on the Included Scheme* by A. R. Orage, Editor of the *New Age*. The whole work, which was a summary of Douglasism with a special application of it to the coal industry, bears the hallmark of Orage's style[1] and ends with a passage which finally marks his departure from Socialism—'veering White' as Beatrice had put it. 'It is impossible', Orage wrote, 'that the present system should continue, and it is no less incredible that any of the ordinary Socialist principles can be realised without a "revolution" that would itself defeat their avowed object. Our desire is to carry on; and to carry forward while still carrying on.' It was a rather uninspiring position, but it had common sense to commend it. The trouble was Douglas's theory.

But Orage's interests, though each of them might seem narrowly focused, were ever-ranging. Some years earlier, just before the outbreak of the war, he had come across a young Russian mathematician, philosopher and journalist called P. D. Ouspensky, who had then returned to Russia after a few weeks in London and a long tour of the East in search of the higher wisdom. But it seems clear that the two remained in touch and late in 1919, from the welter and turmoil of revolution, reaction, and intervention a series of letters appeared in the *New Age*, continuing until the end of 1919. Addressed from Ekaterinodar in the Kuban peninsula of southern Russia (now Krasnodar) they contain a remarkable picture of a society in a state of collapse.

It was a notable journalistic coup; for these letters, unlike anything else Ouspensky wrote, are not about philosophy or mysticism. They are descriptive and political—indeed propagandist. Ekaterinodar lay in the base area from which the White Russian general Denikin was operating—at that time with some success. It is reasonably clear that Ouspensky was connected with Denikin's entourage, and he was certainly in bitter opposition to what he

[1] A word (not perhaps happy, but useful) added to the English language by Orage in this work was 'regionalisation' (p. 152).

called 'the poisonous plant of Bolshevism'.[1] The constant theme of the letters is the need for the British to give greater support to the anti-Bolshevik forces:

> The friends of Bolshevism [he writes on 18 September] have succeeded in assembling such a cloud of lies around it that common sense and reason, all possibility of understanding, have have been completely submerged by it. . . .

But the forces of Denikin, driven back on Rostov, were evacuated with the help of the British to Turkey, early in 1920. At Rostov Orage's old collaborator, Carl Bechhofer Roberts, then a *Times* correspondent, came across Ouspensky in a plague-ridden tenement and arranged for him to get to Constantinople. Thence, under arrangements made by Orage, he made his way to London, but not before he had met an old acquaintance, also running before the storm and finding temporary haven in Constantinople, George Ivanovich Gurdjieff.

Ouspensky's arrival in London in the autumn of 1920 may thus have been sudden (as most narratives have it) but it was not un-expected by Orage, who in all probability prepared the ground in advance. At any rate a group, centred on Ouspensky, for the purpose of psychological study, rapidly came into existence. Its finance came from Lady Rothermere, at whose elegant studio at 58 Circus Road, St. John's Wood the circle usually met, though it sometimes assembled at the Harley Street consulting rooms of the psychiatrist James Young. It was a far from contemptible group, for it included not only Lady Rothermere and Orage but four of the most dis-tinguished British exponents of the new doctrines of psycho-analysis, Young, J. M. Alcock, M. D. Eder, and Maurice Nicoll; together with J. D. Beresford the novelist, Rowland Kenney, originally a working-class socialist, a contributor to the *New Age* and the first editor of the *Daily Herald*, and for a time Clifford Sharp of the *New Statesman*. In spring 1920 Kenney had obtained a post in the Political Intelligence Department of the Foreign Office, where he was to remain for the rest of his career. Others occasionally

---

[1] It seems (*see* C. S. Nott, *Teachings of Gurdjieff*, p. 27) that Ouspensky's presence with Denikin was due to Orage's putting him in touch with the British engineer and intelligence agent F. S. Pinder, who later appears in the entourage of Gurdjieff.

attending the séances were T. S. Eliot, David Garnett and Herbert Read who was Orage's latest literary pupil.

Ouspensky, though strikingly large and blond almost to the point of albinism, was in some ways unimpressive. 'When sitting in reflection or repose', writes Kenney, 'he hunched himself together and looked like a dejected bird huddling up in a rainstorm.' Garnett thought he looked rather like Woodrow Wilson: 'the same lavish display of false teeth, the same baffled, unseeing eye, the same spiritual aura of high thinking and patent medicines.' But he had an overwhelming effect on Orage. 'Why, Kenney', he said, 'I may find that all I have regarded as the real me, the literary man, the artist, the philosopher, all is artificial. Perhaps my real bent is cobbling old boots.' This remark gives the clue to the impact of the doctrines of Ouspensky and Gurdjieff. They taught that by certain spiritual and physical exercises the artificial and mechanical personality could be stripped bare, the true personality discovered, and the way opened to a new kind of awareness through which lay access to genuine humanity and the higher wisdom. It had affinities too with some aspects of psychoanalysis, but made higher claims and was based on theory, not scientific observation.

It may at first sight seem strange that a group of liberal, sceptical, western European literary people should have been so impressed, especially when this doctrine was wrapped in a cocoon of cabalistic, numerological, gymnosophistical jargon about the fourth dimension and the true ratio of zero to infinity. 'To these meditations', as Dr. Johnson said, 'humanity is unequal.'[1] Part of the reason was the trauma of the war itself, which had devastated the world in which they had been brought up and cast darkness over their future. Then there was the fascination with all things Russian which marked the western intellectual world ever since their youth, making Tchekov, Dostoevsky and Tolstoy hardly less important names in English literary conversation than Shakespeare or Milton, and giving the Russian ballet a higher brow than the Italian opera. Yet though they admired Russian culture they detested the Russian autocracy more than any authority in Europe. Tolstoy could be

---

[1] A selection of Gurdjieffian terms may here be given: Legominism, park-dolgduty, helkdonis, hamolinadir, choongarry, akhaldan, iramsamkeep, and Kundabuffer.

admired, but not the Tsar. In a sense they were prepared emotionally for the convulsion of 1917, and whether they welcomed the Revolution or opposed it, Russia seemed a natural place to look for the intellectual lead they so desperately wanted.

Why the quest for a higher wisdom among such rational beings? Here one must remember that even those who had most deliberately shed traditional religion had been brought up in the shelter of its comfortable certainties. Nietzsche still brooded over them. Beatrice speculated on the next world gazing into her coronetted fireplace. And as Katherine put it almost at this time in a letter to Brett, 'It seems to me there is a great change come over the world since people like US believed in God. God is now gone for all of us. Yet we must believe and not only that, we must carry our weakness and our sin and our devilishness to somebody.' An approach such as Ouspensky's to this need was especially well adapted to appeal to those of the intelligentsia (to use a Russian word then just coming into vogue) who owed their claim to culture to their own efforts, as was the case with Orage and Katherine. The more intense the effort had been, and the more solitary, the greater the ease of demonstrating the artificiality of the achievement: such was the perception of Ouspensky and Gurdjieff and the secret of their power.

One cannot doubt that Orage was genuinely impressed by Ouspensky. But there was another reason as well for Orage to be looking for a new life. The *New Age* was dying, and Orage himself was on the rocks financially. 'Getting advts for the N.A. is such a bore lately', he wrote to Read, 'I haven't got any. This contracts space, and, by the same token, reduces my need for MSS.' Some of the backers who had seen him through earlier difficulties had withdrawn their subsidies, and in the bleak economic climate of 1921 others were hard to find. The readers attracted by the now shattered Guild Socialist movement had turned elsewhere. His curiously eclectic paper, dominated by Douglasite propaganda but with strong dashes of psychoanalysis, now had a circulation of barely 2,000 and offered its purchaser only twelve pages. Pound had gone to Paris. After fifteen years of editorship, and at the age of forty-seven, Orage was ripe for change.

✤ 12 ✤

The Harmonious Development of Man

The stay at the more comfortable Villa Flora improved Katherine's health, but in April 1920, after less than three months, she escaped to England, alarmed by Jinnie Fullerton's plans to convert her to Roman Catholicism. Her arrival cannot have been very welcome to Murry, who had embarked on a complicated affair with Brett, and was at the height of the period of editorship for which he is justly renowned. He had spotted that Katherine's daily letters from abroad, though superficially as loving as ever, were forced; and her own insights and discipline were becoming sharper. They resumed residence together at East Heath Road, but it was an arm's-length affair and after some otherwise unrecorded quarrel he found a letter from her on the kitchen table:

> Forgive me. I believe I always do 'start it'. It's become a half-unconscious habit with me to exaggerate my opinions whenever I speak to you just to provoke your attention—to stir you—to rouse you. It is simply horrid. I never talk in that extreme dogmatic way to others you know [she was forgetting about L.M.] I hear myself even *lying* to you to bring you out of your cave. . . . It all narrows down to the old evil. No time to talk anything *out* or to think or to be gently poised. No time for that long breath. So we are both unjust to each other very often, and sometimes I *know* I am unjust in my criticism. It's so difficult to explain: we have to take things on trust. A whole book wouldn't explain it fully. But let's try and get free and write—live and write. Anything else isn't worth living. You see we are both abnormal: I have too much vitality—and you not enough.

Just before she came back to England they had played the game of deciding who their real friends were, and Murry had suggested Virginia Woolf as one for the list. Katherine had been more hesitant, perhaps because she was conscious of a rather malicious review she had written of Virginia's latest novel *Night and Day*, which had led Virginia in her turn to declare, 'I'm not going to call this a success—or if I must, I'll call it the wrong kind of success.' Nor, on the whole, though Katherine and Virginia arranged to meet, was their meeting a success. Katherine seemed to show no surprise or pleasure after eight months of absence, and struck Virginia as 'entirely self-centred: although concentrated upon her art'. The relationship, Virginia felt, was intimate and intense, rather than open; they did not meet again after August 1920, nor did they correspond.

In a sense Katherine had already given Murry his freedom, while retaining the right to address love-letters to him and be cross with him when the spirit moved her. She admired his work, too, though she criticised it penetratingly, and without avail. She told him that if he *cried* for God's sake to just cry, not to be a voice crying in the wilderness. But he could never escape the parsonical note. Burlap, Huxley's picture of Murry at about this time, is a caricature, but an extremely convincing one, which its victim himself was quick to recognise when *Point Counter Point* came out in 1929: moist, sanctimonious, high-flown and libidinous. The affair with Brett, which was to lead to much sorrow, was soon to be succeeded by an attachment to Asquith's daughter Princess Bibesco, who was married to the Roumanian minister in London. As so often, Murry's offer of love was mingled with literature, and in due course Elizabeth Bibesco was to be printed in the *Athenaeum*, much to Katherine's indignation.

There was a kind of rhythm to Katherine's life now, though she would never have admitted it; and it was rhythm with increasing funds behind it as her literary income increased. September found her once more in Menton looked after by L.M. but this time in a separate establishment from Jinnie Fullerton, the Villa Isola Bella. Murry was left behind to deal with his editorial responsibilities. The dream of 'The Heron' had passed, but although Katherine now appeared happy and productive she had bad dreams. In one of them the long unseen Beatrice led a rout of vile, drunken Bohemians who swarmed round her bed. 'You don't take me in old dear', screamed the visionary Beatrice; 'You've played the lady once too often . . .

coming it over me . . . femme marquée.' Then she found herself in a theatre where the play slowly drifted to a standstill and a black, iron curtain was slowly lowered. The world was coming to an end. At Christmas Murry came out to visit her.

These Christmas visits were always moments of crisis. That of 1919 had produced 'The Man Without a Temperament'. Christmas 1920 was worse—it spelt the end of the *Athenaeum* and an open breach between the two. There was a financial as well as a psychological background, though in Katherine's case the two were readily confused. She used money and financial affairs generally as a weapon in the endless war she waged with Murry, whose feelings about finance were extremely conventional, not to say stingy. Now they were both reasonably prosperous, which made them more inclined than ever to take it out of one another. Murry in particular had done well that year. His name was now in *Who's Who*. Apart from his substantial salary he had received advances for two books, and he had other journalistic earnings as well. But the *Athenaeum* was losing money, in spite of its distinguished contributors. It paid the contributors[1] and the staff too well, unlike the *New Age*, and it was over-officered. Rowntree could not stand the pace. Worst of all, Katherine was sick of it, and on 8 December she wrote ending her contributions: 'I have sent back the books today. My dear Bogey, it is with the most extreme reluctance that I am writing to tell you K.M. can't go on.'

It was not that she found it hard to write. Her health was worse but her pen was flowing freely on stories. It also flowed in criticism of Murry, though the criticism contained some helpful suggestions as well: 'You ought to write a book on Keats . . . there are still traces of what I call your sham personality in this book . . . can't you see what a *farce* it makes of you preaching the good life . . . how *can* you lay your sweat up in a phial for future generations?' This was stimulated by his collection of essays, *The Evolution of an Intellectual*. But when she had heard about Princess Bibesco, first

---

[1] Admittedly the pay was not high by modern standards. The marked copies still preserved at Great Turnstile show pieces by Lytton Strachey (£5); Santayana (£3); Eliot (£4 4s); Clive Bell (£5); D. H. Lawrence (£4); Bertrand Russell (£2 12s); Julian Huxley (£3 3s); Paul Valéry (£5); Virginia Woolf (£3 13s 6d). For short reviews Murry paid 7s 6d–12s. It was all measured by the inch, including Katherine's contributions.

from Murry and then, just before Murry came for Christmas, from Elizabeth Bibesco herself, her detachment from the editor of the *Athenaeum* became an alienation from Bogey. 'What happens to your personal life', she informed him on getting a letter from him saying he was 'annihilated', 'does NOT affect me. I have of you what I want—a relationship which is unique, but it is not what the world understands by *marriage*. That is to say I do not in any way *depend* on you, neither can you shake me. Nobody can.'

When he arrived at Menton the faithful L.M. was turned out of the villa to provide him with a separate bedroom; and when he tried to get his own back in the new world of independence by charging her not only half a cab fare but half the tip for a journey together he was pilloried for intolerable meanness. But a great many things were settled about their joint lives. East Heath Road and 'Broomies' (the cottage in Sussex which was the last pale gleam of the 'Heron' dream) were to be sold. The *Athenaeum* was to be given up—it is highly probable that Rowntree had already virtually taken this decision for them. Now that they were both reasonably well known they would be free-lances, living abroad in company but not together. It was as sensible an arrangement as any they had ever made. When Murry had returned to England to carry out this programme her letters back to him became briefer than before, and less pretentious: the protective playfulness and whimsicality is much less evident.

Lawrence heard all about it from Kot. 'A nice little kettle of old fish', he wrote from Taormina on learning of the death of the *Athenaeum*, 'I hear the *Athenaeum* lost £5,000 under our friend the mudworm . . . two mudworms they are, playing into one another's bellies.' Savage indeed, but no more so than what Katherine had written to Murry only a month before about Lawrence's latest publication *The Lost Girl*: 'I feel privately as though Lawrence had possessed an animal and fallen under a curse.'

The Murrys and L.M. left Menton in the spring for Switzerland where the two women established themselves first at Baugy, near Montreux, then at Sierre in the Valais, and then, climbing still higher, at the Chalet des Sapins, Montana. Murry returned for a time to England to deliver a series of lectures which ultimately became one of his most successful and frequently reprinted books,

The Problem of Style. The invitation had come from Walter Raleigh, Professor of English Literature at Oxford, and Murry had at first been nervous about accepting: but he need not have been. The lectures were crowded, and his audiences, far from falling away as the summer weeks passed, increased to over two hundred. For Murry it was not only a success but an important discovery of unsuspected power as a public speaker.

Katherine was cheered by the appearance of her latest story in the *Athenaeum*'s old rival the *London Mercury*, but she was now almost unable to walk. 'I can only walk from the kerridge to the door and from the door to the kerridge.' According to the doctors she was now seeing, both her lungs were infected, one very seriously. All they would say was that she still had a chance. 'I tried to get the word "Guéri" but it was no good.' The protective whimsicality was returning to her letters, though sometimes it almost achieved greatness: 'The FOOD. It's got no nerves. You know what I mean? It seems to lie down and wait for you; the very steaks are meek . . . the asparagus is always stone dead. As to the purée de pommes de terre, you are inclined to call it "uncle".' Creative writing, despite her weakness, was coming more easily again. Sadleir's firm Constable, seizing on the fashion for her stories, had commissioned another volume and the title-piece (originally called 'At the Bay' but published as 'The Garden Party') which was one of her longest, was finished in September. 'Thanks be to God', she wrote when it was complete, 'I wish there was a God.' A little earlier she had told Murry, 'No, one can't believe in *God*. But I must believe in something more *nearly* than I do.'

But Murry was at Montana himself for a good part of the time, often living separately, tapping away at his Corona portable for the beginning of yet another work—*Keats and Shakespeare*. The Woolfs were sure he would end as Professor at either Oxford or Cambridge. 'The Murrain', commented Lawrence, 'is renewing his bald youth like the vulture, and stuffing himself with Oxford garbage.'[1] Truly his output was enormous, and never greater than in 1920 and 1921, during which he published no fewer than four books, apart from his journalism and the composition of his lectures.

[1] Murry's extremely hostile review of *Women in Love*, virtually denouncing it as obscene, had just appeared.

But as between him and Katherine the position was completely false, and no formula of independence would really cure it. He was now convinced she could never recover, but was unable either to console her or detach himself. He could only lament in private his own inadequacy, act (until early in 1921, when she appointed Pinker) as her literary agent, and hope despondently for the best. 'As things were', he wrote later about this period, 'the burden of my unfaith became to Katherine too grievous to be borne . . . we knew ourselves to be travelling different paths. The ways, at last, really had parted.'

Katherine turned elsewhere for consolation: and to whom but to Kot, through whose letter-box at Acacia Road dropped Lawrence's tirades about the Murrys, Brett's agonisings over her love for Murry and her devotion to Katherine, and now Katherine's own melodramatic appeal. 'Not a day passes but I think of you. It is sad that we are enemies. If only you would accept my love. It is *good* love—not the erotic bag kind. But no . . . when my name is mentioned you cross yourself and touch wood.' She enclosed a photograph of herself, demanding he should burn it if he still hated her. Of course he kept it. It is still among his papers. His devotion to her had never been, and never would be in doubt. But when he looked at all his other letters is it surprising that he had not kept up his correspondence with her, which is what she meant by his enmity?

But this time he did write, and from his contact with all things Russian told her about a certain Doctor Ivan Manoukhine, on whom for a time Katherine's hopes of a cure came to be fixed. Manoukhine had been Gorky's doctor and personal friend until, after a period of imprisonment in Russia, he had escaped and established himself in Paris. In November 1921 Gorky himself, in an interview at Stockholm, told the world press that Manoukhine had 'at last discovered the remedy' for tuberculosis, and that the actual manuscript of Manoukhine's work was in Gorky's luggage.[1]

But Katherine had been looking for a spiritual cure also—a

---

[1] Manoukhine's treatment consisted of irradiation of the spleen to increase the production of leucocytes, in which he considered there were powers of resistance to the bacillus (*Lancet*, 2 April 1921). The treatment was expensive, and though it improved the weight of the patient it did not check the disease.

spiritual cure above all. Even before her letter to Kot, and unknown to Murry, she had resumed her correspondence with her first editor, Orage, and in a remarkable letter which is almost the only paper Orage seems to have preserved, she acknowledged her debt to the man who, as he once put it, 'wrote writers':

11 June 1921

Dear Orage,
    This letter has been on the tip of my pen for many months.
    I want to tell you how sensible I am of your wonderful unfailing kindness to me in the 'old days'. And to thank you for all you let me learn from you. I am still—more shame to me—very low down in the school. But you taught me to write, you taught me to think; you showed me what there was to be done and what *not* to do.
    My dear Orage, I cannot tell you how often I call to mind your conversation or how often, in *writing*, I remember my master. Does that sound impertinent? Forgive me if it does.
    But let me thank you, Orage—*Thank you for everything.* If only one day I might write a book of stories good enough to 'offer' you. . . . If I don't succeed in keeping the coffin from the door you will know this was my ambition.
Yours in admiration and gratitude
Katherine Mansfield

I haven't said a bit of what I wanted to say. This letter sounds as if it was written by a screw-driver, and I wanted it to sound like an admiring, respectful but warm piping beneath your windows. I'd like to send my love, too, if I wasn't so frightened. K.M.

Coming as it does so close to the appeal to Koteliansky, this letter's motivation is evident. She was growing desperate for firm ground, and her cry could not go unanswered, even if the answer was a strange one. Kot had suggested Manoukhine. Orage sent a copy of *Cosmic Anatomy* (it bore the name of Lewis Wallace, but there are reasons for thinking Orage had a hand in it) which had just been published. The covering letter, which is now lost, was addressed not to Katherine but to Murry, and requested a review for the *New Age*. It must have been written almost exactly at the time Ouspensky was making his first impact on London, and it was under Ouspensky's influence that Orage dealt with Katherine's cry for help.[1]

At this crisis, excited by hopes of a physical cure and increasingly fascinated by the semi-occult spiritual possibilities she found in *Cosmic Anatomy*, Katherine also received a disturbing letter—'almost frightening'—which 'brought back the inexplicable past'. It is difficult to doubt that the correspondent was Beatrice.[2] 'In some way I fear her. I feared her at Chancery Lane. There was a peculiar recklessness in her manner and in her tones which made me feel she would recognise no barriers at all. At the same time, of course, one is fascinated.' It also flashed through her mind that Beatrice must 'have a large number of letters of mine which don't bear thinking about'.

At the end of January, with the intermediacy of Kot and the service of L.M., Katherine set out for Paris to 'see if that Russian can bake me or boil me or serve me up in some more satisfying way'. At the same time she was full of *Cosmic Anatomy*. On 1 February she was writing to Kot with delight about Manoukhine: 'Yes, one has every confidence in such a man.' She had achieved almost the

[1] Murry's version of these events (*God* 23-4) is that Wallace's book reached him in Switzerland 'just before Christmas' simply in the course of literary business, and he 'put it aside' as uninteresting, indeed not the sort of book he cared for; and Katherine unfortunately picked it up. He does not refer to (perhaps did not know of) Katherine's letter to Orage; or to the fact that he did write a review of it, though this is recorded in K.M.'s Journal. Murry had not written for the *New Age* for many years, and the conclusion that Orage meant the book to reach Katherine in this roundabout way seems inescapable. The surviving letter from Katherine to Orage is only part of their correspondence. Her Journal records another letter to him on 29 January 1922. The only words to survive from this (or possibly a later) letter are given by Orage in his *Talks with Katherine Mansfield*: after a rereading of her stories she felt, 'There is not one that I dare show to God.'

[2] The first edition of the *Journal* (1927) attributes this letter to 'B—' and has 'rue de Tournon' instead of 'Chancery Lane'. The definitive edition of the *Journal* (1954) follows the original text of Katherine's Journal by giving the letter to 'Mimi'. There is a mystery here, made more complex by some pencilled notes in Murry's handwriting in the London Library copy of Carco's *Montmartre à Vingt Ans* correcting Carco's quotation from the 1927 edition to conform with the 1954 edition, and identifying 'Mimi' as Vere Bartrick-Baker. Yet no correspondence, let alone intimate relationship, between K.M. and Vere Bartrick-Baker is elsewhere on record; the feelings expressed are characteristic of K.M.'s about Beatrice. The departure from the original text in the 1927 edition must have been deliberate—it is impossible to mistake the words. The motive remains obscure; and Beatrice (in Chancery Lane) remains the strongest candidate for 'Mimi'.

last of a further volume of stories, later published as *The Dove's Nest*, but now the moods were swinging faster and faster. In the course of less than a fortnight Murry, who had stayed behind, was both urged to come and told that he must stay away. He had no faith in Manoukhine and his system. But in the middle of February 1922 they were together again in Paris, reading the enthusiastic reviews of *The Garden Party*.

It must have been about this time[1] that one of the strangest passages in Katherine's past was sardonically rounded off. Murry unexpectedly ran into Carco, now an established literary man with a fine collection of Modiglianis, in the café d'Harcourt where they had first met. They had not crossed for ten years. Carco noted Murry had lost the freshness of youth that had attracted him at their first meeting. His face was lined, his chin sharpened, his greenish eyes (Katherine in a moment of inspiration had called them 'reine claude eyes') had lost their gleam. They strolled together finding less to say than they had expected, and parted with a hesitant arrangement to meet again: Murry particularly wanted to see Carco's Modiglianis. Katherine had been mentioned, but Murry had made it clear that he had no intention Carco should meet her again; and when they had parted Carco was by no means sure he wanted to meet Murry again—'c'était comme en cachette, qu'il entendait me revoir'.

That evening Carco took a walk—so he tells us—reflecting on the whole story which had led to 'Je ne Parle pas Français' and what Katherine might be like now in her hour of success. 'Je l'avais connue réellement telle que le lecteur du conte devait se la représenter.' Then he found himself outside the café de l'Univers in the Place du Théâtre-Français, and there, just inside, were Katherine and Murry. There were embarrassed greetings, with the two men unable to admit their earlier encounter. Carco was horrified by her appearance. 'Her handsome dark eyes flashed with the old ardour

[1] *Bohème d'Artiste* 253–60 and *Montmartre à Vingt Ans* 204–5. Carco, of course, as a professional writer about Bohemia, heightens everything. He even suggests, in describing these encounters, that they took place on the eve of Katherine's entry into Gurdjieff's Institute some months later, and puts a reference to it into Katherine's mouth. This could not have been so because Murry was not with her at that time. But the substance of Carco's account can hardly be invented.

and the old feverishness. She exerted a kind of magnetism, but she looked ill and her poor little hands, so pale and shrunken, filled me with agony. I tried to talk. She hid her hands under the table.' After a few minutes, refusing Murry's offer of a drink, he pleaded an engagement, and hurried away.

The Manoukhine treatment was disagreeable but seemed to strengthen her and in June they returned to Switzerland—an agonizing journey on which Murry behaved with exceptional incompetence, according to Katherine—lost the tickets, gave 500 francs to the porter in mistake for 50, left Katherine's favourite carriage clock in the train, lost his fountain pen; and when at last they arrived at the rooms they had arranged at Randogne, near Sierre, they had to fend for themselves; L.M. had gone back to England at Katherine's request, to fit in with a new plan for Katherine's life: 'Until I am well it's foolishness for us to be together.' When Katherine was stronger she would divide her time between Murry (cottage together in Sussex) and L.M. (travelling on the Continent and writing). In the meantime L.M. should get a job, which she proceeded to do, searching for a suitable tea-shop to keep on the south coast of England, and finding a home for Katherine's cat Wingly, whose pilgrimage had started in East Heath Road and carried him to half the mountain resorts in the Valais.

Instead there was Brett, who had joined them in Paris and was utterly overwhelmed by Katherine's greatness and beauty:

She means so much to me [she had written to Kot early in June] and after all this while—after nearly two years of silence to find her gentle, beautiful, and holding out both hands to me—overwhelms me . . . there she was standing at the foot of the stairs—small, fragile, and wonderfully beautiful. . . . It's no good Kot—Katherine is so loveable that there can be no half measures. One loves her passionately, because it is impossible to do otherwise. She *understands* beyond all understanding—and she has won so complete a victory over herself that one could almost worship . . . Katherine has come through it all, to the other side—she has discarded much of all that was bad in her. She has put herself up before herself—judged herself and cut out the bad. . . .

Indeed, during that short summer at Randogne Katherine had succeeded in surrounding herself with as much absolute devotion as she ever achieved. She had wholly mastered Murry, reconquered Kot, and commanded the adoration of Brett. To complete it she now resummoned L.M. by the curiously elaborate stratagem of priming her to write offering her services as a paid companion—a device adopted to soothe Murry's pride.

Early in August 1922, avoiding an invitation to meet her father, she announced a decision to return to England, and on 14 August made a will, saying to one of the beneficiaries, 'Whenever I prepare for a journey I prepare as though for death.'[1] She left her wardrobe and a gold watch to L.M. and asked that a book each by way of keepsake should be sent to Walter de la Mare, H. M. Tomlinson, J. D. Fergusson Murry's mentor in Paris, Gordon Campbell, the Schiffs, Sorapure, Orage, and D. H. Lawrence, whose latest novel *Aaron's Rod* she had just been reading with admiration and forgiveness. Koteliansky and Brett were not remembered by books but by trinkets. Murry was appointed her literary heir and executor with specific directions to publish as little as possible of what she left behind, and to tear up and burn as much as he felt able. 'He will understand that I desire to leave as few traces of my camping ground as possible.' On 14 August she set out alone, and on the 16th, without having told any of her friends except Brett, she was staying in Pond Street.

In February of that year the work of Ouspensky had been reinforced and to some extent confused by the advent of the second sage from Eastern Europe, George Ivanovich Gurdjieff.

Ouspensky's earlier career can be traced with some precision, but not Gurdjieff's. One person who knew him well commented that he never gave a direct answer to a straightforward question, and he was particularly reserved about his origins. He was in fact an Armenian, born at Kars, on the frontier between Russia and Turkey in 1877. His youth had certainly been spent in Central Asia, where he gained an entry on the files of British intelligence as a Russian agent; but he was also concerned in hypnotism, occult studies, and trading in carpets. Katherine saw more shrewdly than she knew

[1] *See* Appendix.

when, in a mordant moment, she said he reminded her of a carpet-merchant. The first reliable account of him is Ouspensky's description of an encounter with him early in 1915 in the capacity of manager of a 'Hindu Ballet' in Moscow. At the time of his arrival in London Gurdjieff was in his early forties; and his whole style was very much more that of a ballet-master than of a sage or mystic. His build was stocky, his actions energetic and cat-like, and he wore a heavy, black, almost military moustache. Above it were caverned, piercing eyes and a completely shaven head which was often concealed by an astrakhan cap.

Gurdjieff was not an intellectual. His command of English or any other west European language was negligible, and even his Russian —the tongue he usually spoke—was incorrect. His teachings do not suggest extensive reading or formal education. What he possessed, and in abnormal measure, were energy, self-confidence and control over his passions. He lived in the world of physical movement, and the organisation of dancing was at the centre—not the periphery— of his life. If his career had taken a slightly different turn he would be famous in the annals of ballet rather than in the dubious world of the occult. He was a choreographer who had stumbled on mysticism for his *mise en scène*. He had the power of controlled fury which commands instant obedience.

Although Ouspensky knew Gurdjieff well, and considered himself in some sort as his disciple, he had reservations about this extraordinary man: and well he might. Ouspensky sought the truth through esoteric study: Gurdjieff had no hesitation in claiming he had found it. There is a robustness, an earthiness, even a ruthlessness about Gurdjieff which is wholly absent from the tortured, over-intellectual Ouspensky. Ouspensky was a lecturer and a sage, but Gurdjieff led a troupe—in the literal sense, for they constituted his *corps de ballet* as well as his disciples—and he was their undisputed master. 'When Gurdjieff spoke to you', a pupil records, 'it impressed not only your mind but your feeling.' *'Merde de la merde'*, he would sometimes roar at his appreciative squad.[1] He had led them under the banner of 'The Institute for the Harmonious

---

[1] 'He not peacock or crow, but turkey', Gurdjieff once observed genially of a pupil. The downcast object of this remark was quite cheered up on being told afterwards that really the master was very fond of turkey (Nott, *Teachings of Gurdjieff*, p. 63).

Development of Man' through innumerable hardships over plains and mountains in revolutionary Russia, establishing them successively at Essentuki, Tiflis, and Constantinople, and trained them with iron discipline in Eastern dances for his and their benefit.

From Constantinople he had led them to Berlin, where for a time, he had plans to settle; but his proposed purchase of the Dalcroze building there broke down and in February 1922 he had arrived in England with the purpose of establishing his Institute in London. But despite representations to the Home Office, in which Orage took a part, this was not allowed and Gurdjieff returned to the Continent where he acquired from the widow of Maître Labori, former counsel to Dreyfus, a large estate called the Château du Prieuré at Fontainebleau-Avon. It is said that the arrangement was encouraged by President Poincaré himself. However that may be, in the late summer of 1922 Gurdjieff was gathering his flock at Fontainebleau.

Katherine's arrival in London therefore coincided with critical moments in the lives of Gurdjieff, launching his new institute; and Ouspensky, who was resolved that he could not collaborate with Gurdjieff though he was prepared to recommend to his discipline those pupils who asked for 'a short cut'. It also coincided with a crisis in the life of Orage who by that time had decided to give up the *New Age* and, with others of Ouspensky's circle, throw in his lot with Gurdjieff. Four days before Katherine reached London he had written in strict confidence to Herbert Read wondering whether he would 'feel disposed to "edit" the N.A. for a year for a couple of guineas a week? Your duties would really be rather small, because practically everything would be arranged.' The offer was not taken up.

Katherine made immediate contact with Orage whom Brett saw briefly at Pond Street soon afterwards and 'did not like the back of his neck'; and Orage introduced her to Ouspensky. An entry in her *Journal* records that: 'My first conversation with O[rage] took place on 30 August 1922'; and at least three more talks between them followed, as well as several conversations with Kot. She also saw Sorapure, Sullivan and Edward Garnett; and records a lecture at Warwick Gardens on 14 September, which was the home of Lady Rothermere. This lecture, though she does not say so, was given by Ouspensky. For the first time for more than two years the letters to Murry (who had returned also, but was living with friends in Sussex)[1] cease to be daily, and those there are neither wheedle, cajole, flirt nor scold. She had ceased to live by the mail, though it now brought her, in September, the first personal reminder she had had for more than two years from Lawrence in the shape of a postcard, sent via Ottoline, which carried the one word 'Ricordi'. Of course he had heard of her adventure from Kot, and there was little more that he could say.

She had travelled first class from France and 'lived in taxis', nursing the illness that she still called 'my heart'. It had always been 'her heart' ever since she was a girl in New Zealand. Her letters, apart from a brilliant characterisation of Joyce's *Ulysses* as 'a portentous warning' have an apprehensive, almost at times scatterbrained note about them, and none of them mention either Orage or Ouspensky until the very end of that last stay in London. With Kot she discussed 'ideas', but as she came away she felt she had not told him the real truth, that she was incapable of telling the truth, perhaps that she hardly existed at all. They had talked of being single and of growing. 'I believe it. I try to act up to it. But the reality is far different.'

The *New Age* for 28 September 1922 marked the end of Orage's fifteen years of editorship and he announced bravely that he would 'shortly be leaving London in connection with work of general and special interest'. The editor's chair and proprietorship were to be taken over by Major Arthur Moore, late R.A.F.[2] So, in a rumble of mysticism and financial monomania ended the enterprise launched

[1] At Ditchling, with Vivian Locke-Ellis. Also in the house was a mystic named W. J. Dunning, a practitioner of yoga.

[2] Moore was much more highly qualified for editorship than this announcement might suggest. He had been a classical scholar at Oxford and President of the Union, and had then covered the revolution in Turkey and the Balkan Wars for *The Times*. After fighting through the whole war, including Mons and the Dardanelles, he had resumed his career with *The Times* as correspondent in India and Afghanistan, and had written the novel *Orient Express*. His editorship of the *New Age* was brief, for in 1924 he became assistant editor of the Calcutta daily the *Statesman*, rising in due course to be its editor. The succession of this Buchanesque character, almost straight out of *Greenmantle*, to the editorship of the *New Age* together with the affiliations of both Ouspensky and Gurdjieff with the British Intelligence officer F. S. Pinder almost suggests, without any direct evidence, that in its latter days under Orage the paper was closer to Government agencies than might be supposed.

by Shaw, which had in its turn launched more considerable writers than any periodical this century. Early in October Drs. James Young, J. M. Alcock, Nicoll, and a number of others, departed among sensational whispers to take up residence at Gurdjieff's Institute. A few days earlier, on 27 September, Katherine wrote a strange letter to Murry announcing her intention to go to Paris in a few days to resume treatment under Manoukhine and inviting 'Dear Bogey' to come up to London the Sunday night before her departure. But, she went on, 'There is no need to . . . I'm seeing Orage Saturday or Sunday evening, but otherwise I am free. I don't expect you to come and don't even recommend the suggestion . . . I think I'd better say—it's fairer—that I am engaged on Saturday from 8 to 10.30 and on Sunday from 8 to 10.30, even though the engagement is only provisional. Otherwise I am free.' He did not come. And Katherine had her interview with Orage within a day or two of the last number of his *New Age*.

Two or three days later, on 2 October, she set out for Paris with L.M. and established herself at her old wartime haunt, the Select Hotel in the rue de la Sorbonne. Orage remained behind in London, and it appears that for a week or so she had no contact with him or any of Gurdjieff's circle. She had further treatment by Manoukhine, to whom it seems she mentioned the possibility of entering Gurdjieff's Institute—something which so alarmed the doctor that he wrote privately to Fontainebleau warning them not to accept her. She was also completing her latest work on a Koteliansky translation of Dostoevsky's letters, which was posted to him on 9 October.

Then comes the extraordinary, almost schizophrenic journal entry of 10 October in which she convinced herself that she should submit herself to Gurdjieff. 'Convinced herself' is literally true, because much of the passage is cast in the form of a dialogue between Katherine and herself as if they were two separate people. But none of the arguments against the desperate step being proposed is given the chance of prevailing. The dialogue is bogus, the mind was already made up. The true split revealed is between herself and a picture of herself struggling with herself in that hotel bedroom. 'It's simply incredible', she wrote to Murry only a day or two later, 'watching K.M. to see how little causes a panic. . . .'

Never, in that long agonised entry, does she mention the success which had crowned her literary struggle—not even to reject it. She saw herself as a prisoner, an invalid growing worse and worse, whom nobody could help. Her illness was beyond the reach of medicine or science—a fact proved by the argument 'how can one be cured like a cow if one is not a cow'.[1] No: she must become 'a child of the sun' who would live a warm, ardent living life. Then follows what is in some ways the saddest note of all because for a moment the veil of make-believe was lifted: 'it would be a lie to say even a single word of any desire to love other people or to bring light to other, similar aspirations. That's enough. To be a child of the sun.'

On 14 October, her thirty-fourth birthday, Dr. Young came to Paris from Fontainebleau, and it must have been on this occasion that he gave her a medical examination, which had probably been requested by Gurdjieff after receiving Manoukhine's letter. In view of what happened, much responsibility rests on Dr. Young. In the evening Orage arrived from London on his way to the Prieuré; and in the course of the next day or two Katherine appears to have had an interview with Gurdjieff himself, who is said to have suggested a spell on the Riviera as likely to do her most good. However that may have been, on 17 October she took up residence at the Prieuré, making sure that none of her correspondents knew her intentions beforehand.

There were about a hundred inhabitants, and for most of them life was exceedingly rigorous. Early rising, hard physical labour in the extensive grounds, dancing under draconian discipline in the evening, brief slumber and short commons, were the order of the day. Bechhofer Roberts, who visited the place more than once at this time, noticed positive hatred in the eyes of those inmates who were restricted to soup when they looked at those to whom Gurdjieff permitted pudding. To the master, as he often put it, human beings were no more than machines. Only by discipline could the soul escape from its mechanical prison and achieve contentment and immortality. Habits must be broken, since they were the responses to external stimuli which worked the human machine. Orage, for instance, as a chain smoker, was forbidden to smoke, and it seems probable that Katherine was discouraged from writing.

[1] An odd piece of insight in view of the ultimate treatment she was to receive. Or did this thought occur to her in conversation with Gurdjieff?

Some of the dances were contrived, in a way a drill-sergeant could hardly have improved upon, to produce the utmost discomfort and exhaustion—above all the celebrated technique of 'Stop', on the cry of which, uttered by the master at any moment, everyone within earshot had to remain frozen in precisely the position he had assumed. Some, in consequence, fell flat on their faces, and one man, who had just inhaled a cigarette, is recorded by Ouspensky himself as sitting with tears trickling down his cheeks while the tobacco-smoke slowly escaped from his mouth and nostrils. So far as the English contingent was concerned the Institute for the Harmonious Development of Man closely resembled a glasshouse (in the military sense of that phrase) with the curious qualification that its inmates were volunteers. As Gurdjieff admitted, there was something sinister about his establishment, 'et cela est nécessaire'.

His treatment of Katherine, at any rate to begin with, was cautious, and for about six weeks she was allowed the comparative comfort accorded to visitors. Her first letters from Fontainebleau to Brett, Kot, and of course Murry are receptive, almost optimistic. But in November she too was assigned to a modest cell and midnight dancing, and to washing up. 'My hands are ruined for the present with scraping carrots and peeling onions', she wrote to L.M. at the beginning of December. Her letters to Murry were less frequent than on any previous separation, and her submission to Gurdjieff was absolute. 'Mr. Gurdjieff', she wrote to Murry, 'is there to do to us what we wish to do to ourselves but are afraid to do. Well, theoretically, that is all very wonderful, but practically it must mean suffering, because one cannot always understand. . . . Oh Bogey how I love this place! It is like a dream—or a miracle.'

She had long intense conversations with Orage when he could be spared from digging, building, wood-cutting, and other exercises to which the ex-editor had been put in this purgatory on earth. 'Are we dead?' she asked him, 'or was our love of literature an affectation which has dropped off like a mask?' But she could not resist trying to write, and Bechhofer Roberts, on a visit at that time considered she was happy: 'a frail, doomed silhouette watching the dancing . . . so confident in her ultimate cure that she told me the plan for her next book. She did not say that Gurdjieff and his colony would be in it but it seemed to me, perhaps mistakenly, that the respectful but sardonic smile in her eyes hinted that sooner or later she would make fun of these experiences.'

The outer world was certainly kept at a distance. Poor L.M., after a bit, got a job on a farm in Normandy, and received hints that her destiny was to 'join Jack on a farm'. Katherine's letters to him were written in a curiously flat key, at first. 'You think I am like other people—I mean: *normal*. I'm not. I don't know which is the ill me or the well me. I am simply one pretence after another. Only now I recognise it.' At one moment she urged him to come out and follow the teaching: 'You could learn the banjo here and if the worst came to the worst always make enough to keep you with playing it.' At least he might ask Ouspensky out to dinner. But Murry, who had got so far as to converse with a mystic named Dunning, only wrote, gloomily and tactlessly, saying he would see her 'on the other side'. Then, in a much more loving and realistic letter, he learned that Gurdjieff was buying some cows, and was 'going to build a high couch in the stable where I can sit and inhale their breath! I know later on that I shall be put in charge of these cows. Everyone calls them already "Mrs. Murry's cows!"'

That was late in November, and in due course the high couch was installed on a gallery constructed above the cowshed, reached by a narrow stair. It was carpeted, and the walls and ceiling were elaborately decorated with paintings, among which was one of Orage with the body of an elephant. On the ceiling was the 'enneagram'—a mysterious figure conveying Gurdjieff's teaching. In the end it was to be her bedroom, but for the time being the master cautiously moved that from the cell to which she had been assigned to more comfortable quarters, earning a grateful entry in her *Journal* for his penetration in realising she had learned whatever the cell had to teach her. The thought that perhaps 'we "make up" Mr. Gurdjieff's wonderful understanding' was instantly banished. She forbade Murry to come out to see her for Christmas.

One can only guess at Gurdjieff's real motives in his treatment of Katherine, but he must have considered her attachment to Orage, for whom it is probable he already had plans. Gurdjieff was ambitious. He was proposing to capture Paris with his ballet, and his eyes were on America. A well-known woman writer was clearly a valuable disciple, but his knowledge of human nature, which was considerable, must have suggested to him that Katherine, even apart from her state of health, would present problems. The solution of making her a kind of show-piece for the Prieuré's many visitors, while bizarre, was also ingenious.

Did he have any premonition that she was going to die? Early in January Murry had a letter from Katherine dated 31 December which, without so much as wishing him a happy New Year, demanded he should come at once. 'Mr. Gurdjieff approves my plan and says will you come as his guest?' Though the words are brief and hurried they show no sign that anything may be amiss nor, in a way, did there seem to be when Murry arrived in the afternoon of 9 January 1923. He and Katherine had a long and serious interview. Their relationship, she explained, had been false; she had never been able to express her true anxieties; he had never been any help; he had even turned away as if in horror; the time had come for her to be free of that old love; and—the paradox was still there—to enter in a new one, a cottage in Cornwall together, where he would work on the land. It was all true except the last persistent dream which they both knew was hopeless. The picture of an almost saintly, ethereal Katherine is not quite correct. 'She had not, she said, really made up her mind about Mr. Gurdjieff.'

Murry does not seem to have met Gurdjieff that afternoon. At any rate he does not mention him in the two accounts he has given of that visit. But he met Orage 'for the first time for many years; and he seemed to me a changed man, much gentler and sweeter . . .'. Fairly early in the evening about ten o'clock, she said she was going to bed, and began making her way up the main staircase of the château, accompanied by Murry. He says she moved slowly, another witness that she ran up quickly, without touching the banisters. But half-way up she was seized with a fit of coughing, and by the time she reached her room blood was gushing from her mouth. Murry seemed to hear her say she was dying and rushed for help which arrived in the form of two doctors, probably Young and Nicoll. Both were psychiatrists, but even if they had been cardio-thoracic surgeons the results of that disastrous haemorrhage would have been the same, and at half-past ten she died. She was buried a day or two later at the municipal cemetery, and Orage and Murry were both at the graveside. So were Brett and L.M.. Gurdjieff distributed cornets of nuts and raisins, some of which he threw into the grave saying they contained the germs of renewal. But whenever, afterwards, he was asked about Katherine he would slowly repeat her name and reply: 'Katherine Mansfield. . . . Not remember.'

❧ 13 ❧

The *Adelphi*

Before the funeral, which was arranged by Murry with the municipal undertakers, there had been a kind of wake at the Prieuré at which speculative discussion was brought to a passionate close by the intervention of L.M. And after the ceremony at the grave Gurdjieff offered one of his oriental entertainments at which Murry became far too talkative, 'laughing hysterically', and Orage, who had seen much of L.M. in the day or two since she had rushed to be with her heroine, suggested she should take the widower to his bedroom. Next day she escorted Murry back across the Channel and deposited him at Ditchling with the mystic Dunning, whence he had set out. With him he took the whole of Katherine's papers, including her journal, and all the letters he had addressed to her over the years.

He was shattered and yet, like Bishop Proudie, relieved in a kind of way; and had to bear much blame from his friends for allowing Katherine to die in such strange circumstances, about which quite exaggerated rumours circulated. Lawrence, who had received 'your note via Kot' was generous. 'What is going to happen to us all?' he wrote. 'Perhaps it is good for Katherine not to have seen the next phase. We will unite up again when I come to England. It has been a savage enough pilgrimage. . . . The dead don't die. They look on and help.' In spite of the shock the pressure was off Murry. He was no longer monitored. Katherine's reputation and the whole of her work, published and unpublished, was in his keeping. More-over the Burlap in him was emancipated. His hostess at Ditchling treated him 'in a simple womanly way', and 'may have known what I needed better than I'. But when as a result he was confronted by her husband 'with the simple seriousness that made him attractive to me'; and by her declaration that 'I must come to her as myself,

not as the bereaved husband of Katherine Mansfield', he was
bewildered and out of his depth, and took refuge in Pond Street.

There, in 'the flat where the ceiling was so low that we had to
live on pancakes' he found Brett and L.M.—one in love with both
him and the dead Katherine, and the other trying against odds to
monopolise Katherine's memory. It was a strange though brief
triangle, with Brett developing a degree of hostility towards L.M.
(now rechristened 'Bill') almost equal to Katherine's: 'I feel a large
cushion is being pressed down on me.' At the same time Brett was
pouring out her feelings to Kot about Murry, with whom she
clearly, at this time, contemplated marriage. Never was Kot's
capacity as a father confessor more thoroughly tried. 'I pound all
the bad things', wrote Brett, 'superficial bad things, out of myself
against you and it does me good—they break and vanish—because
I know you will never let me down and pretend bad thoughts and
feelings are good ones in me.' It is hardly surprising that in this
painful situation Murry occasionally had recourse to the services of
a prostitute.

He had to consider his own future livelihood as well as his complex personal relationships, and here there was a measure of comfort. In one of the letters Katherine had written him from Fontainebleau she had suggested he should 'realise his capital', for he now
certainly had enough money set aside to make him more secure than
the ordinary literary man of his acquaintance, lifting him into the
rank of someone others would instinctively look to. Katherine's
books were selling well, with three (including the recently published
The Dove's Nest) in print; and there were several of his own producing royalties. As a literary journalist he could command the substantial income of £800 a year or so. 'I doubt', he had written about
a year earlier to an ambitious young literary man, 'whether there
are half a dozen men who make a living out of reputable criticism.
Luckily I happen to be one of them.' And then there were
Katherine's papers, all carefully husbanded despite her express wish
to the contrary. It is strange that someone who flitted so much from
place to place as Katherine did should have accumulated so many
papers, but she must have travelled with an archive.

Katherine's heritage: Murry was never to escape it or allow it to
escape him in either his literary or his private life. Her letters to

him, covering not much more than ten years, take up more than 700 pages of print. Her *Journal* covers 300. And then there were stories and fragments of stories, poems and sketches of poems, and all the workshop floor of a craftsman who rejected far more material than she used. It was being sorted out at Pond Street that summer and L.M. threw a shawl over it when Brett came into the room— or so Brett thought.

Then there was Lawrence. In his letter of condolence to Murry he had said he was asking his publisher to send his latest work, *Fantasia of the Unconscious*, which he wished Katherine could have read.[1] It had a massive effect on Murry. In February, mounting his motorbike (the 'half-motor car' Katherine had teased him about a few months earlier when he had bought it) he fled on it from the complexities of Pond Street and chugged off to a lonely farmhouse at Twyford, on the edge of Ashdown Forest. 'I was going to be, I was determined to be, really alone.'

Among Murry's many spiritual experiences it is difficult to emphasise one in particular, but he certainly regarded what happened to him at the Old Farm, Twyford, as overwhelmingly important. He sat down in the deserted living-room. 'Slowly and with an effort I made myself conscious that I was physically alone ... I tried to force that consciousness into every part of my body ... I at last had the sensation that I *was* in my hands and feet, that where they ended I also ended ... and beyond that frontier stretched out vast immensities ... where I ended it began—other, strange, terrible, menacing ... yet out upon this from the fragile rampart of my own body, I found the courage to peer. ... Somehow in that moment I knew that I had reached the pinnacle of personal being. I was as I had never been before. ... A moment came when the darkness changed to light ... the room was filled with a presence, and I knew that I was not alone—that I never could be alone any more, that the universe beyond held no menace, for I was part of it.' The passage, which runs to about 500 words, uses the personal pronoun more than fifty times.

[1] D.H.L. to Seltzer 3 February 1924: 'I just heard from Murry that Katherine Mansfield, his wife, died suddenly. I'm sorry. Would you post him a copy of *Fantasia* ... to c/o S. Koteliansky 5 Acacia Rd.' It is significant that the one work by Lawrence which Murry praised unreservedly was a book sent him in the context of Katherine Mansfield's death.

He stayed some time at the Old Farm, but not entirely in solitude. Not far from Twyford, at Chobham, lived a woman he had met in the days of *Rhythm* called Vere Bartrick-Baker, whom he now felt was 'a captive princess, whom I longed to set free'. Between 6 March and early April he discussed *Fantasia of the Unconscious* with her, and came to the brink of marriage for the second time in three months. 'Will it really be any fun for you to hide in a hole with me?' But in April he decided he could not commit himself. 'That's where I am, my dear, waiting for something to happen inside me.' Later Vere was to marry J. W. N. Sullivan and play a part as mediator in a later episode of Murry's life. Well might he say, of the few months after Katherine's death that, 'I entangled myself with women, not in the ordinary sense of that phrase, but as it were touching them with my feelers.'

The experience at Twyford, coming on top of the *Fantasia* and the drama of Katherine's death, precipitated the venture with which Murry's name will always be associated. He decided to launch an entirely new periodical in which he would challenge, with the aid of Lawrence and of Katherine's heritage,[1] and for a wide audience, the growing authority of Bloomsbury and the recently founded *Criterion* edited by Eliot. He moved with astonishing speed, though at the end of February he was telling Kot he was in no hurry and was rather sorry he had mentioned such a thing to Lawrence. He approached a firm called British Periodicals Limited (in Cursitor Street, a few doors away from where the *New Age* had been edited) and Vivian Locke-Ellis, who put up £400 for preliminary expenses. Koteliansky was summoned to Pond Street for a reconciliation and the post of business manager: 'I see him now with a piece of string in his hands, knotting and unknotting it as he told me of his new-born faith.' H. M. Tomlinson was recruited, as was his brother Philip, and the genial, clever Sullivan.

Murry's first idea was to call it the *New English Weekly*, a title which as it happened, was owned by Orage, and in April Murry made another pilgrimage to Fontainebleau to negotiate permission; but although the conversation was friendly the plan was dropped, and in any case Murry had come to prefer the idea of a monthly.

[1] He proved her will on 23 April. Apart from personal possessions her estate came to £232. *See* Appendix.

The Adelphi

Early in May he sent Lawrence the prospectus of the *Adelphi*. The name had been suggested by Sullivan to symbolise the band of brothers who would run the magazine. Its yellow cover bore a woodcut—not easily recognisable—of the Inigo Jones watergate just below the offices in the Adelphi where so many of the editorial staff had worked on the *Athenaeum*, and before that in M.I.7.

Lawrence's reaction from New Mexico was cautious. 'I like the idea of a shilling monthly', he wrote on 26 May, 'but it's no good saying how I shall feel about it till I come.' And that was not to be for some time yet. By the time that letter was received the first number was in the press. It would not be a high-brow magazine, said the prospectus. 'We are bored to death by modern dilettantism. We are sick of "Art" . . . although the contents of the *Adelphi* may not be "literary", they will be literature.' Above all, 'the standards by which the standards of the *Adelphi* will be decided is significance for life'. That was far more important than any 'philosophy', which nevertheless was too big a word for Murry to disregard entirely:

> We believe there is no such thing. There is science, and there is literature . . . but true literature and true science are always in a sense philosophical: they are occupied with reality. In this sense THE ADELPHI also will be philosophical.

Shaw, to whom a copy of this prospectus was sent, commented that the editors had forgotten to mention that the magazine would be printed on paper with black ink and would be dependent for survival on either advertisements or charity.

The *Adelphi*, in fact, was to be high-minded without being too difficult or too exclusive: in a way the same recipe as John Reith was writing for the B.B.C. almost at the same time:

> Shall I say [exclaimed Murry] read 'Antony and Cleopatra' till the bugle-call of that unearthly challenge to human loyalty echoes in the remotest chambers of the soul? Or listen to the last piano sonatas of Beethoven till you feel that on the high B of Op. 109 all that human desire can imagine of the crystalline perfection of the ideal is cracked and shattered with a faint, far-away sound of breaking that stabs the very quick of being . . . or shall I say, read Tchekhov's 'Cherry Orchard'?

The passage is hardly exaggerated by Joyce's spoof purple on Michelangelo's Moses in *Ulysses*.

The star piece of the first number was an instalment of Lawrence's *Fantasia*, and altogether there were nearly eighty pages of material, much of it by well-known hands. Getting it together in three months was a tremendous achievement of literary journalism. Hopefully they printed 4,000 copies.

Far more were needed. The magazine was a sensational success. Total sales of that first number were 15,240, requiring four successive printings. No literary monthly had touched such a figure before. After allowing for booksellers' discounts on the one hand and advertising revenue on the other, the takings from that one number ran to over £700, out of which the contributors' account took £71 3s 6d, and Murry paid himself £26 16s 6d. Kot was voted a salary of £200 a year, and Locke-Ellis recovered a substantial part of his loan.

The next number, for July, was almost equally successful, and contained a large budget of advertisements. It sold 12,000 copies. But thereafter there was a steady decline to between five and six thousand at which the circulation steadied after about six months. Even so the achievement was far from negligible. During its first year of life the *Adelphi* circulated more than 100,000 copies and paid its outside contributors about £1,100. Murry took no salary as editor, but was paid a well-deserved £386 10s 10d, assessed on his own measured wordage.[1]

The main effect of the *Adelphi*, as of the *New Age*, was outside London, and especially in the north of England where its vaguely religious and cultural message, mixed with modernity, struck home for those with a chapel childhood and an adolescence of doubt mingled with regret. Some of those we know of were in much the same circumstances as Edwin Muir when he first picked up the *New Age* in Glasgow as a clerk in a beer-bottling factory: J. P. Hogan, a clerk in Manchester, J. H. Watson, a blastfurnaceman in Durham, and a signalman who swore Murry was his archpriest. In an industrial street a man, tugging the *Adelphi* from his pocket, told someone he met that 'a new asceticism is upon us'. Murry had enough

[1] These figures are taken from the Stoye papers. By July 1924 the circulation is recorded as 5,604.

of the evangelical to reach many who could never have tolerated Virginia Woolf or E. M. Forster or the curl of the lip associated with the poetry of 'the damp souls of housemaids'. The heavy drop in the circulation was attributed to Lawrence's unfortunate observation in the second instalment of the *Fantasia* that 'Jesus was a failure'.

Lawrence was in any case far from enthusiastic about the *Adelphi*. 'It seemed to me', he wrote to Kot on receiving the first number, 'so weak, apologetic, knock-kneed, with really nothing to justify its existence. . . . A sort of beggar's whine through it all. Mr. Wells's parsnips floating on warm butter.' He was in no hurry, he told Murry, to leave America—'though I suppose I'll come back and stand on the old ground'. Yet he was not wholly unsympathetic: 'You'll make a success of the thing; so what does it matter what I say?' The trouble was that whatever Murry said or implied about his intention that the *Adelphi* should be a vehicle for Lawrence, there is no evidence whatever that Lawrence ever seriously contemplated joining the band of brothers.

Frieda Lawrence, however, was longing to come back to England, and towards the end of August she arrived there without her husband. 'I wish you'd look after her a bit', Lawrence had written to Murry: 'Would it be a nuisance?' The apparently naïve words concealed a furious quarrel which had brought them to the verge of separation, and Frieda was thoroughly out of temper. 'She will be alone,' Lawrence's letter went on, 'I ought to come, but I can't.' Very soon afterwards Murry set off on a Continental journey which took him first to Freiburg, and then to the Valais, where he had stayed with Katherine. Frieda went with him.

Undoubtedly 1923 was the most crowded year in Murry's life. Katherine had died; his affair with Brett had come to a head and been resolved; he had escaped from Mrs. Dunning's perception of 'what he needed'; he had become engaged and disengaged to Vere Bartrick-Baker; following on a mystical experience he had launched a successful literary magazine, and had now set out on a Continental tour with his 'blood brother's' wife. In addition, just before setting out for Freiburg he had dealt politely with a manuscript which had arrived at the *Adelphi* office from an enthusiastic but unknown young lady called Violet le Maistre who lived at Oxshott, in Surrey. Unknown to him she had already told a friend, on the strength of a reading of the *Adelphi*, 'That's the man I'm going to marry.'

The excursion to Freiburg was discussed between Murry and Frieda long afterwards, in 1955. 'Tell me Frieda', he wrote, 'for my private satisfaction it shall be buried afterwards—did you love me as much as I loved you in those queer days? It drove me crazy— really crazy, I think, wanting you so badly; the comfort and delight of you and then feeling Oh God, but Lorenzo would never get over it. I mustn't, I must *not*. And I sometimes wonder what would have happened if I had not had that awful feeling of friendship and loyalty to L. . . .' 'I trusted you', she replied, 'and what you would do. Of course I wanted to hear from you but not so much. No, you did the right thing, Lawrence was already very ill. I think you averted an ugly tragedy.' It was nearly, but not quite, the note he would have wanted to elicit thirty years afterwards.

That October, from Randogne, Murry wrote an uncomfortable little postcard to Kot saying he was not quite sure they saw eye to eye about the *Adelphi*. Whatever may have been their differences of opinion on that account Kot's passionate loyalty to Lawrence had worked him into a fury of indignation over what he considered to be Murry's adulterous journey with Frieda. When she returned to England (without Murry) Kot immediately quarrelled with her, and of course poured out his anger to Lawrence, so setting the scene for Lawrence's return to London.

Early in December Lawrence arrived. His journey had been preceded by a letter to Murry in which the postscript recorded his feelings on reading Katherine's last collection of stories in *The Dove's Nest*. 'Poor Katherine! she is delicate and touching—but not *great*! Why say great?' An anxious group consisting of Frieda, Murry and Kot met him at Waterloo off the Southampton train. According to Murry his first words were 'I can't bear it', and they took him back to Hampstead where Frieda had been staying with my parents since her return from Germany.

Not long afterwards, and now fully recovered, Lawrence assembled a group of his friends for dinner in a private room at the Café Royal. The gesture was uncharacteristic, and the motive not altogether clear. The guests were seven in number, making a total of nine including Lawrence and Frieda: Murry, Kot, Gertler, Brett, Mary Cannan, who had been successively the wife of J. M. Barrie and the novelist Gilbert Cannan, and my two parents. The fluctuating and complicated relationships of these guests was known only dimly by the host. Three of them were haunted by a passion for the dead Katherine. Two had been Murry's partners in recent adventures. Murry's partnership with Kot in the *Adelphi* was beginning to crumble. Several of those present, including Brett, Kot, and my mother, felt an intense and competitive friendship for Lawrence, which in the case of Brett was increased by the marked attention Lawrence paid her during the meal. My mother and Frieda were jealous of Mary Cannan, and Kot took an instant dislike to my father, who was placed next to him. Murry was wondering whether he could act as literary impresario for Lawrence, as he had done for Katherine, and he had already, in muted terms which could be taken back, offered Lawrence the editorial chair of the *Adelphi*. Everyone present, except the two who knew the truth, had drawn the obvious inference from Frieda's trip with Murry to Germany.

Altogether they were an unlikely band to follow their host to New Mexico and found the ideal community, which was what he invited them to do as soon as the plates were cleared away. Some of them (my mother was one) he had sounded earlier, and now he solemnly asked them in turn, getting only one downright refusal—Mary Cannan's—in the words, 'No, I like you Lawrence, but not so much as all that, and I think you are asking what no human being has a right to ask from another.' All the other answers were affirmative, but all, with the exception of Brett's, had spoken or unspoken reservations.

Despite this virtual unanimity they did not go on to discuss the practicalities of the plan—how Donald Carswell should give up his ambitions as a barrister to go with his wife and five-year-old son to New Mexico; what Gertler would do in relation to Carrington; how Murry and Kot would dispose of the *Adelphi* and what the rest of their brotherhood would say about it. All of them had fresh in their minds the alarming example of the flight to Fontainebleau which Lawrence was to describe only a week or two later as 'a rotten, false, self-conscious place of people playing a sickly stunt'. Indeed in that letter he seems to be laughing at his own scheme as over-serious, and during the interval several of his fellow-guests had been imploring him to stay in England. The dinner-party itself was brought to a head by a maudlin Murry embracing his host and saying this was an affair between men—which led to protests and Murry's celebrated utterance: 'I *have* betrayed you old chap I confess it . . . but never again.'[1] At which point Lawrence, overcome by emotion, illness, and port (to which he was not accustomed), was sick, and the party broke up in disorder. Murry seems to have vanished in the confusion. Kot and my father took the insensible Lawrence back to Hampstead whence after a short time he and Frieda left for the Continent and then, after a very brief visit to England, for America.

Brett went with them. Alone of all the guests at the Café Royal her problems could be and were solved by doing so. Murry, though he did not go, still proclaimed his discipleship to an unappreciative Lawrence. For a short time even Lawrence, as we learn from his letters to his American publisher Seltzer, expected Murry to come and even to transplant the *Adelphi* to America 'as a little world-magazine'. But the notion was vetoed by Seltzer as the intended publisher: 'I don't want him, flatly', Lawrence wrote to Kot. 'You keep him in London and do businesses with him.'

This was probably a reference to a publishing venture in which the comparatively prosperous Murry was proposing to put £500. Kot was to provide £200, and Lawrence was asked to make the total up to £1,000. No more was heard of this scheme because Murry, and in due course the funds he had intended for it, were otherwise occupied. Within a few days of seeing Lawrence and his party off at Waterloo for America Murry found himself involved for the third time in twelve months in a personal adventure which this time did lead to marriage. The young lady from Oxshott, having studied Tchekov as suggested in the autumn, presented herself at Pond Street in response to an invitation to dine on a *filet* cooked by Murry himself. Love, he insisted (for he had met this girl only once in his life before) was not in his mind. He was worried about his cooking. 'I looked out of the window for her again and again', he wrote afterwards, 'so anxiously that I began to wonder whether it

---

[1] Murry says his words were, 'I love you Lorenzo, but I won't promise not to betray you' (*Reminiscences etc.* p. 175).

was the *filet* after all. Why was I so anxious that this girl should come? Why was I feeling that if she did not come a spark would go out of my heart?' She declared her love as soon as the *filet* was eaten: 'The only question,' she insisted, 'is, do you love me?' His rather lame reply was, 'I didn't know I did, but now I do.'

So, at any rate, ran his recollection twenty years later. Those words spoken over the remains of the *filet* opened a history so strange and even fearful in its symmetry that one wishes there were some evidence about the meeting from her side. All we know is that she was the daughter of an electrical engineer in prosperous circumstances who had been decorated with the C.B.E. for his services during the war, and later became Director of the British Standards Institution.

In describing the scene with Violet at Pond Street Murry was reminded of the climactic moment thirteen years earlier at Clovelly Mansions when Katherine had proposed to him. 'Even at that time it struck me as strange that precisely the same thing had happened again. Once again I had been entirely ignorant that I was in love; once again the woman had spoken, and only that had revealed it to me.' What was still to be revealed was that Violet was not only to succeed Katherine but was to personify her and re-enact the tragedy with terrifying fidelity: 'The show without the art', to transpose Johnson's line.

Murry cannot escape blame for turning Violet into a second Katherine, since Katherine's character and talents were never allowed to be forgotten for a moment. More and more the *Adelphi* became Katherine's mausoleum, containing copious fragments of her writings in nearly every number, and sedulously promoting the cult of her heroic literary life. Violet was encouraged to write stories on the model of Katherine's. She dressed like Katherine and did her hair like Katherine. The engagement ring Murry gave her had been Katherine's. Yet she was not really like Katherine at all.

The wedding was on 24 April 1924 at a church in Belsize Park, and finally put an end to any ideas Murry may have had for joining Lawrence in America. Indeed, between the engagement and the marriage he had already found a new home for his bride, and invested most of his savings in it. Early in April he had taken a holiday in Dorset, and after paying his respects to Thomas Hardy had noticed the Old Coastguard Station on Chesil Beach, which was up for auction. He bought it for £950, which was nearly all he had saved; and almost immediately afterwards he was reinforced by the biggest cheque he had ever received—over £1,000—on account of Katherine's royalties. Ironically enough he had at last acquired 'The Heron', and indeed almost says so in writing of his new home. 'I felt that Katherine's blessing was on our marriage and our tamarisk-girded house by the sea, over which the swans came honking every day. They were, at least, the next best birds to herons.' 'Next best' was the sad epitaph for Violet.

The success of his lectures on style at Oxford in 1922 had led to an invitation from Cambridge to deliver the Clark Lectures in the summer of 1924; and these, on which he was working that spring, were to lead to the book he had long been meditating and became the most celebrated he ever wrote: *Keats and Shakespeare*. It is impossible not to admire and respect his literary energy, as in the midst of personal quarrels, a new marriage, and the editorship of a monthly magazine, his Corona portable tapped away and his neat handwriting covered page after page, wherever he happened to be.

But that summer the *Adelphi* was moving towards a crisis, and it came to a head in the autumn. Murry had fostered the idea that it was owned and run by a brotherhood consisting of himself (editor), Kot (who looked after the day-to-day affairs at Cursitor Street and collected the advertisements), H. M. and Philip Tomlinson, and J. W. N. Sullivan, with Lawrence as a kind of honorary member. H. M. Tomlinson, with whom Murry had now become very close, had rented part of the Old Coastguard Station as his family home, and much of the management of the *Adelphi* apart from the decisions about what went into it, was left to Philip Tomlinson and Kot, who did not care for each other.

The crisis which blew up in October was partly financial, partly literary, and partly personal. At the paper's existing level of circulation the printing costs were just about covered by the revenue from sales, so advertisement income was the only fund for the payment of contributors and Kot's salary of £200 a year. For the last quarter that revenue was £55, of which Murry considered £40 was the minimum he required for contributors. Accordingly there was not enough to pay Kot's salary.

Early in October, just when these figures had emerged, Kot wrote criticising a contribution in the last number (by Mrs. Millin) and pressing for a policy which would improve the circulation. Murry clearly regarded this as an attack on his editorship:

> You don't think about anything else but the A. I do. It would be a good thing if you thought about something else . . . then perhaps you would make up your mind that the A never will be a BIG MAGAZINE, for indeed it won't. . . . I don't intend to keep it alive by artificial respiration. It will either live its own life or none at all. . . . You and I have at bottom quite different attitudes to life. The mere fact that I do most sincerely believe in absolute truth will convince you how different they are . . . I want the A to be successful of course—and I fancy that in the long run it will be successful—but it must be successful on my own terms. I am not going to change myself to suit the A. The A will have to change to suit me. That isn't vanity at all. But I am convinced that I have a work to do, a function to perform, in the world; and the Adelphi is the instrument. . . .

Kot replied hotly accusing Murry of wanting to turn the paper into his personal platform and betraying the principles on which it had been founded. 'When we founded the A we had a quite definite idea of creating a paper which would have a life of its own, irrespective of the views, beliefs, and convictions of any one of its contributors.' Far from it, came the answer from Chesil Beach: 'So long as I edited it it was bound to be *my* paper, not in any personal or egotistical sense . . . I am not interested in a "good magazine" for its own sake. I can't help it. It is so: I'm sorry: but that is the fact.' This meant of course that Murry and in a measure the Tomlinsons were to be the masters. 'Phil [Tomlinson] and yourself [Kot] supply the mortar to our exiguous bricks—a perfectly good arrangement so far as I am concerned.'

On 18 October, when this correspondence was in full spate, Murry learned the advertising figures for the last quarter, and informed Kot that 'something drastic must be done'. Either publication must cease or expenses must be reduced (i.e., though Murry did not say so, Kot's salary must be cut). Then came an extraordinary gesture:

However, rather than that you should feel that I have not acted squarely by you, I make this offer. If you like, you can take over the *Adelphi* entirely yourself. I will consider as completely abolished the considerable nominal debt that A owes me; and hand over the magazine to you completely. In that case my name must disappear as editor. But that is all. I will promise to write as well as I can for *your* magazine month by month without payment until you are in a position to pay me.

The alternative posed was that Kot should leave and Murry continue to run the paper with the Tomlinsons. A reply was asked for by the end of the month.

Kot's reply, which came by return of post, seems not to have been what Murry expected. It accepted the offer of the *Adelphi* on the terms proposed, and taxed even Murry's powers of manoeuvre. Writing on 24 October he withdrew an important, indeed essential, part of his offer:

If you take control of the A it will be *impossible* for me to write in it. I'm very sorry. It is due to my peculiar and personal feeling about the A. This feeling you have, quite naturally, never shared. . . . It is difficult for me to explain this feeling to you, above all because it has been the fundamental cause of our disagreement . . . I'm sorry I didn't realise this when I wrote to you. For some reason I could not take the idea of giving up the *Adelphi* seriously . . . I'm sorry you won't understand this feeling. I wish you could. But imagine it to be something like your feeling of the impossibility of even indirectly serving the Soviet Government.

This was too much for Kot—especially the analogy between Murry working for an *Adelphi* controlled by Kot, and Kot working for the Soviets, of whom he deeply disapproved; and on 3 November he wrote saying he washed his hands of the paper, and 'our friendship too must end'. But Murry was not letting him off so easily as that, and no doubt Kot had already begun to talk to other literary friends about what he regarded as Murry's double dealing. The next letter from the Old Coastguard Station was couched in soothing terms. 'Whether I had the right to offer it to you, or you to accept the offer, the situation between me and you is clear. You cannot run the A alone. Therefore it reverts to me.' And therefore, on this subtle line of reasoning, the whole future of the paper should, on Murry's authority, be referred to 'the brotherhood' for settlement— 'amicably if possible, if not by majority vote'. It is an extraordinary letter, in which Murry shows that he could have amply fulfilled his father's dream of a civil service career. In it he solemnly resigned the editorship and appointed himself interim editor. 'In the meantime', he informed Kot, 'I will receive no salary. Neither will you.' Nor was he willing to come to London to discuss matters. Violet could not be left alone, he had a lot of work to do, and the journey to London would mean 'two fares and a room in a hotel'.

Of course Kot would have none of this. He had said he would resign, and no procedural devices or references to other authorities were going to stop him. Murry's excuses about the expense of coming to London he regarded as 'just humiliating', and despite agonised letters from Murry saying they were both in the wrong and begging him not to take irrevocable decisions, Kot's mind was unchanged. He was unmoved even by the cry, 'I do not *want* you to leave the A, nor do I want the A to become my personal magazine.' The end came on 10 November when Kot wrote:

To John Middleton Murry.

Complying with the request in your letter dated (wrongly) Nov 6 to hand over the keys to P. G. Tomlinson, I placed the keys in an envelope with covering letter and took it down to the Savage Club.

There is cash left in the money box £6 10s 4d.

I declare again and finally that I have nothing more to do with the Adelphi in any way whatever, nor with you personally. Finis.

S. S. Koteliansky

I want the Dostoevsky letter back. I do not want anything of mine to appear in the Adelphi.

This time the breach between Murry and Kot was final.[1] Murry

[1] Mr. F. A. Lea, in his *Life of John Middleton Murry*, suggests that the quarrel between Murry and Kot was in fact decided by 'the brotherhood' as Murry had proposed. There is no evidence in the Koteliansky papers, on which the present account is based, that there was ever any such collective expression of opinion. Indeed time was far too short. The idea was proposed on 24 October and Kot finally resigned on 10 November.

wrote off to Lawrence about the quarrel but received little consolation. Replying to what he described as the 'little yellow cry from
your liver' Lawrence observed that 'You were bound to hate Kot,
and he you, after a while. . . . The Adelphi was bound to dwindle;
though why not fatten it up a bit. Why in the name of Hell didn't
you rouse up a bit, last January, and put a bit of gunpowder in your
stuff and fire a shot or two? But you preferred to be soft, and go on
stirring your own finger in your own vitals. . . . Spunk is what one
wants, not introspective sentiment. The last is your vice. You rot
your manhood to the roots with it.'

Lawrence thought Murry and Kot would make it up after a while
but he was wrong. Such subsequent correspondence as they had
was strictly about business and entirely impersonal. 'I assure you',
Kot wrote in November to his friend Sidney Waterlow, 'that my
resolution to free myself of everything connected with M does not
arise from spite or revenge: it is a kind of inner need to free oneself
of an evil that for years and years has been playing most terrible
tricks on oneself.' But Lawrence was right in thinking Murry was
now set in his style. The dignified missionary tone, the mannered
precision, the high-minded huffiness, were now permanent. However many doctrines commanded his enthusiasm and his fertile
pen (and there were to be many) Murry would never loosen up;
'Apparently it's what you want' Lawrence had written of the
Adelphi. Even now, after three editorships and a mountain of literary
and emotional experience, he was only thirty-five. But he was set
firmly in his ways.

❧ 14 ❧

The *New English Weekly* and its Shadows

Orage entered his fiftieth year at Fontainebleau soon after the drama of Katherine's death, hewing wood and drawing water under the spiritual direction of Gurdjieff. Other English disciples might drop away and turn to less taxing mystics or even, like Nicoll, start esoteric groups of their own as they made their way in the changed post-war world; but Orage gritted his teeth and remained loyal. Gurdjieff treated him with a mixture of severity and consideration, commanding him at one point to dig in the grounds at night until further notice, leaving him to struggle on to the point of exhaustion and virtual mutiny, and then summoning him to a room where a handsome dinner and ample wine were in readiness.

For Gurdjieff was very far from being an ascetic. He loved good food and armagnac, and was a skilful cook. He loved to talk with a drink in his hand at the café Henri Deux at Fontainebleau, or to take company to the café de la Paix or l'Ecrévisse, a fish restaurant in Montmartre. His remarkable powers over himself enabled him to interrupt a tirade of what seemed ungovernable abuse with a cup of coffee and a glass of armagnac and then resume it where he had left off. One of his pupils tells of his terror, on entering with the welcome tray, at finding his master heaping wrath on a crumpled and distraught Orage. For a few minutes the torrent ceased and the scowl subsided into a cheerful smile. But as the pupil closed the door behind him his ear caught the renewed wave of obscenity and denunciation.

In spite of the outlandish nonsense with which Gurdjieff surrounded the substance of his teaching, and the enforced dancing which Orage confessed he was unable to enjoy, the strange regime seems to have benefited the ex-editor. Those who came to see him at the Prieuré remarked on his sparer frame, his better colour, the absence of strain in his manner. As he struggled through the menial work imposed on him he invented mental exercises of a pelmanistic kind, compiled elaborate number sequences, and tried to analyse logical problems.

Gurdjieff's fame was growing and the success of his ballet which he presented at the Théâtre des Champs-Elysées in the autumn of 1923 made a considerable, if temporary, impression. But it brought no French pupils to take the places of the deserting English, and no patron emerged comparable to Lady Rothermere, who had now transferred her attention and funds to other causes—among them help to T. S. Eliot for launching the *Criterion*. So Gurdjieff's eye turned towards America for financial support and the expansion of his doctrine; and for the necessary mission he selected Orage as his aptest and most distinguished disciple, over whose mind, at that time, he exercised almost complete domination.

Orage reached New York in December 1923. His editorial reputation was still fresh, his startling transition had caused a stir, and the United States was just starting on a period of lush, excitable growth in which European literature played an important part. His skill as a lecturer was unimpaired in spite of the strangeness of the doctrines he now had to preach, and he quickly found an audience. What was more it was a paying audience whose dollars he duly remitted to Fontainebleau.

One of the earliest of his meetings was held in a small room in a bookshop on East 44th Street which sold advanced literature— 'Lawrence on the shelves and Joyce under the counter' as one of those who worked there has put it. It was called 'The Sunwise Turn' and was run by two young women of progressive views. Orage's audience, according to one who was present, consisted of 'well-dressed, intellectual men and women' among whom Orage must have been astonished to notice Katherine's first husband, the former St. John's Wood tenor, George Bowden, who had introduced her to that even smaller room at Cursitor Street and her literary career.

Nor was that the only theme to recur at that lecture. Just as Beatrice had first been drawn to him lecturing at the Theosophical Society seventeen years before and had been glad to meet him afterwards, so now Jessie Dwight, one of the two proprietors of the Sunwise Turn found herself after the lecture being asked by the lecturer how she had enjoyed it. Her answer was 'Not much', but the friendship ripened nevertheless and she became Orage's secretary; and some four years later, in 1927, his wife. But her interest in the lecturer did not extend to whole-hearted sympathy with the doctrines he preached, even when she got to know more about them; and later experience of Gurdjieff himself and of the life at the Prieuré which she sampled, confirmed this emancipated young American woman's distaste for the Gurdjieffian system. She noted that although the master himself was married he allowed his wife no particular recognition. 'A man must not be a slave to a woman', Gurdjieff once observed. 'If you are the first, your wife is second.' American men, in his opinion, failed in this respect. Jessie and some others of the more freedom-loving women defied him by organising a party from which men were excluded, eliciting afterwards from the poetess Anna Wickham the quatrain:

> *In the house of the Sphinx*
> *The whores*
> *Do the chores*
> *And buy their own drinks.*

By then Gurdjieff had personal experience of America, for he had not been slow in following up his missionary and in January 1924, accompanied by a large part of his troupe, he made his debut in New York. The tour received a good deal of notice, but on the whole it was a disappointment. Even in New York many of the seats for the displays of dancing and conjuring (at which Orage acted as compère) remained unfilled, and at Boston and Chicago there was even less support. Gurdjieff had returned to Europe in March, very much out of temper.

However, he continued to receive substantial remittances from or thanks to Orage, who must have raised far more money for the Institute for the Harmonious Development of Man than he ever achieved for the *New Age*. And along with this he was comparatively prosperous himself, and lived a good deal more comfortably in his apartment in Gramercy Park than he had done in Chancery Lane. He gave first place to his propaganda on behalf of Gurdjieff, but inevitably acquired a group for whom he himself was the sage, and also turned his editorial talents to the teaching of journalism with considerable success. His circle of friends in America became almost as wide as it had been in London, and among others whom he drew to Fontainebleau were the editor of the *Little Review*, Margaret Anderson and her friend Jane Heap. They had been at his first New York lecture, and had been deeply impressed.

Yet the seven years of his bondage to Gurdjieff produced hardly any written work under his own name. Most of the summers were spent at the Prieuré, where he would stay for two months or so. Not once did he return to England, though he continued to correspond with friends there, notably Dyson and Douglas. Apart from a curious textbook of numerical exercises and a few articles, he published nothing. The most notable English editor of his time had become a mysterious exile owing obedience to an Armenian magus.

As early as 1925 Orage was finding the master's incessant and bullying demands for money burdensome, and the strain was increased by Jessie's unwillingness to be impressed by Gurdjieff. That summer there was a serious quarrel between master and pupil over Orage's insistence on keeping to his time-table for returning to New York in defiance of Gurdjieff's wish to detain him until some pencillings in Armenian of his latest reflections had been transcribed into acceptable English. Another pupil describes the scene in the courtyard of the château where the cars were drawn up to take Gurdjieff and his companions to a feast at l'Ecrévisse: 'He came down into the courtyard and began to storm at Orage for leaving his work at the Prieuré and going back to nonentities in New York. The air became charged with electricity. Orage said nothing, then, rather white, took his suitcase out of Gurdjieff's car and went to his room.' That quarrel was made up, but on the basis that Orage would go back to New York next day, as he had said he would.

Three years later an important event occurred in Orage's life which still further diminished the influence of Gurdjieff. His eldest child was born and at the age of fifty-five he became a family man for the first time in his life. He proved devoted and affectionate, and that summer the pilgrimage to Fontainebleau was omitted. 'I shall not go to the Prieuré this year', he told the departing C. S. Nott. 'As a matter of fact I feel that my work here is coming to an end: another two or three years perhaps, and we shall meet in England.' Even so it was to be a long and agonizing process for the man of whom his friend de Maeztu said, 'he knew the shape of everything and the weight of nothing'. The estimate of three years to shake himself fully free was accurate, and to the end of his life the marks of his time, with Gurdjieff, and his struggle to reduce Gurdjieff's doctrines to acceptable English prose, remained. To the end of his life, for instance, he distinguished between 'essence' promises, which were unbreakable, and ordinary ones; and he could be moved to tears at hearing the music of Fontainebleau played on a cottage piano in the next room.

Gurdjieff, however, helped with the process of detachment by behaving more and more outrageously, and some have claimed that he too had decided he and Orage must part for their own good. The master disliked competition, and perhaps felt threatened by the circle which Orage had now created. He also taught that every man should follow his own bent, all of which goes in favour of believing his behaviour was calculated. But it seems doubtful whether even Gurdjieff, great actor though he was, could by himself have contrived the parting scene or spoken of Orage afterwards as he did, if his conduct had been wholly objective.

In the summer of 1930 Orage visited England for the first time for seven years, and stayed at Bramber with C. S. Nott and his wife, who was teaching music at the experimental school on Telegraph Hill kept by Bertrand and Dora Russell.[1] He had already made up his mind to start once more in journalism, for he made enquiries about resuming the editorship of the *New Age*, which still survived, though now reduced to eight pages. He dined with the group of Anglican socialists (known as the Chandos Group) which controlled it. The meal must have been rather like dining with Holmes after his return from the fatal struggle with Moriarty on the Reichenbach Falls, and was an uncomfortable one. They already had an editor, Arthur Brenton, whom they could not well dismiss at a mere turn of chance. Mairet, who was present and had not seen Orage for some years, remarked on his 'greater strength and dignity . . . a

---

[1] Nott, who has published two books about his association with Gurdjieff and Orage, was by turns a soldier, a bookseller, a traveller in felt hats, and a publisher. There was something of Boswell in him, and he contrived a meeting between Orage and Russell on the beach at Rye to observe the effects. Unfortunately Orage was delayed by a puncture and Russell had to leave before he arrived.

heightened self-consciousness and self-command', but the embarrassment could not be dispelled and Orage made things worse by
employing the mysterious language of Gurdjieff, talking of 'twenty-
seven psychological types of men, of whom only one is decisive for
such action as we are discussing. If a man of the twenty-seventh
type is present, but not otherwise, a group can arrive at an effective
decision.' The effective decision was however taken: he could not
again be editor of his old paper.

Disappointed, but still determined to break with Gurdjieff, he
returned to an America which was now in a state of economic
collapse. But the master had preceded him and had taken command
of Orage's group of pupils, denouncing his former disciple and
extracting from each a written promise to have nothing more to do
with him. Orage behaved with dignity and wit in face of this hostile
action by the man he had reverenced for years, and demanded a copy
of the renunciation his pupils had been asked to sign. Then he
signed it himself and told Gurdjieff that he too repudiated the man
Gurdjieff had made him.

Gurdjieff left New York for Europe on 13 March 1931 and next
day Orage wrote to Nott:

> Gurdjieff sailed last midnight, leaving behind him an almost
> hopelessly scattered and hostile group. He has given the impres-
> sion, as never before, that he cares for money only and thinks of
> the NY people in that light alone. Of course it is not so: but I
> despair of pointing to any evidence in support . . . *I* am not willing
> to tax for him.

The most Orage would do was execute Gurdjieff's commission to
find a New York publisher for *Beelzebub's Tales*, for whose English
form he was himself largely responsible. Then he would emerge
from servitude, buckle on his old armour, and fight one last crusade
under the banner of Major Douglas.

The idea was at once apt and absurd—both for the same reason.
The economic collapse in New York had spread to the whole western
world so that by 1931 there was a ready audience for critics of orthodox finance and for profferers of new remedies, however puzzling
they might seem. But at the same time no moment could have been
less propitious for launching any new enterprise, least of all a literary

and political journal. Just the same, with some help from an American backer and, it appears, from Michael Arlen, whom he had once helped and who now, as the result of *The Green Hat*, was prosperous, Orage set to work. He established himself and his family at 6 Keats Close, a quiet modern precinct off Keats Grove, near the lower end of Hampstead Heath. In the same close lived Robert Lynd, the *New Statesman* essayist and his wife Sylvia; and across the way my journalist parents. Round the corner in Downshire Hill was Orage's old protégé Edwin Muir and his wife Willa, now established as the introducers of Kafka to the English scene. It was a congenial world, but a far cry from the days of Liberal triumph in 1906 when he had launched himself with the *New Age*. That November, on the evening of the general election that swept the National Government into power with the biggest Conservative majority of the century my father returned home out of the fog and wearily confessed that the desperate state of the country had made him give the Conservative his vote for the first time in his Liberal life.

Opinions differed about the new Orage. The man whom his old admirer of the Chandos Group had thought more confident than ever struck his old friend Will Dyson as having grown more sombre and less communicative. The light touch had gone. But he persevered with his plans for a new paper and defied a summons from Gurdjieff for reconciliation with a curt telegram: 'Once I crossed the Atlantic for you. Now I wouldn't even cross the Channel.'

Parties and meetings with possible supporters went on all that autumn. At first he seems to have thought of the new paper as a monthly—'The New English Monthly'; but then courageously though perhaps unwisely decided to make it a weekly, and in April 1932 the first number of the *New English Weekly* appeared, edited from an office in Cursitor Street not far from his old one and overflowing, as in the old days, into the A.B.C. and the Kardomah in the Strand.

But it was not at all the same paper as the *New Age*. The most obvious difference was the nagging social credit propaganda which from the first made it seem eccentric and alienated many of the editor's former admirers. And it lacked the same freshness, for Orage was much more ready to give space to established names, whether they wrote well or not, provided they supported his ideas. As a whole the paper lacked bite and Orage himself confessed he sometimes found it hard work to produce his weekly quota of political notes.

He was disappointed too. To Mairet he confided that he found the literary world of London less fertile than the one he had left in the early twenties. There was less originality, less sustained industry; and the political outlook was gloomy. Mairet rallied him with criticisms of the pessimism of Spengler. 'It's not the pessimism that's wrong with Spengler', mused Orage. 'To those who know and understand, it is all too clear that the present outlook for human beings is precarious and ominous in the extreme.' To Nott, who had been so bold as to say he could not believe monetary reform could be Orage's chief interest in life, he made the even more disheartening admission: 'No. It is a pseudo-interest.'

But much of the old vitality and the peculiar talent of perceiving talent was still there. Murry, who met him again in 1933 after ten years' intermission, reported a 'lively and unembarrassed conversation'. Some of his early discoveries he took up again for further development—Ruth Pitter, for instance, C. M. Grieve ('Hugh MacDiarmid'), and Ezra Pound who as in the old days provided more copy than even Orage was prepared to print. And he brought forward one completely fresh discovery. On 18 May 1933 the *New English Weekly* published the first poem to appear in the national press by Dylan Thomas, then aged nineteen.[1] He also had an encounter with Frieda Lawrence: it must have been in the autumn of 1932 when she came to England to establish Lawrence's lost will. They had never met before and wanted to meet: 'by one of those sad mistakes of life he had never met Lawrence'. The conversation was a long one, saying 'nakedly much what we had felt and not said before', above all, one may guess, about Katherine's strange end.

On most Wednesdays at the Kardomah a group would gather to listen to Orage converse with George Russell ('AE') the Irish poet and mystic. Perhaps a dozen would be present as the talk roamed

---

1 'And Death Shall Have No Dominion.' Murry quickly picked him up for the *Adelphi* (September 1933) but Mr. Rayner Heppenstall (*Four Absentees*, p. 43) is mistaken in claiming this as Thomas's first appearance in serious print.

over such topics as the decay of the Greek tradition and the need to turn once more to the Hindu scriptures for inspiration. C. S. Nott noticed that these discussions often degenerated into a monologue by 'AE'. Once, leaving the café by a revolving door after such a colloquy, a friend caught a wink from one of Orage's flashing eyes. Orage in fact was growing weary. His fireside, his wife, and his children were now his true pleasures. He was not well off, but he was as prosperous as he had ever been and his simple will, made in favour of his wife in 1928, was to show modest but perceptible assets of some £2,000. By 1933 the *New English Weekly*, as we learn from a letter to Wells, was in serious financial difficulty. Orage himself had sunk £1,000 in it and other friends another £1,000. Did Wells think the paper 'worth supporting'? The answer clearly was 'No'. 'That's all right!' was the brave reply. 'I've no doubt I shall find means of carrying on. . . . Send me an outside once, won't you?'

In April 1934 he was sixty-one, and for the first time in his life was invited to broadcast—an invitation he treated with great seriousness. Broadcasting was still almost a novelty but he had insight enough to see its immense potentialities in supplementing and perhaps even in the end superseding the printed word. What is more, he was a skilled and professional speaker and if he had been born a generation later his power to rivet attention would have made him famous on television. The proposed talk was in a series called 'Poverty in Plenty' and he eagerly seized on it as an opportunity to expound a simplified version of Douglas credit.

The piece was delivered on 5 November and contains passages which show both his magisterial gift of description and his acute insight. He is describing the economic system, starting with the shop. Behind it was a line of warehouses

and, behind the line of warehouses, a line of factories and workshops; and behind those, quarries, and mines and farms; and behind these, laboratories and research schools; and finally behind them all, the British people themselves, with their character, industry, genius, and history.

One notes how he moves from the familiar, via the concrete, to the abstract, avoiding any word that could be criticised as 'jargon' or 'talking down'. One phrase in the talk was heard for the first time by a large audience:

> Applied science seems to have made it its mission in life to lift the curse laid on Adam and to transfer work from the backs of Men to the broader backs of Nature's other forces—steam, electricity, and ultimately, perhaps, to atomic energy. . . .

It was only a year or two since the physicists of Cambridge had achieved the experiment of splitting the atom.

Those who listened noted a measured delivery, an occasional pause as if for effect, but each time a little longer than one might have expected. It was in fact due to spasms of pain which had developed from a discomfort he had been feeling in his chest for the past few weeks. He went home to his house, now on The Mount, at the very top of Hampstead, feeling tired and uneasy, and wondering if this new venture in speaking his mind had been a success. He was never to find out, for in the morning he was dead.

At least he had kept to what he had once said was his motto in life: 'Always keep a trot for the drive'—the coachman's rule for sparing the horses to make a show on arrival. But his old friend Paul Selver wrote sadly that 'If Orage had to die through over-exerting himself in the quest for an ideal, I could have borne the bereavement more submissively if the ideal had been worthier of him.'

The funeral was arranged by Will Dyson and C. S. Nott and conducted by the Anglo-Catholic socialist Hewlett Johnson whom Ramsay MacDonald had made Dean of Canterbury a year or two earlier. Orage is buried in the graveyard of Hampstead parish church under a stone on which Gurdjieff's symbol of the enneagram has been carved by Eric Gill. The next number of the *New English Weekly* was devoted to a spectacular tribute from the literary world —one of the most spectacular of its kind, perhaps, that has ever been offered. Shaw, Chesterton, T. S. Eliot and 'AE' wrote at length and there were no fewer than forty-five other notices among which were pieces from Wells and Llewellyn Powys, Augustus John and Ezra Pound, G. D. H. Cole and St. John Ervine. 'He was', declared Chesterton, 'the first fruits of a new sort of freedom.' Shaw, after describing how Orage had begun as an editor and commenting that 'no doubt the paper attracted occasional subsidies as well as contributors from the causes to which it gave a piquant hearing ... but never became a kept paper ...' declared that Orage was 'interested in everything except vulgarity ... there was neither beginning middle nor end to him: in fact this was his fault as a literary and oratorical artist'. Eliot, in what was almost the warmest of the tributes, said that as R.H.C. in the *New Age* Orage had been the best critic in London, and as editor of the *New English Weekly* the best of London's leader-writers: 'a man who could be both perfectly right and perfectly wrong'.

From the writers whom Orage himself had brought forward— Muir, Dyson, Jackson, Penty, Herbert Read, Storm Jameson, Ruth Pitter, Richard Aldington—there was in most cases unashamed emotion. For Bechhofer Roberts the loss of Orage 'was like the death of a father'. A rather different voice was Middleton Murry's, which recalled the days of *Rhythm* and of Fontainebleau[1] in words that paid tribute to the 'essential nobility' of the deceased but fell short of idolatry. 'I was always conscious', wrote Murry, 'of the existence of a barrier between Orage's mind and my own. ... In Orage there was an obstinate substratum of belief that there was some secret of control over the universe ... I happen to belong, by nature, to the other side.'

Only a month later a similar supplement, complete with photograph and thirty-two tributes was published on the other side of the Atlantic as a special number of the *New Democrat*. Many of the writers had clearly been his pupils in the Gurdjieff days, but among them one can note those of the poet William Carlos Williams, the patroness of D. H. Lawrence Mabel Dodge Luhan, and a former governor of New Mexico.

Few men have been offered something like a hundred printed homages on leaving the world. What comes out of a general reading of them is his captivatingness—a power to fix the attention which was not on the surface but was genuinely disinterested. They had felt in encountering Orage that for each of them there had been

[1] Murry claims in this passage that Orage begged him to take over the *New Age* from him at his second visit to Fontainebleau. This cannot be right, for the paper had already been taken over and was not in Orage's gift. The correct version of this recollection is given on page 197.

nothing in the world for him but him or her. In not seeking their admiration it had been freely given.

And yet he was quite quickly forgotten. In spite of his powerful personality, his vast journalistic achievement, his wide acquaintance and his strange adventures he has never since his death been listed among the familiar or even the half-familiar literary names of his period. For a year or two there was an annual dinner in his memory, attended by forty or fifty of his friends, but it died away. A collection of his best work was put together by Denis Saurat and Herbert Read, but it had a recollected look. Had there been something forced about it all? It would be better to say that his best quality, disinterestedness, was responsible also for his glide into obscurity.

Beatrice, of course, was absent from these tributes and dinners, though in fact she had returned to England at much the same time as Orage and settled only ten minutes' walk away from him.

There had been many adventures since she left the Clinique Tarnier in 1920, her affair with Raymond Radiguet being the most extraordinary, for it was complicated by her lover's simultaneous homosexual relationship with Jean Cocteau and ended with his abandoning both Cocteau and Beatrice for another mistress. The poems and letters she sent him in the course of 1921 show her considerable command, if not complete mastery, of French, and a mixture of passion, bravado, and frankness which has its pathos when one remembers that she was well over forty and he was only only just eighteen. 'Je te fais l'aveu que depuis le soir chez Brancusi je te suis fidèle. Mais ne le dis à personne, je perdrais mon prestige.' Or again:

J'ai fait un poème. Il y a sûrement des fautes, mais mon talent dépendant évidemment sur le degré d'espoir qu'on a de coucher avec moi, et personne n'ayant cet espoir pour l'instant, je ne saurai à qui faire appel comme correcteur.

When in the summer of 1921 Cocteau went with Radiguet to the seaside she mischievously wrote that she was consoling herself with the thought of their sitting together on a rock by moonlight and each wishing Beatrice was there. Radiguet was also the recipient of her uncompleted novel *Minnie Pinnikin* and eventually of a long poem in the classical French manner which brought a stately end to the whole strange affair. Cocteau also got a copy. It consists of twenty-five alexandrine quatrains:

> *Tu partis avec lui, l'aimé de tout amour.*
> *Dieu m'aurait pardonnée une ombe de rancune.*
> *Eh bien, non. Je n'avais qu'une peine de coeur—*
> *Que, de mes espérances, il ne restait aucune.*
>
> *Je vous envoie ce mot. Je vous aime tous deux.*
> *J'erre dans le désert. . . . Je songe avec effroi*
> *A nos coeurs sourds, muets, aveugles, amoureux,*
> *Je sais que chacun aime—et je pleure tous trois.*

That had been in December 1921, and since then she had indeed wandered in the desert. She quarrelled with her old ally Roch Grey, met Pound briefly at Dieppe, mounted an unsuccessful exhibition of her own paintings in Paris, and 'il parait que j'ai déjà couché une fois avec André Breton, rue de Bourgogne'. In 1925 she visited London where Clifford Sharp, still editor of the *New Statesman*, told her she was regarded as 'dangerous', and Ruth Pitter remembers her living in a shabby room in Charlotte Street subsisting on porridge turned up with jam and topped up with condensed milk. Then she wandered back to the Continent, brooding more and more and committing her thoughts and dreams to a journal (subsequently offered to, but declined by, the Society for Psychical Research) in which recollections of real people she had known were entangled with experience of a spiritual lover called 'George Letterin'.

It is difficult to believe she did not hear something of Orage's wanderings and of his return to England. At any rate she had returned there at almost the same time and established herself in a flat at 21 Fellows Road N.W.3 in 1931. But it was a sad wreck of former beauty that now haunted the Sir Richard Steele Tavern and yarned about her bohemian experiences to anyone that would listen.

Of course she had to write, and started a paper to print her output and show what she thought of the *New English Weekly* and what she regarded as Orage's betrayal of the principle of her beloved *New Age*. Her *Straight Thinker* began publication in January 1932 and tottered on (after transmutation into the less regular *Straight Thinker Bulletin*) for about two years, so that it was almost coterminous with Orage's editorship of the *New English Weekly*. She wrote it nearly all herself, drawing freely on her journals kept in the Clinique Tarnier (under the title 'Madame Six') and the later 'psychic diary' which has far less biographical interest and was given the fanciful heading, 'The Picnic of the Babes in the Wood'. For some reason, too, she had come to have an interest in and an intense dislike for St. Thérèse of Lisieux, and long columns of anti-hagiography were devoted to her. The paper was rounded off with little articles on Beatrice's idiosyncratic method of teaching Russian, attacks on poverty ('an outworn tyranny, a modern anomaly') and anti-colonialism, on which she provided a poem called 'The Stolen Lands'. This went along with a marked admiration for the Soviet Union: 'It is Russia who, saying—LOOK! holds the world's sanity steady.' Crazy as the paper was it identified some longer-term issues more surely than the *New English Weekly*.

Her old friends of course did not escape. The little note on Katherine Mansfield headed 'A Correction' is one of the most effective pieces of malice in 500 words that was ever written about the Katherine Murry had now sanctified. Nor was Murry spared. 'Our National Publarist' was her heading for a comment on a lecture he had recently given in Bradford:

Burlap has been pal rubbing up at Bradford.

'Oh Comrades! Oh dear hearts! We have found ourselves. We are one and our peace passeth understanding. . . . I believe that the step I took in joining the I.L.P. [as Murry had recently done] was historically important, therefore the conference was historically important. . . . A door in is good: a door out is good. Ah comrades among many uncertainties this is certain that the new road is the road of sacrifice. Rhymes with price. And indeed there be cozeners abroad, it behoves all men to be wary. Comrades let us have a clean party! He, he, he, he, I am positive that I am too positive to express myself positively, but, sometimes, in these dream moments when the soul &c &c. . . . Comrades I will pulrub with you all, all. I will pulrub and laprub and blarrup and plabber and publarise Burlappery wherever the spirit leadeth.'

The obsequies of Orage filled her with rage. The *Straight Thinker Bulletin* had been some months discontinued owing to the illness of its editor, but that did not stop her finding a publisher in the 'Blue Moon Press', which concealed the identity of Charles Lahr, a bohemian bookseller who kept a shabby but interesting bookshop in Red Lion Square. The pamphlet was entitled *The Old New Age. Orage—and Others*, by *Beatrice Hastings* and ran to some forty pages written in a fury of jealousy and literary deprivation. She tore the memorial tributes to ribbons, listed the sheaves of contributions (under thirteen different pseudonyms) she had made to the *New Age*, to raise a cry which is at once outrageous and pitiable:

> And who am I, unknown Beatrice Hastings, to make such an assertion in the teeth of a whole small cosmos that has cried Heil! and Evviva!...A woman who knew Orage intimately for six years between 1907 and 1914, who knew him as well as anyone else ever knew.
>
> A sub-editor of the *New Age* who for all but a few months of those six years, had entire charge of, and responsibility for, the literary direction of the paper....
>
> A writer who contributed in a dozen various styles....
>
> A woman who offended Orage's masculine amour-propre, and for this was made the victim of a social cabale.... In Paris some years ago a well-known author tried to organise a campaign against his former *amie* and colleague. Paris laughed.... Mais ce coquin érige en juge littéraire son lingam dépité!

She had decided to print Katherine's first stories; *she* had fought to get Pound a place in the paper. 'I invite anyone to count those who got in after I was no longer consulted.' As for Orage's celebrated style, 'butting in with his flat, ponderous pen (and what a flat, ponderous, stilted, maundering when not coy, conceited and facetious when not plagiaristic or outright thievish "literary" pen he had)'—the very sentence shows the immense distance between them.

But the scolding—'Iago himself', 'under the shine and dazzle and loquacity there was—a rustic, a lout, a snob' is only part of the importance of this pamphlet. Beatrice had transformed her love from love for the man to love for the paper she had helped him to create—

that hard-hitting adventurous paper in which her gifts and emotions had had free play:

> I sense that since the deplorable attempt to pass off the *New English Weekly* as a 'revival' of the old *New Age* . . . an idea has been gaining ground that the *New Age* was overrated. I declare that this is not so. I have been going through the volumes lately, after twenty years, and I am inclined to marvel. . . . There are hundreds of contributions that have no date and never will have any date because they belong to the ray of the liberal mind. . . .

Of course the man and the paper were inseparable in her mind and underneath it all was the sense of having been betrayed by the combination of love and letters to which the most important part of her life had been devoted. Literary fame had been Orage's bait for many, and the many had included her. And she had given more than good copy for no pay: she had taken on the man as well as the magazine. At the time it had seemed glorious and now, twenty years later, it was misery.

Her claims to have had an important influence on what was printed in the *New Age* cannot altogether be dismissed. Her claims to her own voluminous contributions are valid and there is considerable evidence that Orage himself recognised her in her hey-day as a great deal more than a contributor. Orage's devoted secretary, Miss Marks, who had no cause to like Beatrice, is recorded as saying that 'Orage considered Katherine Mansfield's writing as precious. B.H. did not agree with this, but could not alter O's verdict. This and many other affairs ended her association with the *New Age*.' But looking back she could see that as a journalist in her own right she had made no impact. The style of alias and ambuscade in which she had delighted and no doubt been encouraged had robbed her of a public personality.

After this outburst there is a long blank in the record of Beatrice's life. On 29 April 1936 she wrote to H. G. Wells in a letter which lacks salutation, farewell or address, so that one must suppose no reply was expected. The handwriting is elegant, even distinguished, and is the only specimen I have found. It records that she had been rereading *Mr. Polly* and 'wept and shivered. It is a book for artists. Many times as I was reading my fingers became light as feathers fluttered, afraid of touching.' At more or less the same time she was trying to rehabilitate Madame Blavatsky in a short-lived paper called the *New Universe*.[1] Beatrice's feelings about spiritualism were ambiguous. The rationalist left-winger in her rejected it as nonsense but she had a nagging belief, none the less, in the materiality of dreams and the possibility of reincarnation. And for Madame Blavatsky she felt a sisterhood—she too had been impugned and rejected.

By the beginning of the Second World War she had left London and settled in a little house at Worthing, 4 Bedford Gardens, whence she issued the last of her periodicals, the *Democrat*, Editor Beatrice Hastings, printed and published by Beatrice Hastings, price two pence.[2] The first number must have appeared in the summer of 1941, and again it was an attempt to recapture the spirit of the old *New Age* of which it was a pathetic parody: political opinion without information, attacks on the Vatican, the Government, and the Jews, and curious slogans printed vertically in the margins. The underlying mood is despair and her stiff-necked gift for words suffers a kind of cancerous distortion. Yet just as Orage had hit on a phrase of the future in his last broadcast, so did Beatrice in the very last number of the *Democrat* (January 1943):

> What we will not do is to join up with any tinkering economic-construction party for we have outworn at least any romantic notions as to reforming Mammon. The present current of loathing by men of mines, luxury trades, pearl-fishing and such cruel occupations, mass-production, office-slogging and counter-jumping holds some prospect of a trend towards rational thinking strictly limited population, and women's liberation. . . .

That last number contained a note saying she had been ill for eighteen months and could not promise another *Democrat* imme-

---

[1] And in *Defence of Madame Blavatsky* of which at least two volumes were published. On the flyleaf of each she records sadly that 'Mrs. Beatrice Hastings is a writer well-known in literary circles, but having written mostly anonymously, is unknown to the general public.' This is followed by three tributes—from *Everyman*, from Victor Neuburg in the *Sunday Referee*, and the *Evening Standard* 'Londoner's Diary' for 1 June 1933.

[2] It is rather handsomely printed on a hand press and bears no printer's name except her own.

diately. As for this one it was 'all my own work' and finished with a
sad little epigram:

> *Little country, don't go modern!*
> *If you do, the end of you*
> *Will be to go—that's modern.*

She had a friend called Doris Green who worked as nurse for an
osteopath in Worthing and looked after the increasingly invalid
Beatrice who, it is fairly clear, had cancer. Death must already have
been in her mind in October 1943 when she offered her papers
(including, no doubt, the letters Katherine Mansfield had remembered with such embarrassment) to the British Museum and received
a refusal in a re-used buff envelope. On Saturday, 30 October
she was 'checking a manuscript' and Doris Green thought her in
better health than she had been in for some time. But that evening
(for her body was quite cold when it was found next morning) she
stuffed a towel under the door, put the tube of the gas-fire in her
mouth, and committed suicide along with her pet mouse, which
was found near her body. She left all she possessed, which was £314
and an accumulation of papers that has not survived, to Miss Green,
together with two sketches of her by Modigliani. Apart from an
account of the inquest in the *Worthing Gazette* her death was not
noticed by the press or the literary world, and her will observed that
'if Miss Green will kindly throw the ashes down a hill or in a field,
I shall be obliged'. The idiosyncratic syntax survives even there.
It was a bitter end, but in the last number of the *Democrat* she came
near forgiving Orage in a momentary recollection of him. 'He used
to call me Pippa and say that I looked at things as if I came from
another star.'

❧ 15 ❧

The Adelphi Hero

As for Orage, so for Murry the two years that followed Katherine's death brought a complete change in personal relationships and reputation. 1923, which had begun with the tragedy of Fontainebleau, ended with the drama at the café Royal; and the year that followed saw the departure of Lawrence and Brett for America and the severance of Murry from Kot. All these events were in turn part of Murry's growing estrangement from Lawrence whom he was to meet only once more, and briefly, after that fatal dinner-party.

Katherine's death, he admitted afterwards, had liberated something in him which her desperate demands had always imprisoned. To put a name to it, it was the conventional streak in him. During the two years after her death he forsook Bohemia for the dignity of letters. The Clark Lectures which he delivered to a crowded and respectful audience at Cambridge in the summer of 1924 were extended to become the most admired of all his works, *Keats and Shakespeare*, which was published in 1925. In it he modestly but confidently assumed the toga of a major literary critic and quoted deferentially, but with the implication of speaking on equal terms, from the views of the Poet Laureate, Robert Bridges, and Bradley, the great Shakespearean scholar. 'For my own part', he declared, after quoting Bradley on Keats, 'I subscribe to that limitation with reluctance, though I know that it is inevitable.' The tone of voice is authoritative and that of an insider, and that of an insider not unduly intimidated by authority.

Like some of Murry's other books *Keats and Shakespeare* offers a magnificent entrance to what turns out to be a modest if well-designed house. It was indeed, as he himself said, only a small segment of the mighty task he had now set himself—'the history of the human soul since the Renaissance as seen in the lives and achievements of the greatest poets of the last three centuries'. He was to return to the task, and on a more ambitious scale, more than ten years later in *Heaven—and Earth* which was to display his semi-historical approach to criticism at far greater advantage and with a much greater wealth of reading. *Keats and Shakespeare* suffers from the fact that very little is known about Shakespeare apart from his works, so Murry 'instinctively decided to approach him through Keats'; or, put another way, studied the influence of Shakespeare on Keats. While the outcome contains little of a factual kind which a careful reading of Keats's poems and letters would not provide, it is rich in that pervasively stimulating quality which Murry made his own, with its bold generalisations about 'truth', 'beauty', 'negative capability', and 'pure poetry'.

It has been suggested that in this 'instinctive' evocation of the tubercular Keats Murry was glancing at the history of Katherine. This would be unjust to him as a critic, but he certainly did claim, in a notable passage, that his personal experience gave him peculiar qualifications to interpret the life and work of Keats:

> Nothing more powerfully prepares a man's instinctive and unconscious nature for passionate love than continuing contact with hopeless illness in a loved intimate. The deep unconscious being reacts away from the presence of death and the aching pain of beholding it. The consciousness may strive to suppress this motion as callous or heartless, but the motion persists. The instinctive man turns away from physical death and longs to be renewed by plunging into the instinctive life of which passionate love is the consummation.

So, he argued, it had been with Keats and his love for Fanny Brawne after the death of his much-loved brother. So had it been with Murry after the death of Katherine. The proposition makes little allowance for altruism, but it is certainly the case that Murry knew what it was to be prepared by a deathbed for consummation elsewhere.

His marriage to Violet had been a strange episode from the beginning. She was no Katherine. Even Murry quickly came to see that the stories on which she laboured so hard had none of the fire or force. But to be like Katherine was her one desire and she threw herself into the role almost with desperation. She changed his pet name, but only from 'Bogey' to 'Golly'. She imitated Katherine as closely as she possibly could. The very table-cloths at the Old Coastguard Station were embroidered with Katherine's initials. But it was not the true 'Heron' for all that, and in spite of the piles of Katherine's letters and papers on Murry's desk as he prepared them for publication in successive numbers of the *Adelphi*.

When, soon after their marriage, Violet became pregnant for the first time she was possessed by misery and apprehension. This, Murry had told her, was to be the 'Ribni' Katherine had longed for, and she was overwhelmed with a sense that the child would not be hers at all, but Murry's and Katherine's. 'I always felt', he wrote long afterwards, 'quite simply, that Violet's daughter was Katherine's daughter.' The child was born in April 1925 and he named her Katherine accordingly, though she has always been known as 'Weg', the name Violet gave her soon afterwards: and even this was very nearly 'Wig'. The christening took place in the neighbouring parish church and Thomas Hardy and his wife were the god-parents.

It was four months before Violet could be brought to nurse the new Katherine and for the whole summer Murry had to perform the tasks of both mother and father while editing the *Adelphi* and working on his latest book as well. It was a *Life of Jesus* commissioned by Jonathan Cape. Only in the autumn was a reconciliation achieved in the family which seemed to restore contentment to the Old Coastguard Station and bring the last brief period of happiness Murry was to know for many years.

The reconciliation, unfortunately, in accordance with Murry's forebodings immediately after it took place, led to another pregnancy and 'Violet wept as though her heart was broken and there was nothing I could say that would comfort her'. In May 1926 Katherine's dream of a perfect family was sorrowfully completed by the birth of a boy to whom Murry gave his own names, drawing from Lawrence the caustic comment, on hearing the news from Kot, 'Another John Middleton, ye Gods!'

Earlier that year when washing and feeding his first child amid his literary labours, Murry had received some advice from the same source. It was couched in terms not unfriendly, but for all that was wholly unacceptable. 'In short', concluded Lawrence, 'shut up.

Throw the *Adelphi* to the devil, throw your own say after it, say goodbye to J. M. M. Filius Meus, Salvatore di nessuno se non di se stesso; and my dear fellow—*give it up!*'[1]

Violet's spirits did not revive after the birth of her second child, even slowly. Rather they grew worse. That winter of 1926–7 Murry himself fell seriously ill with pneumonia and the doctor who attended him examined Violet as well. By one of those coincidences which would be unacceptable in fiction the doctor was the very same James Young who had attended Katherine's deathbed in Fontainebleau, and had now returned from the Institute for the Harmonious Development of Man disenchanted: a hard-drinking, strong-swearing, golf-playing man, but a mystic to boot. His examination showed that Violet was carrying her third child and was suffering from pulmonary tuberculosis.

There was no history of the disease in her family, and there had been no adverse conditions such as Katherine had suffered during the war, though the bleak conditions of the Old Coastguard Station no doubt played their part. It is difficult to dismiss the possibility that Murry, unawares and without ever becoming seriously ill himself, may have transmitted the disease. But Violet's reaction to the news of her illness is far more remarkable than any speculation about its origins:

'O I'm so *glad*', she said. 'I wanted this to happen. . . . You see, Golly,' she explained, 'I wanted you to love me as much as you loved Katherine—and how could you, without this?'

Such is Murry's own record. He went on to record his own state of mind at that extraordinary moment in words which recall his reactions on hearing of 'Chummie's' death:

A far-away voice, cold and crystal, seemed to be saying to me 'Faith in life, my dear. . . . Faith in life?'

The question-mark within the quotation cannot be an accident. What he said to Violet he did not remember.

The pregnancy was brought to an end and Violet entered a

[1] 'Saviour of nobody if not of himself': cf. 'He saved others, himself he cannot save'—a clear allusion to Murry's current work on the *Life of Jesus*.

hospital at Midhurst where she stayed for three months, but as she showed no improvement Murry took her away and the whole family settled once more at the Old Coastguard Station for the next eighteen months. The place was lonely and the weather bleak. Violet did not resist invalidity as Katherine had done, and the whole burden of looking after her and two tiny children fell on Murry. It is not surprising that at the end of his stay in Dorset he looked a great deal older—and although he was only thirty-eight the winter of 1927–8 marks his transition from youth to middle age.

Fortunately he was now quite well off. His royalty and investment income together with Violet's annuity amounted to £1,700 a year, which is the equivalent of some £12,000 today without considering an income tax rate which then stood at about 20 per cent. Most of the royalties were Katherine's inheritance, for her books were selling well in both England and America and her *Journal*, which Murry was currently editing, was one of the literary sensations of 1927. Such an income, to which any payments for current literary work were additional, was quite exceptional for a writer still under forty, and almost unknown for one who was neither a novelist, a play-wright, nor a poet. Nevertheless his acquaintance with established authors brought additional help. Hardy's recommendation to the Royal Literary Fund produced £250 and a recommendation from Edmund Gosse a similar sum—an interesting illustration of the truth of the parable of the talents. Then there was the *Adelphi*, which was transformed in 1927 into a quarterly under the title of the *New Adelphi*. As a consequence of the change Murry assigned himself the balance of the *Adelphi* account, which stood at some £200, as well-deserved arrears for the editorial salary he had never drawn. Altogether his income for 1927–8 must have been more than £2,500, or rather more than double what he would have been earning if he had fulfilled his father's ambition, entered the higher civil service, and achieved rapid promotion.

The long and painful sojourn in Dorset led him to take a more favourable view of Christianity. Till then he had always, and on principle, rejected theism of any kind, and his *Life of Jesus*, though praised by Dean Inge, was the contribution of a non-believer. He had placed Jesus in the same category as Keats and Shakespeare as a man mysteriously endowed so that the claim to be the Son of God was (as Murry might have put it) valid *for* Jesus. But now the mood was changing:

> The life and death of Jesus of Nazareth is the archetype of all tragedy; and the experience which comes through the unflinching contemplation of that life and death, is the experience in which all tragic experience culminates.

That summer of 1927 he was reading Bossuet, and the golden language of the missionary demand for surrender to belief made a powerful impression on his mind: but not a decisive one. He found himself 'trembling on the very verge of Catholicism' as Katherine had once done at Menton: and refusing the plunge for the very same reason:

> It presents itself to me now as one prolonged temptation. How I overcame it I can hardly say. But my resistance focused on one single point: Ought I, J.M.M., to make the effort or not? I knew I *could* make it, which I had never known before. Gradually I reached a kind of peace. I learned that I ought not to make this effort:—that for *me* it would be a self-violation from which I should never recover.

A kind of integrity is associated with the egotism of this significant passage, and it is an integrity of which Murry is a very early example. Its non-religious elevation of style is characteristic of the man and of much since his time. But one can say with certainty on the strength of it that its writer has not trembled on the verge of religious conviction. He had considered whether religion could fill the void he found in himself and had decided that it could not.

He tried to explain his religious dilemma at greater length in T. S. Eliot's *Criterion*, and to hold out the hand of a non-believing romantic towards Eliot's classical (and religious) position. It was partly a defensive move, for the highly regarded *Criterion* was at that time pursuing the romantics with the same kind of well-bred scorn as Murry himself had used so effectively against the post-romantic Georgians. In the essay hopefully entitled 'Towards a Synthesis' Murry contrasted the march of science with a continuing literary tradition 'which could not be denied' yet would not, any more than science, fit in with any religious or metaphysical system.

Surely this must show that the highest in literature could run in harness with religion—have some of religion's numinousness without commitment to belief? But the only result of his effort was a shower of scepticism and well-bred banter in subsequent numbers from more confident believers.

From this point onwards, and despite his firm rejection, the possibility of embracing a more or less orthodox religious faith never left Murry, but hovered in his thoughts, and tempted his rampant pen. He was conscious he had some of the gifts of a theologian. He projected, and actually began, a work on Christianity, but it was delayed by the pressing need to move nearer London, and eventually abandoned. In October 1928 the Old Coastguard Station was sold and the Murrys moved to a bungalow at Yately, a few miles north of Farnborough, called 'South Acre'. The train service to London was good; there was a golf course near by on which James Young came to play; and in a cottage close at hand lived a friend of Young's, Richard Rees.

Rees had means and had inherited a baronetcy. As I remember him long afterwards he was a gentle, melancholy, lanky man who loved literature and speculative thought. He was an odd contrast to the robust outspoken doctor when they gathered with Murry on a week-end evening to talk about Adler and Jung.

To this little circle there was soon added a fourth, Max Plowman. He was Murry's exact contemporary and a literary journalist of some repute working at that time for a weekly called *Everyman*. His hero was William Blake, and a burning Christian faith and conscience had led him, after serving for a time in the trenches as a subaltern, to pacifist convictions, court martial, and imprisonment. There was much common sense in Plowman as well as deep religious conviction. He was built in the heroic Quaker mould and believed that nothing was impossible to faith: even the rescue of someone suffering from a mortal illness.

In spite of his objurgations that it should not be so, Murry's devotion to Violet was giving way, as in the case of Katherine, to alienation. Eddie Marsh's judgement that he habitually took on more than he could bear and then collapsed was being borne out once again. Violet's cough in the room next to his (the cough he had heard before) hacked at the nape of his neck as he tried to sleep,

and be began to long for the ordeal to end. But suffering did not
prevent him from writing. His latest work was entitled *God: an
Introduction to the Science of Metabiology*, and when it came out in
1929 he sent a copy to Shaw, with an earnest request to read it.
Shaw sent the following reply:

> The subject is hackneyed. . . . But I warn you that if you show
> the slightest symptom of sentimentality the book will knock the
> bottom out of the waste paper basket. Your conclusions about
> God don't matter a solitary damn to Him (or It). So buck up and
> carry your convictions lightly and gaily.

There is more than a hint of Lawrence's 'give it up' about this,
and *God* probably hit Shaw's waste paper basket pretty quickly. But
Murry's motive in sending it had not been wholly obtuse, for it had
been written (or that part which was not autobiography had been
written) under the influence of James Young's Nietzscheanism. It
rejected theism and the divinity of Christ—it even questioned the
validity of Murry's own spiritual experience in Ashdown Forest
which is described in the autobiographical portion. It states in its
clearest form Murry's semi-mystical humanism. 'To know reality . . .
is to be freed finally from the need for God. There is no place for
him in the universe; there is no place for him in the unity of man.
There is nothing for him to do.' He dedicated it to Violet.

Writing to Kot from Bandol in November 1929 Lawrence observed that he was glad Murry had decided there was no God: 'It
makes me know that there *is*.' He also made light of his own state
of health and said he simply did not want to make a long journey to
see a doctor who will 'want to talk about lungs'. A few months
earlier Murry himself, breaking a long silence, had offered to come
out to see his ailing friend for a reconciliation. It might, he hinted,
be the last opportunity. He would have done better to go without
notice as L.M. had done in similar circumstances, for the reply to
his letter was a crisp, if fairly good-humoured rebuff which Murry
never forgot. 'I don't understand you', Lawrence wrote, 'your
workings are beyond me. And you don't get me. . . . Let's not
pretend. By pretending a bit, we had some jolly times in the past.
But we all had to pretend a bit—and we could none of us keep it up.
Believe me, we belong to different worlds, different ways of con-

sciousness, you and I, and the best we can do is to let one another alone, for ever and ever. . . . My health is a great nuisance, but by no means as bad as all that, and I have no idea of passing out.'

That had been in May 1929, not long after the publication of *Lady Chatterley's Lover.* Early in March 1930 the news that Lawrence was dead reached Yately, and this time Murry set out for the South of France.

He arrived too late for the funeral, which had been arranged by Huxley, whose savage caricature of Murry in *Point Counter Point* had appeared only the year before; and in advance of setting out he had done two things. He wrote a generous tribute to Lawrence as 'the most remarkable and lovable man I have ever known' whose 'work needs no excuse', which was published in *The Times Literary Supplement* for 13 March. He also wrote briefly to Koteliansky offering reconciliation 'over Lawrence's dead body'—an emotional offer which was almost certainly ignored.

By the second week in March he was in Vence to console Frieda. The reason for the restraint shown seven years earlier on their journey into Germany no longer existed, and the principle he had enunciated in *Keats and Shakespeare* could not have been more clearly exemplified than in what followed. 'With her, and with her for the first time in my life, I knew what fulfilment in love really meant.'

But soon Frieda departed for Italy to join the captain of Bersaglieri, Angelo Ravagli, whom she later married; and Murry had to return to the melancholy world of 'South Acre'. Before doing so he wrote to Lawrence's American agent Pollinger offering himself, with proper reluctance, as Lawrence's literary executor—for Lawrence had left no will.[1] No more seems to have been heard of this offer except that it was relayed to Koteliansky in a furious letter from Huxley urging steps to frustrate it.

The adventure with Frieda was in its way pardonable, despite its strange setting. He had been starved of physical sex for a long time and had recently even thought of trying to trace his Parisian grisette of long ago. In other ways he had had much to bear, including the bad press of *God*, coming as it did in the wake of *Point Counter Point.* But after making all allowances it is difficult to believe that

[1] *See* Appendix.

this conclusion to his long, unhappy relationship with Lawrence did not contain scintillas of both disappointment and triumph, or that on his setting out he had not seen himself as Lawrence's heir. He had set out for Vence as Lawrence's admirer and returned his detractor.

His return to England was followed rapidly by 'Reminiscences of D. H. Lawrence' in six instalments of the *Adelphi*, containing his narrative of the relationship between the two men. But his mind was brooding on something more profound and very soon he was at work on a full-length book of which the central theme must have been conceived very soon after his parting from Frieda. It was to be called *Son of Woman*. 'It was not until after Lawrence was dead', he wrote later, 'that I dared to take this plunge: to fulfil my mission as the destroyer of Lawrence.'

While that work was at its early stages another extraordinary chapter opened in his personal life. In May 1930 Max and Dorothy Plowman engineered a change in the domestic arrangements at 'South Acre'. The saturnine nurse who had looked after Violet was superseded by a good-looking, healthy, country-woman called Betty Cockbayne. She was a farmer's daughter and an excellent cook, and she made no pretence to intellectuality or even literacy. Her speech was frank, free and earthy, and she remarked of her new employer and his friends, with a cheerful smile: 'You people take life too damn seriously.' If one believed in reincarnation one could almost think that just as Katherine had entered into Violet, so Lawrence left something of himself behind in Betty. Like Lawrence in one of his good moods she spread happiness:

> Such laughter as I had not heard for years came echoing from Violet's room. . . . Betty's life seemed to pour into Violet's veins. She worked the live-long day, gaily. . . . She was happy. And she loved Violet with a careless, living love.

But all was not well. Max Plowman had now taken over the formal editorship of the *Adelphi* (once more a monthly) in partnership with Rees, though Murry was still the proprietor and presiding genius; and Plowman and his wife Dorothy were more and more at 'South Acre'. He had formed a plan, a conviction born of his Christian faith which had more than a tinge of Christian Science in it, that

Violet could be cured if only she could, for a spell, be detached
from the agonised scepticism of Murry and the burden of acting
out the part of a deutero-Katherine. Just after Christmas 1930
Murry was persuaded by the Plowmans to go away for a short holiday to Margate, and when he got back from a solitary week on that
wintry esplanade he found his wife to all appearances rather better.
He soon learned from her own lips:

> Golly, I don't want to tell you this. I know it will hurt you. But
> I must tell you because I love you. I don't love you any more.
> I am in love with Max.

Plowman's plan had gone wrong, or at least it had gone further
than he had intended. Violet had decided to live out her pattern as
a second Katherine in her own way, and as Katherine had departed
for the Prieuré she departed to the Plowmans' house at Golders
Green leaving Murry to console himself with the reflection that
while he had not trusted Orage, he did trust Max. There was another
consideration also. Ten days after his return from Margate he had
noted in his diary that he had been 'according to the law rather too
glad' when Betty came back from her Christmas break on her
father's farm at Banbury. By mid-February, only a short time after
Violet's departure, Betty was mistress at 'South Acre'. How Murry
would have resolved these difficulties if Plowman's plan had succeeded and Violet had been restored to him cured, can only be
guessed. But she died at the Plowmans' house on 29 March 1931
just fourteen months after Lawrence. Murry was not present, but
before the cremation he slid Katherine's pearl ring for the second
time from a dead finger.

Soon after the funeral he revealed to Max the decision he had in
fact made before Violet's death—that as soon as he was free to do
so he would marry Betty. His friend tried to hide the shock as best
he could:

> Well, John, you are an enigma. I believe in you all right but I'm
> blest if I understand you. . . . I'm not one to put myself at a gate.

There were, of course, plenty of entirely comprehensible reasons
for Murry's decision, one of them being that Betty was pregnant
by him. She offered, or seemed to offer, health, cheerfulness, vigour,

and practical straightforward support for a fortyish widower left with two young children. It was a vista of good housekeeping, lemon meringue pie, and contented uncomplicated sex in succession to the dark adventurousness and morbidity of his two earlier marriages. But he did not love her, or at least he had to argue himself into a new intellectual position to justify himself on this important point. Lawrence's views, or what he took to be Lawrence's views, were a great help. The spiritual side of man, he decided, was 'utterly impersonal', but he could still love Betty 'as a creature'. 'That creature loves, with a real love, with a commitment of its total self, but what is not-self (the true Spirit) it cannot commit. Believe me, I love Betty with such a total self-commitment of the creature.'

Plowman, to whom all this was addressed, was not an unintelligent man, and he never quite forgave Murry, even though he long remained under his spell. He felt that for Murry 'Violet had died in life, and while she lived you had really given her up. . . .' He reflected that there was something inaccessible about Murry, and perhaps this had been the reason why he had never been able to get on with Lawrence. 'If only he and Lawrence could have agreed. But they couldn't. Their difference was radical. Mine is too. Words fail to express my regret, but there 'tis.' Sometimes he felt, in a phrase that could hardly be bettered, that Murry's 'heart was made of sensitive stone'. 'I believe', he declared, 'that when you were a child you suffered such pain in your love-relation that fear and self-mistrust were constellated with any expression of love.' What we know of Murry's parents supports this reading. His devotion to his mother (who very nearly survived him) was deep. His father, who also lived to a great old age, was a narrow-minded, possessive tyrant.

Plowman's insight into human nature, which was deeper than Murry's, had also produced the phrase about the proposed marriage —'put myself at a gate'; and its meaning was given body in a discussion between Murry and Mr. Cockbayne, his future father-in-law. Even to the name it could be lifted from a Lawrence novel. Did he, Mr. Cockbayne asked, know what he was doing? Receiving no reply, he went on with what he had to say. 'You know she's got the devil of a temper on her. I wouldn't like any man to think I hadn't given him fair warning of what he was letting himself in for.' With these frank village words for convoy Murry pledged himself to Betty in May 1931 at the Odiham Registry Office. It was left to Richard Rees some time afterwards to ram the point home. 'You don't listen to anybody who tells you "There's a brick wall ahead". You look, with your eyes apparently open, and you don't see it. And then comes the crash. You run your head into the brick wall. And you pick yourself up and walk into another.'

And all this time—death of one wife, marriage to another, tortured distinctions between 'spirit' and 'creature'—*Son of Woman* had been going forward. From its conception to its completion was nine months, for Plowman was reading what were probably proofs in February 1931. No wonder it is a strange book. It is neither biography, reminiscence nor criticism but a blend of all three floated on a curiously sophisticated paradox: Murry was the only person who truly understood Lawrence and it was his duty (and his destiny) to destroy his literary reputation while paying tribute to his personal greatness.

The obvious implication of the title was a comparison between Lawrence and Jesus, and the advantage was given to the latter. But this notion, while it raised the dignity of Lawrence (and his disciple), overlay the general tendency of the book which was a sustained and eloquent attack on its subject both as an author and as a man— always excepting *Fantasia of the Unconscious* and *Aaron's Rod*. As early as 1916, Murry said, Lawrence 'wanted to exult in the world's sickeningness', to let himself lapse into an ecstasy of decay and disintegration'. That the war was in progress was merely incidental. But later things grew far worse. Lawrence had shown clear signs of going downhill—for example he had declined the leadership Murry had offered him at the time the *Adelphi* was founded. After that he sank into 'vicious and inverted sentimentality; his pride is become a madness. He cannot admit he is wrong, that he has failed, that he is beaten.' 'He would not accept himself; he would be something that he was not. . . . In the books of this period . . . we are witnessing a lapse from humanity.' 'He wanted to feed his sense of doom and death and corruption . . . he could not make the effort towards a new and fuller life . . . deeper still was his longing for hatred and revenge.'

This general thesis of grandiose but almost diabolical failure was much heightened by treating all the other characters in the story as merely incidental to the epic relationship between Lawrence and Murry.[1] Two other specific lines of attack were also developed. One was depreciation of Lawrence's sexuality—a matter on which Murry had some claims to speak with authority: 'Instead of being strengthened by his relation with a woman, he was weakened by his own vain struggle to be dominant and lacerated by his sense of guilt.' Put more bluntly, he had 'less than normal sexual vitality'. The other was a crisp deflation of Lawrence's literary achievement. 'He was neither a great novelist nor a great poet.' 'I do not think his [creative] capacities were very great. . . . At bottom he was not concerned with art.'

What, then, was the justification for a book which on the whole was a massive condemnation of both Lawrence and his work? Murry's answer was immediate. 'Lawrence was a major soul', 'the great life-adventurer of modern times', a prophet and a leader who at one moment in his career had pointed out the right path. The blending of this theme with the attack on Lawrence's career and achievement was expressed in Murry's final apostrophe:

For truly you were wonderful among the sons of men, and you gave the world a gift beyond price: not a gift of prophecy or wisdom, for truth and falsehood are mingled in utter confusion in your work—but the gift of yourself. Without someone to 'betray' you, it could never have been given. No man in these latter days has given to men so marvellous or so terrible a picture of Man as you have given. No such picture of Man existed in the world before you came. You were a man of destiny, driven to sacrifice yourself in order that men might know themselves, and the eternal laws they must obey, the laws which, even in denying them, they still obey. Two eternal things you denied, two things of which the promise was richer in you than in any other man whom living men have known: Love and the Spirit, which cannot exist apart. You denied them to the end. Yet to those two

[1] A small but characteristic instance is Murry's description of the invitation to join Lawrence in New Mexico. 'Would I not give it all up and go back with him to New Mexico, and there begin a nucleus of a new society?' (*Son of Woman*, p. 331). The statement is true but omits the fact that six other people were asked at the same time.

things your appeal will be enduring. That which you sought to strangle, you are doomed to bring to birth, in men.

Lawrence was not the only character in the book. The other was Murry, the man who alone could claim to understand Lawrence, who alone had failed him, who alone had a destiny to fail him and to fail him in a peculiar way, which it was not given to others to understand, namely to fail to destroy him. This seemingly tortuous theme, developed at great length at a later stage in the inevitable controversy, illustrates what was perhaps Murry's most exceptional characteristic: his power to convince himself of, and then to elaborate with theological ingenuity, an almost religious bond between himself and a selected individual—Katherine, Gaudier, Lawrence—which conferred as much status on the disciple as on the chosen master.

Son of Woman was the first book to appear about Lawrence after his death and its picture of a 'haunted, tortured, divided, devil-angel of a man' in so great contrast to the obituary Murry had himself contributed to *The Times Literary Supplement* just after Lawrence's death[1] caught the imagination and has to some extent endured. But it aroused fury among Lawrence's other friends and supporters. They pointed out that it was at best an impressionistic portrait by a man who had not met Lawrence for five years or seen him more than occasionally for over a decade; that it was based almost entirely on published work and owed nothing to consultation with its subject's other acquaintances or his extensive correspondence; but above all Murry's assumption of the mantle of a noble traitor with peculiar rights over Lawrence produced a mixture of indignation and nausea. 'Malignant hagiography' was Huxley's phrase for it. The book could not fail to receive an answer.

The person chosen to deliver it was my mother, Catherine Carswell, and I well remember, though I was only thirteen at the time, what went on on that side of the firing line. But at this distance of time it should be possible to be objective.

[1] 'I desire (if I can) to correct the impression, which is widespread, that Lawrence was a madman of genius, savagely bent on violating the sanctuaries, and bruising the finer conscience of his fellow men. . . . Lawrence was the most remarkable and most lovable man I have ever known. Contact with him was immediate, intimate, and rich. A radiance of warm life streamed from him. . . .'

As an old friend of Lawrence, who had known him since before the war and had corresponded with him throughout his wanderings, my mother was already involved with Koteliansky and the Huxleys in the project for publishing Lawrence's letters.[1] She had made her own view of Lawrence plain enough in a letter to the magazine *Time and Tide* soon after his death defending him from obituarists who had seen his influence as dark and sinister:

> He wrote something like three dozen books of which even the worst page dances with life that could be mistaken for no other man's, while the best are admitted, even by those who hate him, to be unsurpassed. Without vices, with most human virtues, the husband of one wife, scrupulously honest, this estimable citizen yet managed to keep free from the shackles of civilization and the cant of literary cliques. He would have laughed lightly and cursed venomously in passing at the solemn owls—each one secretly chained by the leg—who now conduct his inquest.

This was the theme and the approach of *The Savage Pilgrimage* which appeared in the spring of 1932. It did not catch the whole of Lawrence but it was based on long personal acquaintance uninterrupted by quarrel, and on access to a large part of Lawrence's correspondence. It contained a blow by blow account of the episode at the Café Royal; and it ferociously contrasted Murry's record in relation to Lawrence with his claim to exclusive, or indeed any, understanding of him or his works.

By the time *The Savage Pilgrimage* appeared 'South Acre' and its unhappy memories had been left behind. After chugging round East Anglia with Betty in the Trojan he had found a handsome old rectory at a village called Larling, not far from Norwich, which he bought for £1,000. It was a late Georgian house standing in nine acres of trees and meadow, with walled garden, lawns and shrubberies. Such things were to be had in the depths of the depression. There was a cellar which Murry stocked with the excellent vintage of 1929. James Young and his dark, clever American wife Helena planned to move to another disused rectory near by. It was to be a new life. Soon it was to be a purgatory.

[1] This appears from a note among Koteliansky's papers.

For a few short weeks Betty's better side was still uppermost. She was well advanced in her pregnancy and was cheerfully frank to her step-children about the facts of life in a manner that left no more to the imagination than *Lady Chatterley*.[1] But from March 1932 onwards, when she had presented Murry with his third child and second daughter, things began to deteriorate. She resented her husband's friends, especially the Youngs, persecuted her step-children, and was given to referring to her husband, in language he was not used to, as 'the old bugger'.[2]

It was at this point that *The Savage Pilgrimage* was published. In form it was a simple biographical study and Lawrence's widow told the author she found it 'as impersonal as reading about Elizabeth and Essex' as well as 'I am *grateful* to you for L's sake and my own—and "our" sake.' But it was unsparing of Murry. It rudely contrasted the record of his reviews of Lawrence's works with his offer of the *Adelphi* as a platform for Lawrence. It disputed the veracity and the validity of Murry's *Reminiscences* and *Son of Woman*. It poured scorn on his claim to be peculiarly qualified as an interpreter of Lawrence, and was especially savage about his offer to visit the sick Lawrence at Bandol.

It was the first time since the days of *Rhythm* that Murry had had to face open public attack by name, and the indirect attack in *Point Counter Point* must still have been rankling. He was goaded into fury. 'It is time to lance that imposthume', he wrote in his Journal, and threatened an action for libel which, since the author refused alteration and apology, resulted in the book's withdrawal and eager preparations for its reissue by another publisher. One such was found, to whom Murry proposed publication of the full text to which he had objected provided it was preceded by 'a prefatory note not exceeding 1,000 words, written by me'. On this being refused the book, with minimal alterations to the passage about Lawrence's last illness, was published by a third publisher, Martin Secker. But even that was not quite the end. Murry had the last word. In 1933 he

[1] Murry had reviewed it in the *Adelphi*, circumspectly but with sympathy and some penetration: '. . . in it is the courage of a new awareness. But it is no use pretending that all the world is fit to read it. If it were, Mr. Lawrence would have no excuse at all for his still smouldering rage. In a sense, therefore, the point of the book is that the world is not quite fit to read it' (*Adelphi*, June 1929).

[2] It seems from his Journal that Murry was not even sure how to spell this word.

published *Reminiscences of D. H. Lawrence* which reprinted the original reminiscences published in the *Adelphi* and all the reviews he had ever written of Lawrence's works, together with an eighty-page reply to *The Savage Pilgrimage* entitled 'Murry and Mrs Carswell' which included the revelation of Lawrence's alleged letter of January/February 1920 to Katherine; as a result of which 'I wrote to him that he had committed the unforgivable crime: that I sincerely hoped that we should never meet again, because if we did meet again, I should thrash him.'

In the midst of all this literary controversy and domestic realignment his inexhaustible fertility of mind was entering a new phase: extreme if unorthodox socialism. In a matter of two months during the autumn of 1932 he produced *The Necessity of Communism* and ushered in a political career which was to last for several years. The new development alarmed Plowman. 'The *cry* of injustice', he wrote to Murry, 'is surely the most moving sound a man can hear; but the *whine* of injustice is surely the most nauseous ... and on and on these professional left-wingers whine till their voices are a permanent falsetto, and their faces—clocks set to strike on the Day of Judgement.' As for Murry's hopes of 'going back to Marx' and working out a synthesis between Marxism and Christianity minus God: 'You preach Marx as a *religion*. What's the result? Every Marxian disowns and abuses you. They see you trying to span the Red Sea, to have one foot in Egypt and the other in Canaan. It's the limit of impossibility. Shut up in finite revolutions—that's how I see Marxism. Round and round the blasted economic mulberry bush go the victims of those who think they can find an economic solution to a spiritual problem.'

Betty had given him one more chance before displaying her true colours. It must have been towards the end of 1931, for it was before her child was born:

> She came to me quite unexpectedly, one day, and staggered me by asking me to let her go away—for ever. If I would give her twenty pounds, that would be enough. She would get a room and go to work as soon as her baby was born. She besought me to say 'Yes!' 'Let me go out of your life—for ever. Please! Please!' She stood before me like a slave before her master, and pleaded.

He did not give her twenty pounds but she ran away just the same:
he pursued her to the railway station and brought her back to
Larling. 'From then on', he records at the end of the passage just
quoted, 'she was never to plead with me again.'

War, unstinting, merciless war became the order of the day at
the Old Rectory. She hated his intellectualism and his intellectual
friends, regarded his socialism with horror, and increasingly despised
his character. Her fury of course extended to his elder children. As
his son records:

> When she was in full spate Betty was awe-inspiring—a truly
> elemental fury. To attempt to reason with her was impossible.
> She despised reason. To try to follow her line of thought when she
> was working herself up into a rage was to risk permanent disloca-
> tion of the intellect. . . . At such times she exuded a kind of black,
> demonic force of pure annihilation like a psychic miasma.

Quarrels, curses, even blows became a matter of every day, and
the Murry household was a byword in the village. The unfortunate
Murry could do nothing right. The man who delivered the paraffin
turned out to be an admirer of his work and was enlisted as a fellow-
socialist: Betty swore about the low company her husband kept.
When James Young and his wife Helena settled nearby Betty
accused Murry of having designs on Helena.

Yet through all his troubles the committed literary man laboured
on. Since the *Dostoevsky* of fifteen years ago only three years had
been without the publication of at least one book: sometimes there
had been two, occasionally even three. And during those infernal
years with Betty he produced not only his two works on Lawrence
but a study of Blake (suggested by Max Plowman and not one of his
best works) and his extremely interesting autobiography *Between
Two Worlds* in which he carried the story of his life down to the
end of the war. With a propitiatory gesture he dedicated it to Betty.
These years were also the crest of his reviewing career in *The Times
Literary Supplement*, which was then exerting great influence under
Bruce Richmond. Study and potting shed were his refuges from the
demon that roamed through the rest of the house.

He also pressed forward his career as an active, if eccentric
socialist. The I.L.P., then a splinter group of the Left, was his

choice as a political base, and he declared that he found in Maxton and Fenner Brockway respectively the British Lenin and the British Stalin. The pages of the *Adelphi* were filled with articles on Marx and Revolution[1] and Murry himself, lean now and round-spectacled, but ever smiling, was often seen in his crumpled grey flannel suit expounding his version of the 'Marxist imaginative vision' on many platforms. Among those who were struck by his oratory was the daughter of a Lincoln architect, Mary Gamble, who long afterwards was to become his fourth wife.

The thirties almost required political attitudes from literary men, but Murry took a bypath to the Left, just as Orage, as one can see in retrospect, took a bypath to the Right. It was the response to the change which had carried western Europe and America into depression, and then, as time passed and dictatorships swelled, opened the prospect of an engulfing war. The certainties about British power and European civilisation that had buoyed them up even when they criticised the apparatus which made them possible, seemed ever less substantial. Both men were temperamentally inclined to hero-worship, and Orage still had Douglas; but Murry could make little of Maxton, and Max Plowman was too common-sensical to follow in the series of Gaudier, Katherine and Lawrence. Just as he scouted Orage's social credit propaganda as 'little better than infallible pills for constipation', so he condemned Murry's socialism as 'putting wolves in pens and calling them sheep'. 'Marxism', he declared, 'is crippled by its own deadly cocksure materialism.'

They mattered still as literary men and editors, though never as politicians. Rayner Heppenstall, as a student from Leeds with literary ambitions, applied for work to both of them. The *New English Weekly* was the first and the *Adelphi* the second to spot the talent and print the work of the unknown Dylan Thomas. Heppenstall, through writing a favourable notice of Murry's *Blake* for the *New English Weekly* (Orage printed it but was very cross) was drawn into his orbit and found himself, at Murry's suggestion, writing an appreciative work with the curious title *Middleton Murry: A Study*

[1] It was in this Marxist phase that the *Adelphi* (3 June 1932) made its polite bow to the appearance of the *New English Weekly*. 'We welcome the re-emergence of Mr. A. R. Orage as editor of a new weekly journal.' But the welcome was combined with a stinging repudiation of Social Credit.

in Excellent Normality which appeared in 1934. In a later work
Heppenstall provides a vivid portrait of Murry at this time:

> ... the curious way of hanging his head and of suddenly turning
> it, with eyes thrown quite out of focus, as if blind. There was
> often a hint of locomotor ataxia about Murry's movements. If he
> became at all eloquent while standing up, he would duck his
> head and roll his eyes, writhe and half turn while making a point,
> stand up to reach his conclusion and only just recover his balance
> in time.

Murry's gifts as a public speaker, though not equal to those of
Orage, were not inconsiderable, and he had already organised one
or two direct encounters with his public through 'Adelphi Summer
Schools' held at Larling. By 1935, finding himself increasingly out
of sympathy with the I.L.P., a more ambitious plan began to take
shape in the idea of an 'Adelphi Centre' which would be a permanent community based on socialist principles where men could
keep themselves fit 'for the real battle of life against death ... in a
quasi-return to monasticism and retreat'. To provide it with a home
he acquired, in the autumn of 1935, a country house called 'The
Oaks' standing in its own grounds at Langham, near Colchester.
    Although 'The Adelphi Centre' was very different in style from
either Lawrence's dream of 'Rananim' or the actuality of Gurdjieff's
Institute for the Harmonious Development of Man, it shared with
them the notion of retreat from a society which had taken the wrong
turning; and it is difficult to believe that Murry was not attracted
to the idea of being master of a community by the experience of
two men who had played so great a part in his own life. There was
of course no tinge of the supernatural about the Centre. But it was
to be a place where intellectual life was to be fortified by the pooled
physical labour of the inhabitants, and the institution was to revolve
round the teachings of the founder. Murry, who had provided half
the money for buying 'The Oaks' in the form of a loan at $4\frac{1}{2}$ per
cent was permanent chairman of the limited company which owned
it and was

> to promote the education of children and adults of any age,
> whether male or female ... in accordance with the philosophy,

principles, and methods heretofore set forth or hereafter to be
set forth in the published writings of John Middleton Murry and
Professor John MacMurray[1] with such modifications thereof
(if any) as may from time to time be determined.

Another, more private, aim was incorporated in the project. This
was to escape from Larling and Betty into the company of Helena
Young, who was now separated from her husband and encoded in
Murry's Journal as 'Nehale'. They had met again in New York in
the early spring of 1935 while Murry was on a lecture tour in
America, and Betty's worst suspicions had been fulfilled. That
autumn Murry left Larling, Betty and his family, as he thought for
ever, registering the fact in a lachrymose Journal entry:

Houses and lands and wife and children. It has come to pass as I
foreknew it would. And nothing will ever take the pain away.
Nor God nor Demon can undo the done.

Nineteen thirty-five was the year of pacifist high tide. The Peace
Pledge Union, under the leadership of the Revd. Dick Sheppard,
had profoundly influenced the results of the general election, and
Sheppard's right-hand man was Max Plowman who, though he
remained on friendly terms with Murry, initially regarded the
Institute as 'a home for stray dogs'. There was something to be said
for the judgement, though it was coloured by Plowman's inveterate
anti-Marxism. The membership of the group assembled by Murry
at 'The Oaks' ranged from a sculptor to a colloidal chemist, from the
ex-paraffin man to a lady textile designer. Heppenstall was the cook.
Under Murry's chairmanship they heard lectures from such diverse
speakers as John MacMurray, the socialist professor, S. L.
Bensusan, the Jewish novelist, and George Orwell—the last an
almost unknown friend of Heppenstall's.

They were riven by doctrinal differences, and while Murry could
be just as authoritarian as Gurdjieff he was not that master's equal
at enforcing discipline. Some were inclined to pacifism but others,
especially after the outbreak of the Spanish Civil War in 1936,

[1] Professor of Philosophy at London University and author of *Freedom in the
Modern World* (1932), *Interpreting the Universe* (1933), *Philosophy of Communism*
(1933), *Creative Society* (1935). MacMurray was a Marxist and a pacifist, and
in these years had considerable influence on Murry.

were for the resistance symbolised by the Popular Front. Nor was the domestic side of his life prospering. Betty ruthlessly used his children to blackmail him. His literary work was crippled by the absence of his library. And his partnership with 'Nehale' was not working out as either of them had hoped.

Another change was inevitable. In the summer of 1936, on a holiday in the Norfolk Broads, Plowman converted him from red revolution to pacifism, so that only five years separate *The Necessity of Communism* (1932) from *The Necessity of Pacifism* (1937). In reality the transition was far more rapid. Early in August he had been telling the Centre that 'I . . . find it difficult to be ruthless: but I think I understand the necessity, and whatever it might cost me personally I should be prepared to obey it.' By the end of the year he was declaring that in English conditions socialism was wholly incompatible with violence of any kind.

And he was back at Larling, with the Atlantic safely between him and 'Nehale' who, he told Plowman, had sent him back to Betty 'with joy'. This was not quite true. Her final rather caustic observation had been that 'the next few years will be a bloodier hell than anything I ever saw at Larling'. She was right.

He was rushing with an emotional welcome headlong towards the hardest brick wall he ever hit. The day of his return to Larling was 14 October—Katherine's birthday—and under the double influence he at once sat down and wrote to Plowman:

> Oh, Max darling, I feel that I can't bear it. I am for ever dissolving into tears of joy, as I am now (such a big tear on the end of my nose!). And more strangely still a big tear of sweat running down my side. And now another. My very body weeping tears of joy.

But after a brief truce over lemon meringue pie and the conception of a fourth child war was resumed on terms yet bloodier and less merciful than before. Betty had not forgiven him, and in his open desertion of her she now had a weapon to be picked up at will. The next two years of domestic war and pacifist propaganda were the unhappiest of his whole life.

The Centre, after a period of confusion and acrimony, during which most of its members, as Popular Front militants, seceded, was captured by a pacifist rump and eventually became a home for

Basque refugee children. To Murry himself the Peace Pledge Union, in whose affairs he was increasingly involved, was far more congenial than the revolutionary violence he had professed for the last few years. A review of his life as a whole shows how much against the grain violent doctrines must have been. Revolutionary violence had been a kind of hair shirt which his peculiar nature impelled him to try on for a season. Pacifism commanded his allegiance through the darkest days of the war against Hitler, despite the Union's rapid slither in only a year or two from apparently massive popular support to an opinion verging on the unacceptable. There were other setbacks too. Sheppard died suddenly, at the height of his fame, in October 1937, and Plowman followed him, worn out, in 1941, leaving Murry as perhaps the best known of the P.P.U.'s leadership.

The return to Larling led him to contemplate once more the intellectual surrender to Christianity which he had always resisted in the past. He took part in seminars with Christian thinkers, conferred with bishops, and even enquired about formal theological training that would qualify him for a quiet country living. The English village, he began to tell his Journal, centring on the parish church for its spiritual life, was surely the ideal form of human organisation. Could he not be such a pastor? He studied 'The Parson's Tale' in Chaucer, attended the village church on Sundays, and found some comfort for his bruises in its simple Shakespearean liturgy. He also reflected that a living would provide for an old age when his literary powers began to flag or his style went out of fashion. But how could such a life be reconciled with his past, and above all his present domestic life? His parsonage would ring with curses and obscenities. He put the idea from him.

Another blow was now to fall. Heppenstall had been shrewd in noticing something strange about Murry's articulation, and in the autumn of 1937 he began to find difficulty in walking. The cause was diagnosed as *endoteritis obliterans*, otherwise Burger's disease, a complaint which, though not fatal, is painful, progressive, and difficult to treat. Yet he wrote on unflaggingly. Writing was not now only a way of life or of gaining an income, but a refuge. When the disease overtook him he was working on one of his best and most mature books. *Heaven—and Earth*, which despite its title is a work of literary criticism, returned to the grand theme he had announced in *Keats and Shakespeare*: 'the history of the human soul since the Renaissance'. Though it still shows the weakness of all Murry's work in offering spectacular generalisations which do not always stand up to reflection, the range of reading and scope of imagination are far broader than ten years earlier. Chaucer and Shakespeare, Cromwell and Milton, Wordsworth and Goethe, Rousseau and Marx, are displayed with insight and impartiality. At last, too, the gush and sentimentality have been brought under control. Of all his books it is the one that best deserves to survive.

Yet the impressive display is not so catholic as appears at first sight. The choice is highly individual. Where, in this parade of human achievement, are Voltaire, Pope, the whole 'enlightenment'? Where are Shelley, Byron, and Scott? Where are Ibsen and Tolstoy? A book can only be so long, so these are unfair questions, but the list does suggest something about Murry as a literary man which he came to realise himself in the last years of his life. Before he could write he needed an emotional interplay between himself and the author he was expounding. The witty, the sceptical, the historical, provided him with no such spark. For Murry it is always twilight, never shafts of sunshine; and in the twilight, gently smiling, he is there in symbiosis with his chosen hero.

About the time he was completing *Heaven—and Earth* he answered an enquiry from two Americans, Kunitz and Haycroft, who were compiling a biographical dictionary of contemporary literature on the plan of asking each contributor not only for the usual details but for a short passage about 'where he felt he stood'. Murry was just completing his fiftieth year and in response wrote:

> With the exception of some far-away novels and a poetic play, *Cinnamon and Angelica*, I do not believe I have ever written a book for its own sake. My final position is non-descript . . . I am now a semi-invalid, living in semi-retirement in the country; and at the present moment wondering more anxiously than ever before how to keep my family afloat during the coming storm.

The passage contains a courageous admission and a forgivable falsehood. He had always found it hard to be frank about himself, as he more than once confessed, but now he conceded that except for the least successful part of his work—the part needing creative imagination—there had been no inner compulsion in his writing. It had been a profession.

The falsehood was perhaps not there when the words were penned, but it was by the time Kunitz and Haycroft published their directory. During the latter part of 1938 and the beginning of 1939 the struggle against the combined forces of Betty and Burger's disease became unendurable. He did what he could to civilise Betty, though in strange ways: read psalms to her at breakfast, persuaded her to read a little poetry. But it was all to no purpose. The elemental fury broke out as blackly and as often as ever, and sometimes—such was the rift between them—it was varied by pathetic reproach. 'It's no use', she cried once. 'Why did you marry me? Why couldn't you let me go? Why did you come after me? Why did you make me come back? I knew what it would be. I knew. I knew.' It was Lawrence without the literature, and in May 1938 there was another baby whom, in memory of Lawrence, he named David.

Gradually he was resolving on a last throw for peace and freedom. At a Peace Pledge Union meeting in 1938 he had for the first time met the Lincoln architect's daughter who had been struck by him some years earlier when speaking from an I.L.P. platform. Mary Gamble's politics were of the well-intentioned kind, socialist yet Christian, among which Murry himself was moving. She has told her own story of the development of their friendship from that point onwards until in July 1939, after reciting the horrors of his domestic life, he offered her his heart and himself, and was accepted.

The new war broke out and then failed to explode, leaving a strange nine months during which Murry, still based on Larling, appeared prominently on pacifist platforms to urge a negotiated peace. To the enormities of the Hitlerite persecutions, as he afterwards confessed, he had closed his mind. Some penalties had to be paid. His long connection with *The Times Literary Supplement* was brought to an end by a new editor who believed in the war, so that an important part of Murry's income disappeared. But pamphlets still poured from his pen. The refurbishing of 'The Oaks' as a pacifist centre was contemplated. Then the war caught fire, and among the lesser sequels of the fall of France was a descent by the police on both 'The Oaks' and the 'Old Rectory'. And by that time Betty had found out about Mary Gamble.

The Blitz in London was as nothing compared to the reinforced domestic tyranny of Larling, and Murry, commuting between the two, suffered both. The outbreak of the bombardment found him sitting three days a week (for £7 and his fares) in the last of the four strangely assorted editorial chairs he was to occupy—that of *Peace News*. Those three nights he had the consolation of spending with Mary, but he had to return for the other four to the better-aimed missiles of his domestic hearth. Still, as he said to Mary with a smile, 'The play in which J.M.M. is cast for a leading role has not been played out yet.' The Nazi system, he was sure, was capable of liberalisation. Russia, he considered, should be left without help to absorb the German onslaught.

Yet it was not for three years after meeting Mary that he decided to depart once more, and for all, from Betty and Larling. The unending struggle had told terribly on the once spruce young man of Dan Rider's bookshop and *Rhythm*. Since then there had been thirty-four books, huge labours in the memory of Katherine and Lawrence, shattering emotional adventures which had tested to the limit even his powers of survival. He had shrunk, his hair was reduced to a tonsure, his body almost writhed as he spoke, his legs dragged pitiably. But his housekeeping had been good, and he had always been careful about money. Apart from Larling he had two or three thousand pounds and an income, apart from the yield of his own writings and royalties, of some £500 a year from Katherine's books and £250 from Violet's annuity (which survived her). Then there was the *Adelphi*, still struggling on under editors he appointed, and 'The Oaks' of which he was chairman and principal creditor. There was the base for one more start when he left Larling in the autumn of 1941. He visited it only once more, when Betty was in her grave and it was to be sold, and even at that distance of time he found that 'each room had its own particular memory of horror'.

At first he and Mary lived on the estate at 'The Oaks' which had been developed for agriculture by a group of conscientious objectors. But a stronger base was needed. He had to provide for Betty (who grimly refused to divorce him), four children, two aged parents, and a new household of his own; and he was haunted, as he had been even in days of greater prosperity, by the fear of poverty. He resolved on systematic and profitable agriculture. Katherine's vision of him as a farmer had seemed absurd when she conceived it, but she had seen more clearly than she herself had realised, and his transition to agriculture in late middle age seems almost natural.

By a piece of good fortune 'The Oaks' was at that point acquired compulsorily for some warlike purpose and the compensation helped Murry and Mary to acquire a substantial, if rather run-down farm at Thelnetham, a village some fifteen miles north of Bury St. Edmunds, to which they moved, with some of the conscientious objectors as a labour force, in 1942. Some violence had to be done in the process to the original idea of community which had underlain the Langham experiment. Now, as expressed in Murry's latest work, *Adam and Eve*, which came out in 1944, the emphasis was not so much on community life as on 'a modest but adequate subsistence' for those who worked and 'a modest but adequate return on the capital employed' for those who provided it. For a time community life of a kind continued, and the proprietor still addressed little sermons to his work-force, but gradually the original group melted away leaving him with hired labour to reflect, in 1948, that 'I have at the Adelphi Centre and here proved the failure of socialism'.

The main theme of *Adam and Eve*, however, was not economics but the celebration of his new-found happiness with Mary and the expression of what proved to be his final views on 'the man–woman question'. Looking back over his varied experience he decided this question had been more important to him than literary achievement—had indeed been central to his life. His conclusion that spiritual and physical love reinforce one another was not, perhaps, especially original, but in emphasising the physical side as strongly as he did Murry struck the authentic note of seriousness, even solemnity, about sex which was characteristic of his intellectual generation.

That book found one of the poles from which he was never again to stray; but politically one more transition had to be made, and required yet another book. As the war ended he discarded pacifism, resigned from the Peace Pledge Union, and abandoned all claims that the totalitarian tiger could be prevailed upon to change his habits. Revelations about the true horrors of Hitlerite Germany played an important part in this change (he had always treated the atrocities of the concentration camps as 'horror stories' like those current in the First World War), but so did a declining taste for controversy and a sapping of the egotistical appetite for brick walls. Peering ahead he saw the coming threat in very much the same terms as Orage long ago in his crusade against Fabian collectivism, and recommended a supra-national authority presiding over a world of small, self-organising communities.

The core of *The Free Society*, indeed, is contained in an article he wrote in 1946 called 'Basis of the New Humanism' in which he specifically recalled Orage as 'the chief of those who saw the coming crash of liberalism and the dangers of the omnipotent state'. Alongside Orage he placed D. H. Lawrence as the seeker for a religion 'based on the instinctual nature of man' to fill the vacuum left by the failure of liberal values; Eliot, as the profferer of a traditional consolation 'over which the Church is still rubbing its drowsy eyes'; and Huxley as a fashionable modern sceptic. The only basis for the new humanism, he declared (glancing perhaps at the turnip fields outside his window) was 'literally and figuratively to put down roots again.'

The Free Society was written—all 100,000 words of it—in three months, almost the same speed as he had achieved with *Fyodor Dostoevsky* more than thirty years earlier. It is possible that such powers of fluent composition over so long a period have never been exceeded. But the effort left him exhausted, and the sales were disappointing. 'Here, it seems', he wrote a little later, 'is where I stop.' He gave away the *Adelphi* (which was losing money) and in 1954 wound up the Adelphi School Company which had owned Langham, so that the only relic left in his possession from the long, variegated Adelphi adventure was the Adelphi herd of red-poll cattle, which was the glory of Thelnetham.

He settled for the quiet life he had never had, and perhaps had never sought, supported by a woman who loved him and had no ambitions of her own. The farm prospered under their management. The tiger of modernism, the adventurer among the artists, the I.L.P. orator, the crusader for community living and pacifist principles, were replaced by the benevolent chairman of the Thelnetham Parish Council, the donor of its village hall, the producer of its Christmas show, and a solid voter for the Conservative cause.

It would be easy, but not quite true, to slip into the idea, which he rather fancied himself as he entered his sixties, that a roseate glow settles over these last years. One by one he pasted into his Journal (now intermitted) photographs of his contemporaries as they died, and resumed nostalgic correspondence with the survivors. It was 'nice to be old' he wrote to Frieda in New Mexico, reminiscing about their affair together. He wrote in a similar strain to T. S. Eliot, and paid a visit to the Campbells in Ireland—they were now Lord and Lady Glenavy. Age, he found, suited him now that ideal and personal gyration had ceased. In 1954 the indomitable Betty died (as she had lived) from malignant hypertension, his family, to whom he was devoted, was reunited, and he was able to marry Mary, with whom his alliance was altogether the longest of his four marriages.

But the evening glow was not all pink and gold. The feud with Kot and many others had been re-envenomed by his decision, in 1949, to publish the whole corpus of Katherine's letters to him. In two years of editorial labour he had to relive that painful and complicated relationship, and the result is a remarkable monument to them both.[1] But many of those who were faced with it felt that it should have been raised, or at any rate unveiled, only after the survivor's death. Among the many paradoxes of Murry's character one may count extreme reserve combined with lack of reticence— a paradox which can only be resolved by pleading a deep-seated need for self-justification.

Nevertheless calm induced greater self-knowledge. He had already decided that 'the true man–woman relationship is, to me, more important than artistic distinction'. But that was only part of the truth because it omitted the fact that some great artists had no such choice thrust upon them, and others could not but choose their art. His trouble, artistically, had not been love of women but the fact that his writing was powered by the need to identify himself with the man or the cause he was writing about. The one invariable character in all his books was Murry—what Murry thought, what Murry felt, about Keats or pacifism, about Shakespeare or Marxism,

---

[1] It is not quite complete. It omits at least eight letters now in the Alexander Turnbull Library at Wellington. Two relate to the disposition of her possessions. The other six all belong to the Casetta–Menton period. There are also an unknown number of unpublished letters in the Turnbull Library covering the whole period 1912–23 (MS Papers 119, 89–95).

about Blake or Christianity. But the achievement of domestic felicity enabled him, with his last book, to write without competing for attention with his hero, and he did it deliberately. He chose a subject from a period he had always avoided as 'a challenge to myself to write a book about someone with whom I could not *possibly* identify myself', and the result was one of his best and most successful works. The subject might just as well have been Pope or Steele, and the fancy crosses the mind that the choice of Swift was wafted by a subconscious recollection of the 'Stephen Swift' who had betrayed him and Katherine long ago and reduced him to the bankruptcy which his Camberwell upbringing had made such a fearful humiliation.

Swift was published in 1954, and in the following year he made his peace with the shade of Lawrence: first in a long review of F. R. Leavis's *D. H. Lawrence* in *The Times Literary Supplement* and then in a more extended treatment of the subject in one of the pieces making up his last major publication, *Love, Freedom, and Society* which appeared in 1957. The theme of *Son of Woman* was still there—Lawrence was more a prophet than an artist—but the intolerance and the competitiveness, amounting almost at times to hatred, which had disfigured the earlier work, had gone.

So, though he was only sixty-four, had most of those he had known best or to whom he had pinned his faith: Gaudier, Katherine, Lawrence, Sullivan, Kot, Plowman, Frieda. He was comfortably off: his will shows assets of nearly £32,000, a considerable fortune for a literary journalist who had started with nothing. He died quite quickly after a heart attack which came on while gardening in March 1957. 'Ripeness is all' with its many reverberations of meaning, is carved on his tombstone. His old mother, whom he survived by only a year or so, once reflected that she always thought of him as 'Anthony Adverse'. His escape from the adversities which had dogged him (and which he had dogged), and the comparative tranquillity of the last years of his life were, as can now be seen, due to his having at last brought himself to follow Lawrence's advice: 'My dear fellow; *give it up.*'

❧ 16 ❧

Acacia Road

Koteliansky died two years before Murry, in March 1955, at the house in St. John's Wood where he had lived for nearly forty years ever since the days when he, Lawrence, and the Murrys had worked together on *Signature*. The continuity was characteristic of the man. The others had flitted from cottage to cottage, from one continent to another, parading their ideas and prejudices: he had lived up to Lawrence's description of him as a 'monolith'.

Legends had gathered round him. There was the wolf story and the story of how, as a young man in Kiev, he had organised a revolution at which nobody had turned up but himself. Long ago in Russia, it was said, he had been engaged but the girl had jilted him, leaving a permanent wound. Certainly he never, so far as is known, made any further gesture towards marriage or even attachment, unless we can so describe his abiding passion for Katherine. He did not hate women, and as his life went on he elicited much love from them. In his later years, old and ill, he happily conversed for hours together with his old friend Beatrice Campbell, with Dilys Powell, and with H. G. Wells's daughter-in-law, Marjorie.

He was excessively house-proud and declined all help of that sort. He not only washed all his clothes himself, but laundered the towels, the sheets, and even the blankets. His furniture and ornaments were arranged with rigid precision and his floors were polished to the point of endangering his visitors. He used a polishing clog, in the Russian manner, which took him with a strange limp over the surface to be polished, while he hummed mournfully. Everything that was needed for self-sufficiency he could manage.

Britain was the country of his positive adoption. Revolutions could not happen in that 'old, ordered, spiritually disciplined nation'. No more patriotic refugee ever came to this nation. Nevertheless his first application for naturalisation (in 1925) was rejected, and he

259

did not obtain British nationality until his request, supported by Leonard Woolf and Mark Gertler, was repeated in 1929. The enquiring detectives asked him if he was a bolshevik and received the answer that he was neither a bolshevik nor a menshevik, 'if only because I dislike the sound of those words'. He had been overjoyed by the revolution that had brought Kerensky to power, but almost from the first had been appalled by the ascendancy of Lenin, Trotsky, and (worst of all) Stalin. As early as 1922 he was sending Leonard Woolf cuttings from *Pravda* to illustrate 'the criminal policy of indiscriminate requisitioning on the part of the government' and 'Soviet guilt for the present state of the famine-stricken provinces'. H. G. Wells also applied for information about the new socialist republic and the connection led to a friendship with Wells's children, to whom he taught Russian, that lasted for the rest of his life.

Kot's connections with Russia, through his family and otherwise, were quite extensive. His regular correspondence with his mother (now in the Hebrew University of Jerusalem) and with a brother whom he later helped to emigrate to Canada gave him first-hand information about the Ukraine on the strength of which he knew of the struggle for existence there and how, as he once said, 'they took the blankets from our beds'. He also had lines to a number of literary figures, traces of which have now been lost. Such was his reputation as a first-hand source that in 1924 his Foreign Office friend Waterlow arranged an interview between him and Victor Wellesley, then head of the Russian Department.

His many friends found it difficult to understand how he lived. Certainly his needs were modest, but his income was tiny. Over the years he produced a number of translations to be polished by other hands, and gave Russian lessons. He also published a Russian reader which had some sale. During the thirties he was a literary adviser to the Cresset Press, whose wealthy proprietor may well have given him some tactful financial help while complaining about the impracticable works which Kot kept suggesting for publication. But when Kot was asked directly by some anxious well-wisher about how he would manage he would reply with shrug, 'I will sell some old trousers.'

Katherine's image was constantly in his mind, almost as if she had still been alive. 'Her' pear-tree in the garden, the guelder rose she had planted, the lock of her hair she had once given him, the chair she used to sit in when she wrote—all were devotedly preserved. It made no difference that he was conscious of her faults. Waterlow accused him of prejudice in favour of her writings, and urged him to apply the principles of justice he imposed on everyone else. But to Kot that was impossible as he frankly admitted. With all her faults he had loved her too much, and her writing, with all its faults, was too much part of her for him not to love that too.

The theme would not leave him, and more than a year after saying he could not judge her fairly he was writing to Waterlow:

> Her division and 'secret sorrow' I felt from the very beginning of my meeting her, but the extent of her suffering I realised only a few months before her death. Oh Sydney! If I could write, I could show you simply and clearly that her flaws—lack of a certain sensibility, disregard for certain things and for people, her conspiratorial 'love' for Murry, her deliberately invented friendships &c. were due to that terrible unhappiness when an individual human being, realising his difference, is made every moment, by everything, to see his loneliness.

This was his distillation of those interviews in Hampstead in the late summer of 1922 when Katherine was gathering herself for the flight to Fontainebleau. The phrase 'secret sorrow' comes from there too. 'This', she wrote to Murry only two months before her death, 'which has been my "secret sorrow" for years, has become everything to me just now. I can't go on pretending to be one person and being another Boge. It is a living death.'

He was not over-possessive in his admiration and kept up a correspondence with L.M. for the rest of his life. But the breach of 1924 with Murry was never repaired. He had recorded at the time that 'my resolution to free myself of everything connected with M does not arise from spite or revenge: it is a kind of inner need to free oneself of an evil that for years and years has been playing the most terrible tricks on oneself.' Eleven years afterwards, in 1935, when he needed Murry's permission to publish some of the letters he had received from Katherine, the negotiations had to be carried on through an intermediary, Vere Sullivan, who had once been Vere

Bartrick-Baker and a potential Mrs. Murry. She and her husband
J. W. N. Sullivan were among the few who were able to sustain
friendly relations with both the founder and the former business
manager of the *Adelphi*.

Though Kot's hostility to Murry was unbending he invariably
qualified any critical remark (usually equating Murry with Dostoevsky's character Smerdyakov) by saying, 'Murry is a *real* writer,
a real literary critic.' Their antipathy, however, was such that on
Kot's death Murry found even conventional sympathy difficult.
'You will miss him very much', he wrote to Beatrice Campbell. 'I
am sorry for that.' In a letter to the same correspondent a little later
he was unable to conceal his enduring possessiveness in relation to
Katherine:

> Kot's view of our relation was quite superficial, and his relation
> to her was quite false. . . . As a matter of fact Kot's influence on
> her was quite pernicious. The one chance of saving (or prolong-
> ing) her life was her staying quiet with me in Switzerland. He
> filled her with the dangerous dream of being completely cured
> by the Russian Manoukhine, from the inevitable failure of which
> she reacted into the spiritual quackery of Gurdjieff—and death.
> Katherine was lovely—much lovelier than Kot ever knew. Her
> suffering, which was great, came not through me, but from her-
> self. Kot fed what was false in her, and what she knew was false.
> Knowing what I know, it would have been impossible for Kot
> and me to be friends, without my telling him the truth. He *would
> never* have taken it. He didn't like truth. It was not his kind of
> meat.

But what was 'the truth'? That Kot had idealised Katherine? Kot
saw her faults and chose deliberately to ignore them. It is difficult
to say that such a love is not genuine and generous.

During the fifteen years ending with the outbreak of war in 1939,
which virtually coincided with a serious illness, Kot gradually came
to occupy a special position in the literary world of London. Murry
had foreseen it as early as 1922 when he told him, 'your opinions,
since you are so greatly respected, carry weight'. It was a position
of influence, even a kind of authority, and depended, along with his
wide reading, on his personal qualities of extreme, even crusty

uprightness. He wrote little, and held no editorial post. He did not even go out much, though for a time in 1926 he attended some lectures given in Fitzroy Square by Orage's old friend Mitrinović— but he found them disappointing and gave the circle up. His life became a closely regulated round in which conversation with friends whom he trusted played the principal part. He was the repository of many confidences about both love and money.

His main forum was a group of chosen friends, all men, who gathered on Thursdays and so came to be called by Kot 'the Thursdayers'. Sometimes it was at his house in Acacia Road, sometimes for tea at Twinings' shop in Oxford Street, sometimes over dinner in a small restaurant off Tottenham Court Road. Membership varied over the years and sometimes they were reduced to only three or four. But from time to time there would be a fresh recruit and at full strength 'the Thursdayers' must have been a dozen or so.

Sydney Waterlow the diplomat and rejected suitor of Virginia Woolf was one when he was in London, but in 1926 his duties took him to a series of posts abroad culminating at the ambassadorship to Greece, and conversation with him was replaced by long letters, written at intervals of a month or so, in which Kot expressed himself at large about current affairs, giving as he did so a very good idea of the range of serious conversation which occupied his Thursdays. The amiable and versatile Sullivan—a typical learned journalist of his time, who could write with equal charm on Beethoven and popular science, was among the most senior Thursdayers till paralysis struck him down and he wasted away in an invalid chair at the Adelphi Centre. Two others were drawn from the scholarly staff of the British Museum: A. S. Fulton, of the Department of Oriental Manuscripts and H. J. M. Milne, of the Department of Western Manuscripts who, like Sullivan, was an old habitué of 'The Elephant'.

Leonard Woolf may perhaps be reckoned among 'the Thursdayers'. Unlike the rest he knew some Russian and Kot corresponded with him in that language, but he was a rare attender. Regular literary men who were more faithful attenders were the poets W. J. Turner and the gnome-like Irishman James Stephens, author of *The Crock of Gold*, who was one of Kot's most intimate friends and correspondents. Kot was inclined to dismiss all literature written by Irishmen as in some curious way synthetic, and conceded respect to Stephens alone among them. Two others in the group were T. A. Levi, professor of jurisprudence at the University College of Aberystwyth, who devoted his life to the development of legal studies in Wales, and the liberal-minded Greek academic, Mavrogordato, who lived not far down the street.

Finally there was the gifted, ebullient painter, Mark Gertler whom Kot had first met in 1915 in the Garsington circle. In some ways Gertler's temperament, alternating between enthusiasm and depression, was not unlike Kot's own, and the bond between them became almost that of father and son. The older man patiently bore the long unhappy affair between Gertler and Carrington, and in 1925, when Gertler suffered a sudden stroke at Garsington, the monolith actually moved from Acacia Road to his bedside to nurse him with tireless devotion.

Under Kot's sombre chairmanship there was little room for the flippant or the sophisticated. He was a passionate opponent of all he felt to be 'not genuine' and anyone he considered to be a 'blight-er'— a word he seems to have adopted in its literal sense of someone with a blighting influence. Very occasionally he would take too much to drink, and his opinions then became furious, his behaviour unpredictably destructive, as at the Café Royal party for Lawrence, when he had hurled glasses to the floor after drinking successive toasts of his own proposing, or a little later when, with Mark Gertler's help, he systematically destroyed an elaborate buffet supper which he considered to be too ostentatious.

'Sophistication', he declared, 'is the greatest obstacle to anything valuable.' Ideas solely acquired through reading and not mediated through thought and experience could do great harm, but 'one's own ideas, the pivotal ideas of one's being—yes that is certainly essential.' The need for veracity and firmness was paramount. 'I am perfectly convinced', he wrote to Waterlow in 1927, 'that the majority of writers cannot write a personal book':

They fear that people may say about them that they are not 'clever' enough, 'refined' &c. . . . I speak of good writers, not of budding Nation and Statesman geniuses. These are simply sickening. It is sickening and horrible that in English literature there should not be writers but literary playboys. . . . The only consolation about England is that somehow one believes—seeing that the people are so much better, firmer, truer than its writers—that somewhere in obscurity, stilly, away from the literary marketplace, there is ripening a writer worthy of the name. In spite of all the obvious evidence to the contrary I personally believe that it is in England that such a writer will come . . . in spite of all the emptiness and beaverbrookism of life here, there is still a definite awareness of what is right, and that is the proper soil for a writer to grow up.

Lawrence was, of course, the writer in whom Kot had most faith, and they saw a great deal of each other during Lawrence's last visit to England in 1926. Kot was delighted to find in his friend a revulsion from 'Mexico and the religion of death' which had repelled him in *The Plumed Serpent*. He found 'a grumbling return to essentials' in a decision by Lawrence to write no more novels until he could restrain himself from using them to announce 'new truths'. 'There is in Lawrence', he reflected, 'a real good writer who is too impatient with the surrounding externals . . . I believe that when Lawrence ceases to lay down laws of truth . . . he will then only be able to be the very fine and real writer that he undoubtedly is.'

Other authors were treated much less enthusiastically. To Huxley, for instance, he was dispassionate, even condescending. 'Personally I think that if he husbands his resources, he could become a useful writer—not creative, but preserving a purified and firm European tradition.' Forster, he was prepared to admit, 'is a writer', but 'not a creator, oh no, but a writer.' He admired Virginia Woolf, and considered *To the Lighthouse* had 'life in it, not mere invention', but he did not hesitate to criticise her when he felt she fell below her best, as happened with *Orlando* in 1928. 'Virginia's *Orlando* is rotten and so stupid and dense in its ready-made cleverness. Why does she not realise she is wasting herself? Wasting a good talent for nothing at all.' As for the professional critic I. A. Richards, he 'missed the mystery' though he could 'distinguish between a literary Ford, Daimler, or Rolls Royce'. Wyndham Lewis was 'trying to clear up rubbish but I am afraid that, in spite of his undoubted talent as a journalist and pamphleteer he has absolutely nothing to say. Nil.' After allowing for the brutality of these judgements their undoubted sanity and durability was due to the detachment in which he managed to place himself both in his way of life and his choice of friends. He was above clique.

Having prescribed a period of inactivity for Lawrence he was alarmed only four months later to hear from Florence that a new novel was already under way; and what was worse it was going to shock the public into accepting new truths. This was the work which eventually became *Lady Chatterley's Lover*. 'The news to me was not pleasant', he wrote to Waterlow in Bangkok, 'for I don't believe L has the peace needed for a novel. I don't believe he will do justice to himself.' But despite his reservations he loyally undertook to act as the London distributor of *Lady Chatterley*, and his accounts of copies sold and remittances to the author are still among his private papers.

All his life he had suffered from recurrent 'dark moods' of unsociability during which he avoided inflicting himself on his friends. They may account for his deliberately solitary household life, for they made him quarrelsome as well as gloomy. Murry's was by no means the only friendship which came to an end in wrath. Another such was with Sydney Schiff, the wealthy American who translated the last volume of Proust under the name of 'Stephen Hudson'. The scene was the Savoy, where Schiff and his wife Violet were staying on a London visit, and to which they invited Kot for a series of evening meals in a well-meant effort to cheer him up. The result was the opposite of that intended, for after two evenings the guest became 'increasingly irritated by Schiff's complacency and self-indulgence'. By the third, with one of his black moods coming on, he found himself in violent opposition to Schiff's comments on a recently published novel; and when his host seemed to insinuate that 'I was against capitalist society' (no doubt he had been attacking the commercialism of the press) 'I rose up and said that, in spite of my dislike for romantic gestures, I must not see him again. I apologised to Violet, shook hands with her, said nothing to Schiff, and went away.'

As he grew older the dark moods developed into black patches of depression which could last for weeks or even months at a time. His melancholy was accelerated by the death of Lawrence, whose greatest achievement, Kot considered, still lay in the future. But worse was to come. He began to reproach himself. Friends persuaded him to undergo electro-therapy, for in a fit of despair he had attempted, and almost achieved, suicide by cutting his throat. Then, almost simultaneously with the outbreak of the war against Hitler, came the further blow of Gertler's death. He was to have come to tea at Acacia Road and when he failed to arrive Kot went to seek him in his studio not far away: he was dead beside the gas fire with his head on a pillow. 'Gertler', he said afterwards, 'who loved life, how could he have killed himself?'

Very soon afterwards he was himself taken suddenly ill with a heart attack from which he nearly died. Recovery found him old and shaken, but much gentler. He still loved to talk endlessly, perched often on a stool in his kitchen. But he still blamed himself. 'I have lived the sort of life I wanted to. I am paying for it now.' Religion in all its forms he rejected. Literature, he declared was Holy Writ, and it was in that sense, perhaps, that he told Lady Glenavy one day that he was God's most humble servant.

He still had one more painful experience to face. Murry had been right in supposing that Katherine had shown only one of her many faces to Kot, and that even if he had detected her faults, the face she had shown him had dazzled him. Murry's publication in 1951 of the full text of Katherine's letters to him broke Kot's heart. His agony was only made worse by Lady Glenavy's well-meant comment that Katherine's sufferings arose from within herself and were not felt for others; and so perhaps were not the worst kind of sufferings. He described his reading the letters as 'a shattering blow'.

Just after Christmas 1954 he had another heart attack, but stayed at home in bed, not even sending for a doctor. Marjorie Wells came to see him and, seeing how ill he was, stayed to look after him. On 21 January Leonard Woolf paid him a visit which, he said, gave him a great deal of pleasure. 'For a quarter of an hour the past came alive again, but now, alas, it is fading very quickly.' Marjorie Wells was with him the next day, Thursday, 22 January, when he died.

Woolf wrote a tribute in the paper Kot had always disliked, the *New Statesman*, honouring his uprightness, his fiery noble character, and his influence in the literary world. The outline of the man, despite his obsessions, is firmly moulded, rare in its integrity, and is instantly recognisable in all that he did. James Stephens once reflected that the greatest book never written about English literature was by Koteliansky. In spite of his decisiveness he remains something of a mystery, perhaps because he liked to be a little mysterious. Even the exact date of his birth is unknown—a blank which he filled in with one of the few flashes of humour ever recorded of him, by entering on all forms against the relevant question, 1 April. There was more than a little jealousy in his character, especially towards the wives and close friends of those he had chosen to admire—a dislike which was reciprocated by Frieda Lawrence when she spoke of Kot's 'little slave legs tucked under the chair' as he 'howled like a wolf at the moon in the Ukraine'. He loved the feeling that as those whom he valued wandered, physically and emotionally through the world, he remained their confidant, almost their recording angel. Though he had none of Ben Jonson's jocularity Drummond of Hawthornden's words about Jonson might almost serve as his epitaph: 'passionately kind and angry, careless either to gain or keep, vindictive, but if he be well answered, at himself'.

❧ 17 ❧

Retrospect

When exploring my parents' world as an only child in the twenties and early thirties I made a discovery which no doubt everyone makes, but it seemed important to me at the time and perhaps living in a literary household brought it home to me early because literary people work and transact business with their colleagues in their own homes. Until I made this discovery I had supposed, as most young children do, that my own and my parents' friends and acquaintances were, so to speak, additive. They were arranged in a circle, or rather a series of concentric circles ranging from dearest friends to the most distant acquaintances, with one's own family in the middle. When these friends were not present they were no doubt (I calculated) at the centres of their own circles, which had nothing to do with mine. But of course these circles must *intersect*. My parents, for instance, lay at the centre of their own system and on the edge of others. Then I found, rather to my surprise, that two people who belonged to the periphery of our own circle, coming rarely to our house—and then separately—were in fact close friends dwelling very near one another's respective centres.

All this sent me to the drawing board, and like some ptolemaic astronomer I sought to contrive ever more complex systems of circles intersecting at the right places so as always to take in *these* people but not *those*. Some of these circles cheated by having wavy edges to bring in *him* but not *him*. It was all in vain. The wealth of knowledge from direct observation and supplementary enquiry was too rich. 'Would you call Mr. Koteliansky a friend or an acquaintance?' 'An acquaintance, I suppose, darling.' 'But he's a *friend* of Mr. Huxley's?' 'Well he does see a lot of Mr. Huxley just now.' 'Mr. Huxley knows Mrs. Lawrence doesn't he? Does Mr. Koteliansky?' 'Not really, dear—not now.'

And then there were enemies. Where did one put them? Because of course I knew they existed. Hugh Goldring, a boy of my own age, was clearly a friend, but his father, Mr. Goldring, I gathered, was to be accounted an enemy. Gradually I abandoned the circle theory. There was, I now knew, no limit to interrelationships.

The people in this book do not make up a circle, nor were they chosen in the hope that they would make one. Long before I knew as much about them as this book gives, their names, and in most cases their personal images had been present to me as forming part of the world in which my parents made their own struggling literary careers. No more than that. 'Oh . . . Orage . . .' my mother said thoughtfully when I asked about the name that had caught my ear: and fell silent. Koteliansky stalks solemnly up the narrow garden path, shaded by his broad-brimmed black hat. Much longer ago the name of Katherine Mansfield 'dying in a cowshed in that insane place—how could he have allowed it?' conjured up a mystery that was not allayed by reading her stories or her *Journal*. Murry was the name that at one time brought the garrison, including me, to the walls, though I had no idea what the war was about, except that it was in some way connected with the Mexican stamps I had patiently soaked off their envelopes and stuck in a sixpenny album. The name floated up to me in my gallery bedroom from the dinner-table where Secker or Charles Prentice, Koteliansky or Aldous Huxley, were sitting with my parents during the months following the publication of *Son of Woman*.

So this book had its origin in a collection of sights and sounds and smells to which I wanted to add accurate knowledge; and thence more broadly, in a desire to explain, after having explored, what that particular kind of literary life was like by describing some inter-related examples about whom there is some evidence.

Beatrice and Orage, Murry and Katherine, were not a group or even the centres of two groups, and their affiliations, though close at some stages of their lives, were no closer than with others in an extensive world whose members had declared their independence of ordinary economic life and embarked on a literary career. The price of this emancipation was competitive struggle. They were not, as was the case with the Bloomsbury Group, borne up by incomes which would have been adequate even if they had never set pen to paper, and they were not salaried journalists. In my house a review ordered over the telephone half-way up the stairs meant the overdue gas bill could be paid. The irregularity of money gave it a special significance. Murry's financial care, Katherine's insistence on having a cheque sent out to her in France so that she could look at it, both reflect this sense of money being not only a necessity but a recognition. The business side of authorship—the contracts and the agencies, the negotiations and sharings of the proceeds of collaboration, were treated with immense solemnity considering how pathetically small most of the sums were. The papers of Koteliansky, the letters of Katherine and Murry are peppered with serious little notes about entitlement to a few pounds or even a few shillings.

Murry and Orage, of course, were literary entrepreneurs as well as authors, which entitled them to a special effulgence in that literary world. Those who wrote and hoped to get printed belonged to their public almost as much as did their readership. More than that. The way in which editorial life provides the stream on which the domestic life of the editor floats was never more clearly illustrated than in their histories. Yet when one is allowed to peep behind the impressive façades in front of which they accepted material for publication and delivered 'our' opinion on almost any issue, one finds a staff and an organisation that would hardly support a modest student newspaper today.

Virginia Woolf called them 'the literary underworld'—a phrase in which there is a mixture of fear, distaste, and admiration. Most of them had not been conventionally educated to a high standard; and yet they were widely read, even learned. They were professional without being academic, dedicated without being organised. The shelves and the reading from which they drew their work were haphazard but copious, and if few of their books would now stand up to a pounding from modern batteries manned by doctors of philosophy, they had a breadth of reading which later generations of literary people lack. My father, for instance, was weak on modern fiction, of which he had read little besides Joyce, Proust, and Lawrence. But from Hardy backwards there was very little of importance which he had not read, whether it was Hume or Cervantes, Montaigne or Chaucer, Balzac or Vergil; and I should be surprised if any of the main characters I have described, including Beatrice, fell far short of him. What they did not read much was commentary, because there was still not much of it to read; and they were not particular about the texts they used, for scholarly editions of notable works were still few.

In spite of their emancipation they were strongly marked by their upbringing among the certainties of religion and the Victorian social order. Both Orage and Murry, in their very different ways, may be said to have spent their lives trying to find some substitute for the Victorian God. Orage sought it in the notion of secret wisdom, to be attained perhaps by internal discipline but residing somewhere outside himself. Murry was the reverse. In all his different doctrinal adoptions he is like a chameleon determined to stay the same colour. He maintained that there was something inside his personality which was peculiarly valuable. Sometimes he dreaded that this was an illusion, that there was nothing inside him at all; and Orage's enemies, notably Beatrice after their parting, suspected nullity in him too. J. W. N. Sullivan might have had them both in mind when he wrote of 'men who seem never to lose the sense that life offers boundless possibilities'. 'I notice', he reflected, 'that such men do nothing, in fact, but repeat their experiences.'

This inward and outward regard was reproduced in a curious way in the appearance of the two men. Murry's greenish eyes hardly looked at you. To some people it almost seemed as if he was blind. Orage's hazel stare was one of the most effective things about him: some of those who were fascinated by it declared his eyes were flecked with gold in the iris. Yet both could hold an audience—Murry by his intellectuality, Orage by an extraordinary warmth and selflessness that seemed to flow from him even when his utterances verged on nonsense.

The literary world of London attracted recruits from far afield, geographically and socially. Murry's Pooterish Camberwell background and subsequent progress through Christ's Hospital to Oxford was among the most orthodox and metropolitan. Orage, the rural elementary schoolteacher, Holbrook Jackson, the Liverpool clerk, Beatrice and Katherine, star-struck and pseudonymous, from South Africa and New Zealand respectively, Koteliansky from the Ukraine, Edwin Muir from the Orkneys, Lawrence from the East Midlands coalfield, all flow together in this 'literary underworld'.

And then explode again over the surface of the earth. They are in constant movement from cottage to cottage, from country to country, from one side of the Channel to the other, in search of new places to sense their emancipation and cheap lodgings to suit their short purses. Only Kot, like a large boulder, having rolled all the way from Ostropol to Acacia Road, remained immovable when he reached his resting place. Most of them pioneered a new form of travel—the unladen, intellectual kind.

Katherine and Beatrice, with their remotely born literary ambitions, were citizenesses of the world, used from childhood to long distances. But they could almost be said to represent a centripetal tendency in British culture, for although they wandered all their lives their trend was always homewards from the circumference, even if it was a homing to criticise not commend what they found. Literary passion, which consumed them both, was in them a combative one, a desire to acquire, elaborate, and employ language to etch the folly and scotch the institutions of the metropolis: because it was only in the metropolis that such language was worth employing.

The relationship and ultimate fates of Katherine and Beatrice are particularly interesting. Both of them intensely, over-consciously feminine, they both also had an ambi-sexual side which drew them to one another yet was a source of horror and embarrassment. Katherine's initial admiration for Beatrice, and conspiratorial dependence on her, gave way to disgust and fear as Beatrice grew older and more desperate in her ways; yet it is possible that the reverence she had felt for Beatrice eventually reinforced her admiration for Orage, leading her in the end to Fontainebleau. As for Beatrice, jealousy of the younger woman's fame, which she lived to see, was an important ingredient in her pathetic descent into craziness.

Katherine's talent, despite the meagreness of her output, was exploited to the full. Beatrice's literary gifts were more abundant and her ambitions ranged wider, but failure of discipline and contempt for obstacles denied her success or even a single first-class piece of work. She was, as she kept on saying in the one poem of hers that has any merit, 'a lost Bacchante':

Retrospect

We rushed from the forest at break of day
The last of our mad god's train.
We had wakened the night in cursing the rite
Of a mortal who loves in vain.

. . . .

My body is red with wounds and rage,
But I'll bathe in the mountain lake,
And I'll ease my spite by blessing the rite
Which the moral maid did make.

It has some of the vigour of a female W. E. Henley, but it is chaotic
and lacks any sensibility. But then Katherine was no poet either.
None of them were.

Murry was tortured by his lack of creative gifts. To be able to
write so freely and so well, yet to be incapable of either poetry or
fiction, deeply distressed him. To the end of his life he tried to soothe
himself with the thought that the trifle he wrote for a Garsington
Christmas charade—'Cinnamon and Angelica'—was an outstanding
work. This absence of creativity in a man essentially literary may
help to explain some of his least attractive traits, notably his tendency
to heroise and then identify himself with a succession of people
whose creative talent was conspicuously great. Indeed his very
success as an editor was due partly to his perception (and a degree of
jealousy) of those with creative talent. His later years were clouded
by a sense of having been deprived of the heroes he had in some
way made his own—Katherine and Lawrence. For Katherine's loss
he blamed Orage, and in a measure Koteliansky: for Lawrence's he
could blame only circumstances and himself. He was never able to
forgive any of them.

Orage was equally lacking in creative power, thus severely
defined, but he had few ambitions in that direction, at least in his
own name. Instead he was one of the greatest 'ghosts' that ever
wielded a pen. Where he had real talent to work on, as with
Katherine Mansfield, Ruth Pitter, Herbert Read and Edwin Muir,
the strictness of his craftsmanship and the warmth of his personality had real effect and went some way towards justifying his
boast that, 'I write writers'. Cliché was the enemy he had recognised
early, and he had enforced his standards even on Beatrice, as she

admitted when, pausing in her dance on his grave, she spoke of 'the young artist who knows only too well what pains and practice, besides his gift, are necessary'. Above all his success as a writer of writers was due to his genuine disinterestedness. 'All these exercises in culture', he once wrote, 'are elementary in comparison with the master problem of "disinterestedness". No word in the English language is more difficult to define . . . in its capacious folds it contains all the ideas of ethics, and even, I should say, of religion.'

As a critic, therefore, he had no need to identify himself with his author, and his range is therefore greater than Murry's. He writes of Scott, for instance (an author Murry would never have tackled):

A writer who has succeeded in successfully competing with actual history in the creation of characters so that posterity can scarcely distinguish between the real and the imagined, is not to be relegated at any time to a lower position than the very highest in literature.

Bolingbroke—'one of the great dark horses of English history'; Kipling—'a strain of mysticism that redeems his work from the vulgarity that otherwise would surely weigh it down'; Landor— 'there is no *virtue* in him'; Bertrand Russell—'He thinks glacially but his style is warm. . . . In a word, I dont believe he believes a word he says! That tone, that style, them there gestures—they betray the stage-player of the spirit.' Not eternal truths in all cases, perhaps, but perceptive dealing with all comers.

Part of the difficulty of coming at the man is that he kept few letters and not many people kept his, though he wrote thousands in that neat, cursive schoolmasterish hand. Nor did he keep a diary. The thing was temperamental, the obverse of Murry's careful archivism and voluminous journals and Kot's obsessive, almost curatorial neatness. For whatever differences there may have been between them Kot and Murry were alike in that they neither of them ever threw away a piece of paper. It is one of the reasons why, though not great in themselves, they still have a place in literary history whereas Orage is almost forgotten. As Frieda Lawrence remarked, he had 'a brave voice and a genuine heart' but when his physical presence was removed his influence quickly faded and even the dinner founded so enthusiastically by his admirers petered out after a year or two.

But all three showed one trait, though it took different forms: the need for a group of chosen spirits. The reality of the mis-heard 'Rananim' turned out to be Kot's rather masculine Thursdays in Acacia Road. For Murry it was the febrile and disorderly Adelphi Centre. And for Orage it can be summed up in the sentence: 'We sat together in a tea-shop close to Gower Street and discussed Plato.'

Religion, or at any rate the supernatural, none of them, except perhaps Kot, ever wholly escaped. Rejection of the formalities simply left them as explorers on the basis of personal experience so that they often became the victims of charlatans and eccentrics. They were, in fact, easily taken in, despite their earnest intellectuality, wide reading, free style of life, and readiness for adventure: one has only to consider such astounding failures of judgement as Murry's decision to marry Betty, Orage's submission to such men as Grayson or Gurdjieff, Katherine's adventure with the St. John's Wood tenor and her rush across France to Carco, Kot's idolisation of Katherine, or Beatrice's innumerable errors, of which perhaps the most ludicrous was her proposal to rehabilitate Madame Blavatsky as the wronged heroine of womanhood.

This mixture of high principles, genuine craftsmanship, and gullibility was characteristic of their world of letters. Their apparent membership of the middle classes is thus illusory. Their waistcoats and their bickerings about money, Katherine's periodic reincarnations as a dove-grey, flower-arranging lady instead of a girl in a Burberry hurrying to meet her lover, even Murry's woodmanship and potting-shed at Larling, cannot conceal the fact that the worlds of business, politics, finance, the whole system in fact of salaries and safety, had nothing to do with them at all. 'The standards of success of that world', as Sullivan remarked, and in this was typical, 'the achievements for which it bestowed fame and wealth, all seemed to me entirely unreal.' The same feeling underlies Frieda's remark about her counsel's tribute, in the dispute over Lawrence's will, to her and Lawrence as 'a devoted couple': 'No, it wasn't like that at all.' Kot's acquaintance with Waterlow and with the Campbells, Murry's and Katherine's intersection with Garsington, were merely incidental. Even Murry, who had the largest share of middle-class qualities, was essentially a voyager, floated onwards by literary study and personal speculation.

Though they were unaware of it, did not think it even possible, they and those like them broke the way for social change in directions which have since become commonplace. Circumstances were such that mobility put extraordinary bargains within their reach. Rural cottages and rectories were beginning to beg for occupants as urban growth thinned the villages, and those who were willing to accept the hardships of paraffin lamps and pumps were welcome to the houses for almost nothing. A cottage in northern Essex was rentable, right down to 1940, for five shillings a week, and buyable not much earlier for twenty-three pounds. Literary people were the first ex-urbanites. It was the same with foreign travel. If one were willing to accept the discomforts and spend the time, very little money was needed. In France, Italy and Germany, hotel accommodation was to be had for shillings, and wine for pence.

All this helped them to live, and to feel themselves to live, outside the main structure of society while accepting as inevitable the economic constraints of their hand-to-mouth existence. And this in turn made them feel, even when they were at their most subjective, that as outsiders their comments had objectivity. However variegated their diagnoses might be—Christocracy or Communism, theosophy or social credit, love or pacifism might be their prescriptions—they could espouse them with a conviction that derived part of its strength from a feeling that they would in practice make very little impression on the towering industrial and political fabric of the British Empire.

The politically inclined generation of the thirties overtook them when they were already middle-aged and state socialism had established itself irreversibly in an important part of the world. The history of Murry's flirtation with Communism demonstrates, more than any anti-socialist polemic could do, how utterly alien mass politics and the manipulation of power were to that literary generation. And yet, jingling about among their many enthusiasms, in the pages of the *New Age* and the *Adelphi* one can find most of the ideas and even most of the campaigns that have since transformed society. Their leaders about women's rights, industrial democracy, penal reform, are all quite dead now. They remind one of the bodies of fallen soldiers who charged the breastwork before the decisive breach was made and the castle fell.

Both Murry and Orage, however, clearly foresaw, towards the end of their careers, what might happen when the penny-farthing publicity machines they had organised were improved and developed. Murry was writing in 1939:

> Thus modern technique is the enemy of democracy, because its insistent tendency is towards diminishing the scope for individual and responsible choice, which is the training ground of the responsible person, while its increasing centralisation of control offers unprecedented opportunities for the seizure of power. That is to say, modern techniques confront democracy with a problem of the utmost urgency, which democracy is making strangely little effort to solve.

A few years earlier Orage had written:

> Radio, it is certain, is only in its mighty beginning. There are worlds before it to conquer of which print can scarcely dream. . . . With a little real imagination, it is not difficult to establish something like a parallel between what is happening today and what happened when letters were first invented.

They were the very men who, a generation later, would have been the personalities demanded by the modern techniques. The difference between them was that Murry, more bookish, feared what he foresaw, but Orage, who could hardly have failed on television, welcomed it. 'It is possible that the Radio, by partially, if not completely, restoring the original relationship of Speaker, Listener, may at the same time improve both writing and reading.'

But the printed word was what they lived by, or rather the written word, for it will be by their letters rather than their works that they will be remembered. Katherine's passion for mail, inward and outward, was only an exaggeration of something that imbued all their lives. Lady Glenavy movingly describes the burning, after Kot's death, of the huge accumulation of letters from her which he had carefully preserved. The whole of Katherine's correspondence has even now not been published, nor have any of Murry's letters to her.

Six huge volumes in the British Museum contain part, and only part, of what reached Kot in Acacia Road.

To them letters were not matters of business or news. They were the link between their professional writing and their personal relationships face to face. Sometimes one can almost believe that they gave more to their letters, to the idea of maintaining relationships by writing, then they did to either the manuscript or the meeting. Bent over café tables, blinking under paraffin lamps, pads on knees as the train bumped from Victoria to Eastbourne or from the Gare de Lyon to Marseilles: and rushing to the Poste Restante, agonising for the delivery, glancing (as the most important moment of the day) towards the space beside their place at breakfast—all this at least gave them the guaranteed audience, the few to whom, rather than for whom, they wrote.

The greatest letter-writer of them all, of course, was Lawrence and his influence, even over Orage who never met him and thought of him as 'subversive', was considerable. 'Mr. Lawrence is one of the few new writers with whom we shall have to reckon.' Katherine could not escape him, quarrel though she would. Koteliansky treated him as if he was a Ming vase. And Murry: if Violet's shadowy life had ended twelve months sooner and the captain of Bersaglieri had not been on the scene, Frieda might well have become the fourth Mrs. Murry, with all that would have implied. There lies the origin of *Son of Woman* and the battle waged over Lawrence's grave.

But Lawrence was a knight-errant, not a free-lance whose works were written for the moment. Katherine wrought, but for art's sake, not for perpetuity. The others wrote for the moment, and freely, but their seriousness and passion one cannot for a moment doubt.

Appendix

The Wills of Katherine Mansfield and D. H. Lawrence

On 7 and 14 August 1921 Katherine Mansfield made two testaments in rapid succession, the first informal and the second formal. The informal testament, in the shape of a letter addressed to Murry, did not reach him until after her death and is not included in his edition of her letters to him, though it is printed in Mr. Lea's *John Middleton Murry*, p. 95. The original is in the Alexander Turnbull Library. It leaves everything to Murry with a few hints of personal keepsakes to friends and, so far as her papers are concerned, the following instruction:

> All my manuscripts I leave entirely to you to do what you like with. Go through them one day, dear love, and destroy all you do not use. Please destroy all letters you do not wish to keep, and all papers. You know my love of tidiness. Have a clean sweep, Bogey, and leave all fair—will you?

It ends: 'I feel no other lovers have walked the earth together more joyfully—in spite of all.' A remark Murry often recalled and usually misquoted by omitting the last four words.

The formal will of a week later is much more specific. Named possessions are left to L.M. ('my gold watch and chain and my clothes'), Anne Estelle Rice, Murry's mother and brother, her father ('my brass pig and my bible'), her sisters, her cousin Elizabeth Russell, and Koteliansky ('my carved walking stick'). Murry was to select books as keepsakes to Walter de la Mare, H. M. Tomlinson, Sorapure, Orage, the Schiffs, Fergusson, Gordon Campbell, and D. H. Lawrence. Everything else is left to Murry but with a much more stringent injunction, namely:

> All manuscripts, papers, letters, I leave to John Middleton Murry likewise I should like him to publish as little as possible and to tear up and burn as much as possible. He will understand that I wish to leave as few traces of my camping ground as possible.

Murry was disposed to give the first testament precedence over the second, and in fact preserved (and published) almost everything.

D. H. Lawrence died intestate. Though his wife had always thought he had made a will in her favour, none could be found. Since his relatives claimed a share in the intestacy the matter eventually came before Lord Merrivale, President of the Probate, Divorce and Admiralty Division in 1932: Mr. T. Bucknill for Frieda, Mr. Walter Frampton for Lawrence's sisters, Ada and Emily, and his brother George. They had had letters of administration granted to them in June 1930.

Frieda's claim was that Lawrence, herself, Murry and Katherine had met on 9 November 1914 at Cholesbury, and the conversation had fallen on the subject of money and how poor they were. There was, too, the anxiety of the war. Lawrence had ended this gloomy discussion by saying, 'We shall all be great men some day, and we must make our wills', whereupon two wills were made by Lawrence and Murry leaving all they possessed to Frieda and Katherine respectively. Each couple then witnessed the will relating to the other couple. Murry, who gave evidence of this meeting, clinched matters by producing his own will of 9 November 1914 bearing the signatures of Lawrence and Frieda as witnesses.

Frieda's evidence was that the will had been seen as late as 1925 when she and Lawrence had been packing for what proved to be their last visit to England. It might, she thought, have been sent with some other papers to New York—doubtless to Thomas Seltzer, Lawrence's agent and American publisher—before they left. If so it was by accident. He had always said, even in his last illness, that she would have everything.

The Lawrences, said Mr. Bucknill, were a devoted couple throughout their married life, and during their later years might be described as 'citoyens du monde', always moving from place to place. The loss of a sheet of paper was easy to suppose. One of the more moving parts of Mr. Bucknill's address is said (mistakenly) to have wrung from Frieda a cry of, 'No! It wasn't like that at all! We fought like HELL!' at which even the judge allowed himself a smile. But the remark was made afterwards.

Lord Merrivale gave unhesitating judgement for Frieda. The evidence was clear and undisputed. She was the widow. Murry's evidence of the execution of the will was convincing and supported by the documentary evidence of his own will made at the same time. The will had been seen more than ten years later, and there was no evidence that Lawrence had ever changed his intentions—indeed there was evidence that on his deathbed they had remained the same. Frieda had offered £500 each to Lawrence's brother and sisters, in goodwill. This was generous. He pronounced in favour of the will.

Nearly half a century later the fairness, justice, and equity of Lord Merrivale's judgement remain beyond dispute. There is nevertheless an irony in the fact that one of its results was the descent of the hereditary interest in Lawrence's estate to the children of Professor Ernest Weekley, of University College, Nottingham, who had been so deeply wronged by one of his most promising students.

References

Abbreviations for main letter-writers and authors are:

KM   Katherine Mansfield
MM   Middleton Murry
BH   Beatrice Hastings
O   A. R. Orage
SK   S. S. Koteliansky
DHL D. H. Lawrence

Abbreviations for frequently used sources are explained in the Bibliography. Otherwise references to books are by author's name followed if necessary by a clue to the book's title. If no clue is given the work is that given against the author's name in the Bibliography.

CHAPTER ONE

For the relevant figures on teachers in training see *Reports of the Privy Council on Education* and *Statistics of Education* (1971) Vol. IV, 2.

'Do you speak . . .' Mairet, 70.

'The last quarter of the nineteenth century . . .' Shaw to Henderson (10.2.05), *Collected Letters*, I, 511.

'In appearance Orage . . .' Mairet, 24–5. The description is by Holbrook Jackson.

The notebook in question is in possession of Mr. J. M. Bunting.

'Do what you will . . .' Mairet, 26–7.

'You will gather . . .' O to Wells (8.10.05), University of Illinois.

CHAPTER TWO

'Aphrodite amused herself . . .' BH, *TONA*, 19

'She looks at me . . .' BH, 'Pages from an Unpublished Novel', *NA* (13.6.12).

'We were a big family . . .' ibid.

'My divine memory . . .' BH in *NA* (27.6.12).

References

'Say so in the right place . . .' O to Wells (10.11.06), University of Illinois.
'The main objection to socialism . . .' O to Wells (23.7.06), University of Illinois.
'The Arts Group . . .' Jackson to Wells (14.3.07), University of Illinois.
'Two tall men . . .' Hobson, 140.
'We all like Ruth's new poems . . .' O to George Pitter (15.4.12).
'Not *articles* . . .' O to Herbert Read (3.6.21), University of Victoria.
'Beware of the valueless business . . .' O to Herbert Read (22.8.21), University of Victoria.
'Desperado of genius . . .' Shaw in *NEW* (15.11.34).

CHAPTER THREE

The 'Chesterbelloc Controversy' can be said to consist of: 'Why I am a Socialist', Bennett, *NA* (30.11.07); 'Thoughts about Modern Thought', Belloc, *NA* (7.12.07); 'Why I am not a Socialist', Chesterton, *NA* (4.1.08); 'About Chesterton and Belloc', Wells, *NA* (11.1.08); 'On Wells and a Glass of Beer', Chesterton, *NA* (25.1.08); 'Not a Reply', Belloc, *NA* (8.2.08); 'Belloc and Chesterton', Shaw, *NA* (15.2.08); 'A Reply to G.B.S.', Chesterton, *NA* (29.2.08); 'On Shaw, Wells, Chesterton and Belloc', Filson Young, *NA* (7.3.08); 'A Question for Socialists', Belloc, *NA* (21.3.08); and 'An Answer', Wells, *NA* (28.3.08).
BH's controversy with Bax and Norman is in *NA* for May, June and July 1908.
Crowley, 'The Pentagram', *NA* (21.3.08).
'Orage abuses me . . .' Shaw to Norman (8.9.08), *Collected Letters*, I, 810.
'Has not become so dogmatic . . .' O to Wells (9.6.07), University of Illinois.
'I hope you will appreciate . . .' O to Wells (7.10.08), University of Illinois.
Bennett's column over the signature Jacob Tonson began on 28.3.08 and continued for three years.

CHAPTER FOUR

'Her childhood had been lonely . . .' Mantz and Murry, 132.
'The view out of the window . . .' *KMJ*, 103.
'When I get to New Zealand . . .' Mantz and Murry, 22.
'9 p.m. Sunday night . . .' *KMJ*, 36.
'As I looked up . . .' Alpers, 118.
'Ich muss streiten . . .' *KMJ*, 43.
'The friendship which now developed . . .' Mantz and Murry, 328.
'Resentment against New Zealand . . .' Mantz and Murry, 3.
'It seems positively dear . . .' *NA* (12.5.10).

'But some things . . .' *NA* (19.5.10).
'Wasn't that Van Gogh . . .' KM to Brett (5.12.21), *KML* II, 160.
'She is exuberant Idie . . .' Alpers, 141–2.
'The test of Nietzsche . . .' A. E. Randall in *NA* (2.2.11).
'They drank to the golden age . . .' BH, *The Maid's Comedy*, 137–8.
'Not by the aid of swords . . .' ibid., 156.
'I believe you are frightened . . .' KM, 'In a German Pension'.
'If it is felt . . .' *NA* (2.6.10).

CHAPTER FIVE

'I left school . . .' MM, *BTW*, 80.
'Si transformé que soit . . .' Carco, *Montmartre*, 16.
'C'était un adolescent . . .' Carco, *Bohème*, 245.
'I have always been taken by surprise . . .' MM, *BTW*, 188.
'Something infinitely plastic . . .' MM, *BTW*, 126.
'After my arrival . . .' LM, 68.
'Miss Mansfield abandons her salt furrow . . .' *NA* (28.3.12).
'Mediocrity is not a product . . .' *NA* (18.4.12).
'He [Orage] named her the marmozet . . .' BH, *STB* (June 1932).
'I understand beauty . . .' Ede, 82.
'My dear Murry . . .' ibid., 147 (the letter may never have been sent).
'Sophie gave a shrill . . .' Brodzky, 45–9.
'I confess I am out of my depth . . .' MM, *BTW*, 245.
'With her hair done in old-fashioned plaits . . .' Roberts, 184.
'The ordinary home life . . .' BH, *NA* (26.2.14).
'He got up as if nothing had happened . . .' BH, *TONA*, 10.
For Marsh and Murry *see* Marsh, *A Number of People*, 225, and Hassall,
    Edward Marsh, 206–7, 215, 271.

CHAPTER SIX

'I entangled myself with women . . .' MM (MS of 1947), L, 115.
'You *must* save your soul . . .' DHL to MM (22.7.13), *Letters*, 214.
'You've tried to satisfy Katherine . . .' DHL to MM (autumn 1913),
    Letters, 239.
'Nous avons beau sortir . . .' Carco, *Montmartre*, 183.
'I feel as fastidious . . .' KM to MM (summer 1913), *KMLM*, 6.
'Elle n'aimait pas le Milord . . .' Carco, *Les Innocents*, 131.
'A damnably sordid business . . .' Marsh, 271.
'All those save Lawrence are dead . . .' MM in Stoye MSS.
'That which struggles . . .' MM in Stoye MSS.
'I have noticed in myself . . .' MM in Stoye MSS.
'He was never a *real* boy . . .' Colin Middleton Murry, 86.

References

'Looked at, through, and over . . .' Leonard Woolf, *New Statesman* (5.2.55).
'Kot, howl like a dog . . .' Lucas, 120.
'I long and long to write . . .' *KMJ* (May 1914), 60.
'We were envious . . .' MM, *BTW*, 286.
'What kind of a wobbly . . .' BH, *TONA*, 11.
'When the train had fairly moved . . .' BH in *NA* (21.5.14).
'I like the Rondeau very much . . .' O to George Pitter (9.4.14).
'Browsing is a rather more advanced regimen . . .' O, *Selected Essays*, 143.
'To criticism, at least . . .' O in *NA* (28.3.12).
'Have you seen the Blue Book . . .' Mairet, 72.
'The next step . . .' O to George Pitter (14.6.14).
'It is not the business of these notes . . .' *NA* (18.6.14).
'I was being tossed . . .' BH in *NA* (21.5.14).
'Last week I was drunk . . .' BH in *NA* (21.5.14).
'The fair and pure English . . .' BH in *NA* (4.6.14).
'A pig and a pearl . . .' Sichel, 270.
'You mustn't go to sleep . . .' BH in *NA* (11.6.14).
'One of Modigliani's stone heads . . .' BH in *NA* (9.7.14).
'Modigliani, someone says . . .' BH in *NA* (16.7.14).
'One of Us, Ladies . . .' BH in *NA* (23.7.14).
'Votes for Women . . .' BH in *NA* (6.8.14).
'We *were* happy . . .' DHL to Lady Cynthia Asquith (31.1.15), *Letters*, 309.

CHAPTER SEVEN

'It is not to be supposed . . .' *NA* (6.8.14).
'I have no belief . . .' *NA* (6.8.14).
'The origins of the war . . .' *NA* (13.8.14).
'Frieda, you have left your children . . .' Leonard Woolf in Nehls I, 258.
'I quite understand . . .' SK to Waterlow (31.6.27), Stoye MSS.
'No dear Koteliansky . . .' KM to SK (n.d.), Stoye MSS.
'Jack, Jack . . .' *KMJ* (18.12.14), 62.
'must beware . . .' *KMJ* (January 1915), 64.
'soupe aux larmes . . .' Carco, *Montmartre*, 187.
'I had not expected it . . .' *KMJ* (16.11.14), 62.
'We gave ourselves our freedom . . .' *KMJ* (9.1.15), 67.
'I rather cling to him . . .' *KMJ* (27.1.15), 72.
'very bad . . .' *KMJ* (4.2.15), 73.
'I was possessed . . .' *KMJ* (18.1.15), 69.
'She came to me in Paris . . .' BH, *STB*, 7.
'Still a dream of town beauty . . .' BH in *NA* (24.9.14).
'He did the Mary portrait of me . . .' BH in *ST* (23.1.32).

References

'If we should lose this war . . .' BH in *NA* (24.9.14).
'I feel as if . . .' BH in *NA* (24.9.14).
'The misery is so quiet . . .' BH in *NA* (8.10.14).
'The generation to come . . .' BH in *NA* (21.1.15).
'less taste for analysis . . .' Carco, *Montmartre*, 196.
'*often, often* . . .' KM to SK (17.3.15), *KML*, 7.
'Un petit homme large . . .' Max Jacob, *Correspondance*, II, 185–6.
'B's flat . . .' KM to MM (21.3.15), *KMLM*, 20.
'Toutes les impressions . . .' Carco, *Montmartre*, 199.
'Strange and really beautiful . . .' KM to MM (21.3.15), *KMLM*, 20.
'But of course . . .' KM to MM (21.3.15), *KMLM*, 20–1.
'Biggy B . . .' KM to MM (20.3.15), *KMLM*, 18.
'sur un ton singulier . . .' Carco, *Montmartre*, 201.
'A very lovely young woman . . .' KM to MM (22.3.15), *KMLM*, 23.
'I think O wants kicking . . .' KM to MM (27.3.15), *KMLM*, 28.
'One of the men of the future . . .' DHL to Lady Ottoline Morrell
  (?22.2.15), *Letters*, I, 321.
'Yes, Koteliansky . . .' KM to SK (29.3.15), *KML*, 21.
'You *must* do something . . .' DHL to SK (8.4.15), *Letters*, 331.
'He took me to see a Russian Jew . . .' Morrell, 57.
'Three months ago . . .' Stoye MSS.
'You know . . .' *KMJ* (29.10.15), 86.
'By the remembered stream . . .' LM, 96.

CHAPTER EIGHT

'He was an odd, remarkable-looking man . . .' Morrell, 84.
'the moment that I knew you . . .' MM to Lady Ottoline Morrell
  (31.12.15), Morrell, 84.
'We might be fifty . . .' Alpers, 211.
'There are times . . .' MM, *Fyodor Dostoevsky*, 33.
'[He] attracted and repelled me . . .' MM, *BTW*, 436–8.
'It is a difficult business . . .' BH in *NA* (18.11.15).
'I was becoming disconsolate . . .' BH in *NA* (4.5.16).
'The same dances and dulcimers . . .' BH in *NA* (13.1.16).
'Everything shows . . .' BH in *NA* (17.2.16).
'There was a great scene . . .' BH in *ST* (6.2.32).
'The apparition of Ezra . . .' BH in *NA* (2.9.15).
'Why democratise it . . .' Mairet, 69.
'to mitigate in it . . .' Muir, 148.
'The endowment of women . . .' BH in *NA* (15.6.16).
'It used to be a stand-by . . .' BH in *NA* (15.6.16).
'But who has brought us . . .' BH in *NA* (3.8.16).
'Our virtues are deep . . .' BH in *NA* (10.8.16).

References

'If Germany is badly beaten . . .' BH in *NA* (27.7.16).
'There is no possibility . . .' BH in *NA* (27.7.16).
'Women should have no employment . . .' BH in *NA* (16.6.16).
'Katherine distrusted the very idea . . .' MM, *BTW*, 402. *See also* DHL
   to MM and KM (7.1.16, 17.1.16, 17.2.16, 24.2.16, 5.3.16, 8.3.16,
   11.3.16), *Letters*, I, 410–2.
'you know that in this . . .' DHL to KM (12.12.15), *Letters*, I, 396.
'The world is gone . . .' DHL to KM (7.1.16), *Letters*, I, 411.
'It is not really a nice place . . .' KM to SK (11.5.16), *KML*, 67.
'They should have a soft valley . . .' DHL to Lady Ottoline Morrell
   (24.5.16), *Letters*, I, 452.
'the large house . . .' For the Murrys at Garsington *see* Morrell, 148–9
   and 189–90.
'Of course it's *not* true . . .' Gertler to SK (29.8.17), BM Add. MSS,
   48969.
'It amazes me . . .' DHL to Catherine Carswell (27.11.16), *Letters*, I, 488.
'My feelings for her . . .' Clark, 308–9.
'I don't believe a nicer set . . .' MM, *BTW*, 428.

CHAPTER NINE

'the doors burst open . . .' Sichel, 404, quoting *Recollections of Modigliani
   by those Who Knew Him* (Los Angeles, 1958).
'That incredibly vulgar stuff . . .' BH in *STB* (June 1932).
'It is really very curious . . .' KM to Virginia Woolf (August 1917), *KML*,
   I, 80.
'I want nobody but you . . .' KM to MM (19.5.17), *KMLM*, 93.
'Sometimes when you write . . .' KM to MM (1917), *KMLM*, 93.
'Rheumatics plus . . .' KM to Virginia Woolf (August 1917), *KML*, I, 75.
'It was in November . . .' MM, *BTW*, 446–8.
'We could both . . .' Bell, II, 45.
'I shall always have a warm memory . . .' MM to SK (1.6.17), Stoye
   MSS.
'The monkey talked . . .' BH in *STB* (June 1932).
'Mouse, my little Mouse . . .' KM, 'Je ne Parle pas Français'.
'Ah! Ah! Vous êtes beaucoup changée . . .' KM to MM (11.1.18),
   KMLM, 115.
'What the HELL . . .' KM to MM (11.2.18), *KMLM*, 162.
'We shall always be "little gentlefolk" . . .' KM to MM (16.2.18), *KMLM*,
   170.
'I woke up early . . .' *KMJ* (18.2.18), 128.
'this is *not* serious . . .' KM to MM (19.2.18), *KMLM*, 173.
'It's a good thing . . .' KM to MM (19.2.18), *KMLM*, 174.

References

CHAPTER TEN

'Behold the gay mosaic of the scene . . .' *NA* (13.4.16).

'lean, hungry-looking . . .' Mairet, 64.

'she had no comparable connection . . .' Mairet, xiii.

'We discovered . . .' *NEW* (15.11.34).

'It is the fortress . . .' KM to MM (11.3.18), *KMLM*, 208.

'She's made me feel again *weak* . . .' KM to MM (13.3.18), *KMLM*, 210.

'When I met her at the station . . .' MM, *God*, 19.

'I listened and suddenly . . .' KM to MM (16.6.18), *KMLM*, 303.

'I, personally . . .' KM to MM (10.6.18), *KMLM*, 296.

'Dear Koteliansky . . .' MM to SK (1918 n.d.), Stoye MSS.

'I did not want . . .' KM to LM (15.7.18). Alpens, 265.

'There was no escape . . .' MM, *BTW*, 490.

'Let her have it . . .' DHL to KM (21.11.18), *Letters*, 565.

'As soon as she came down . . .' LM, 125.

'Murry seemed to wear a paper hat . . .' KM to Brett (1.1.19), *KML*, 221–2.

CHAPTER ELEVEN

'The Cocoa-Pacifist . . .' Ford to Read (19.9.20), *Letters*, 128.

'No, Mr Hamilton will never . . .' *Athenaeum* (16.5.19). I owe all the financial particulars in this passage to the courtesy of the *New Statesman* whose archives include the marked editorial copies of the *Athenaeum*.

'a sworn promise . . .' KM to SK (11.9.19), BM Add. MSS, 48970 fol. 217.

'It is not being ill that matters . . .' ibid.

'built on the slope . . .' KM to MM (9.12.19), *KMLM*, 439.

'Your loneliness is precious . . .' KM to SK (14.12.19), *KML*, I, 315.

'Your Georgian review . . .' KM to MM (9.12.19), *KMLM*, 439.

'Now, Eddie . . .' Hassall, 475.

'These letters . . .' KM to MM (21.11.19). *KMLM*, 400.

'ill and cold . . .' KM to MM (4.12.19), *KMLM*, 427.

'This letter killed the Mouse . . .' Lea, 76.

'It is not only that the hatred has gone . . .' KM to MM (13.1.20), *KMLM*, 455.

'Katherine had *so* wanted . . .' LM, 145.

'If I don't get well here . . .' KM to MM (21.1.20), *KMLM*, 457.

'See it with my own eyes . . .' KM to MM (8.2. 20), *KLMM*, 471.

'It was a question of sympathy . . .' KM to MM (7.2.20), *KMLM*, 469.

'Lawrence sent me a letter . . .' KM to MM (7.2.20), *KMLM*, 469–70.

'My dear Jones, one day . . .' LM, 149.

References

'It is difficult . . .' MM's comment in *KMLM*, 531.

'Darling, your memory . . .' KM to MM (25.3.20), *KMLM*, 504–6.

BH's three contributions in 1918 to *NA* were on 17 January, 31 January and 14 February.

'Modigliani, always suspicious . . .' BH in *ST* (23.1.32).

'All their grand systems. . .' BH in *ST* (20.2.32).

'He criticises too . . .' BH in *ST* (5.3.32).

'A hateful, sniggering letter . . .' KM to MM (24.9.20), *KMLM*, 542.

'Of saucy and audacious eloquence . . .' BH in *ST* (Dec. 1932).

'It is impossible . . .' O, *Credit Power and Democracy*, 212.

'The friends of Bolshevism . . .' *NA* (18.9.19).

'When sitting in reflection . . .' Kenney, 326.

'Why, Kenney . . .' Kenney, 328.

'Getting advts for the *N.A.* . . .' O to Herbert Read (10.2.22), Victoria University Library.

CHAPTER TWELVE

'Forgive me . . .' KM to MM (June 1920), *KMLM*, 532.

'I'm not going to call this a success . . .' Bell, II, 69.

'You don't take me in . . .' KM to MM (1.11.20), *KMLM*, 581.

'I have sent back the books . . .' KM to MM (8.12.20), *KMLM*, 615.

'You ought to write a book on Keats . . .' KM to MM (Dec. 1920), *KMLM*, 618.

'What happens to your personal life . . .' KM to MM (12.12.20), *KMLM*, 621.

'A nice little kettle of old fish . . .' DHL to SK (2.3.21), *Letters*, 643.

'I feel privately . . .' KM to MM (Dec. 1920), *KMLM*, 621.

'I can only walk . . .' KM to Anne Estelle Rice (May 1921), *KML*, II, 102.

'I tried to get the word . . .' KM to Anne Estelle Rice (19.5.21), *KML*, II, 111.

'The FOOD . . .' KM to Anne Estelle Rice (May 1921), *KML*, II, 103.

'Thanks be to God . . .' K.M. to Brett (Sept. 1921), *KML*, II, 134.

'No, one can't believe in *God* . . .' KM to MM (23.5.21) *KMLM*, 637.

'The Murrain . . .' DHL to SK (27.5.21), *Letters*, 654.

'As things were . . .' MM's commentary in *KMLM*, 643.

'Not a day passes . . .' KM to SK (18.10.21), *KML*, II, 145.

'Dear Orage . . .' Mairet, 59 (original in possession of Mrs. Jessie Orage which shows that Mairet misdated the letter, for some reason making it 9 November 1921.

'In some way I fear her . . . *KMJ* (13.1.22), 285.

'She means so much to me . . .' Brett to SK (June 1922), Stoye MSS.

'There is no need . . .' KM to MM (27.9.22), *KMLM*, 663–4.

'It's simply incredible . . .' KM to MM (11.10.22), *KMLM*, 670.

References

'Mr. Gurdjieff . . .' KM to MM (19.11.22), *KMLM*, 687.
'Are we dead . . .' O, *Selected Essays*, 127.
'a frail doomed silhouette . . .' Pauwels, 156.
'You think I am like other people . . .' KM to MM (27.10.22), *KMLM*, 679.
'You could learn the banjo . . .' KM to MM (27.10.22), *KMLM*, 681.
'going to build a high couch . . .' KM to MM (2.11.22), *KMLM*, 683.
For accounts of Katherine's death *see* MM *God*, 29–31 *and* Adèle Kafian, *Adelphi* (Oct.–Dec. 1946).

CHAPTER THIRTEEN

For KM's funeral *see* LM 229–31 *and* Pauwels, 280–3.
'What is going to happen . . .' DHL to MM (2.2.23), *Letters*, 736
Brett's correspondence with Koteliansky is in Stoye MSS, and is partly printed in *D. H. Lawrence Review*, Vol. 7, No. 3 (1974), edited by George J. Zytaruk.
'I doubt whether there are . . .' MM to H. P. Collins (29.3.22); L, 105.
'Slowly and with an effort . . .' MM, *God*, 35.
'I entangled myself with women . . .' MM (MS 1947), L, 115.
'Tell me, Frieda . . .' MM to Frieda Lawrence (27.11.55), Frieda Lawrence, *Memoirs and Correspondence*, 367.
For the Café Royal dinner-party *see* Carswell, *Savage Pilgrimage*, 215–23.
'A rotten false self-conscious place . . .' DHL to Mabel Luhan (9.1.24), *Letters*, 770.
'I don't want him . . .' DHL to SK (9.2.24), *Letters*, 777.
'I looked out of the window for her . . .' MM (MS. 1936) L, 123.
The letters recording the crisis between SK and MM are in the Stoye MSS.
'little yellow cry . . .' DHL to MM (17.11.24), *Letters*, 821.

CHAPTER FOURTEEN

One of his pupils . . . Peters, *Boyhood*, 31.
'Well-dressed, intellectual men . . .' Nott, *Teachings*, 1.
'A man must not be a slave . . .' Nott, *Teachings*, 114.
'In the house of the Sphinx . . .' I owe this to the recollection of Mrs. Jessie Orage.
'He came down into the court-yard . . .' Nott, *Teachings*, 121.
'I shall not go to the Prieuré . . .' Nott, *Teachings*, 216.
'he knew the shape of everything . . .' Nott, *Journey*, 14.
He dined with the group . . . Mairet, 107–9.
'Gurdjieff sailed last midnight . . .' Nott, *Journey*, 14.
'Once I crossed the Atlantic . . .' Recollection of Mrs. Jessie Orage.

'It's not the pessimism . . .' Mairet, 113.
'No. It is a pseudo-interest . . .' Nott, *Journey*, 30.
'by one of those sad mistakes . . .' Frieda Lawrence, *Memoirs,* 149.
The letters to Wells are at the University of Illinois (26.1.33 and 2.2.33).
Orage's last broadcast is printed in full in *NEW* (15.11.34).
'Always keep a trot for the drive . . .' Mrs. Jean Orage to Holbrook
    Jackson (letter in possession of author).
The *New Democrat* (15.12.34).
'The one single person . . .' *Adam*, 300, 16.
Crosland, 98–105 and Odouard, 74–87.
'It is Russia . . .' BH in *ST* (3.1.32).
'Burlap has been pal rubbing . . .' BH in *STB*, Sept. 1932.
'And who am I . . .' BH, *TONA*, 3.
'I sense that . . .' BH, *TONA*, 8.
'Orage considered Katherine Mansfield's writing . . .' *Adam*, 300, 12.
'wept and shivered . . .' BH to Wells (29.4.36), University of Illinois.
    Worthing Gazette (10.11.43).

CHAPTER FIFTEEN

'For my own part . . .' MM, *Keats and Shakespeare*, 9.
'the history of the human soul . . .' MM, *Keats and Shakespeare*, 1.
'Nothing more powerfully . . .' MM, *Keats and Shakespeare*, 98.
'I always felt . . .' MM, (Journal, 9.10.50), L, 329.
'Violet wept . . .' Colin Middleton Murry, 14.
'Another John Middleton . . .' DHL to SK (28.6.26), *Letters*, 923.
'In short, shut up . . .' DHL to MM (4.1.26), *Letters*, 875.
'O I'm so glad . . .' MM (MSS of 1947), L, 144.
'The life and death of Jesus . . .' MM in *Adelphi* (April 1927).
'It presents itself to me now . . .' MM to C. du Bois (31.7.29), L, 250.
'Towards a Synthesis' appeared in the *Criterion* for June 1927.
'The subject is hackneyed . . .' Shaw to MM (26.9.29), L, 158.
'To know reality . . .' MM, *God*, 250.
'It makes me know . . .' DHL to SK (23.11.29), *Letters*, 1217.
'I don't understand you . . .' DHL to MM (20.5.29), *Letters*, 1154.
The letters to SK from MM (4.3.30) and from Aldous Huxley (8.5.30)
    are both in the Stoye MSS.
'With her . . .' MM (Journal, 12.3.53), L, 165.
'You people . . .', L, 177.
'Such laughter as I had not heard . . .' MM (MS of 1936), L, 170.
'Golly, I don't want to tell you . . .' MM (MS of 1936), L, 174.
'according to the law . . .' MM (Journal, 19.1.31), L, 177.
'Well, John, you're an enigma . . .' MM (Journal, 25.4.31), L, 182.
'utterly impersonal . . .' MM to Plowman (30.5.31), L, 184.

References

'If only he and Lawrence . . .' Plowman to Mary Marr (17.6.31), *Bridge*, 385.

'sensitive stone . . .' Plowman to MM (21.5.31), *Bridge*, 374.

'You know she's got the devil of a temper . . .' Colin Middleton Murry, 36.

'wanted to exult . . .' MM, *SOW*, 128.

'his pride is become a madness . . .' MM, *SOW*, 334–5.

'Instead of being strengthened . . .' MM, *SOW*, 123.

'less than normal . . .' MM, *SOW*, 123.

'He was neither a great novelist . . .' MM, *SOW*, 174.

'Lawrence was a major soul . . .' MM, *SOW*, 174.

'For truly you were wonderful . . .' MM, *SOW*, 389.

'haunted, tortured, divided . . .' MM, *SOW*, 130.

'as impersonal as reading about Elizabeth . . .' Frieda Lawrence to Catherine Carswell (n.d. but 1932) in possession of the author.

'it is time to lance . . .' MM (Journal, 7.7.32), L, 214.

'a prefatory note . . .' Boriswood and Co. to Catherine Carswell (28.9.32) in possession of the author.

'I wrote to him . . .' MM, *Reminiscences of D. H. Lawrence*, 165.

'the *cry* of injustice . . .' Plowman to MM (1.2.32), *Bridge*, 417.

'You preach Marx . . .' Plowman to MM (30.5. 32), *Bridge*, 434.

'She came to me quite unexpectedly . . .' MM (MS of 1947), L, 187.

'When she was in full spate . . .' Colin Middleton Murry, 41.

'little better than infallible pills . . .' Plowman to Geoffrey West (1.8.34), *Bridge*, 509.

'Marxism is crippled . . .' Plowman to Geoffrey West (3.6.32), *Bridge*, 439.

'the curious way . . .' Heppenstall, *Four Absentees*, 37.

'for the real battle of life . . .' *Adelphi* (October 1935).

'to promote the education . . .' L, 223–4.

'I . . . find it difficult to be ruthless . . .' MM, *Adelphi* (September 1936).

'the next few years . . .' L, 236. The 'Nehale' of Murry's Journals and the 'Hetty' of Mr. Heppenstall's *Four Absentees* both refer to Helena Young.

'Oh, Max darling . . .' L, 237.

'With the exception . . .' Kunitz and Haycroft, *Twentieth Century Authors*, 1002–3.

'It's no use . . .' MM (MS of 1947), L, 259.

'The play in which J.M.M. is cast . . .' Mary Middleton Murry, 69.

'each room . . .' MM (Journal, 8.11.49), L, 328.

'a modest but adequate subsistence . . .' MM, *Adam and Eve*, 55.

'Basis of the New Humanism', *Cavalcade*, (1946).

'Here, it seems, is where I stop . . .' MM (Journal, 31.5.48), L, 319.

'nice to be old . . .' MM to Frieda Lawrence (9.12.51), *Memoirs*, 311.

'the true man-woman relationship . . .' MM (Journal, 14.2.53), L, 332.

References

CHAPTER SIXTEEN

Many of the details in this chapter come from conversations with Miss Dilys Powell and Mrs. Catherine Stoye.

'Neither a bolshevik nor a menshevik . . .' SK to Leonard Woolf (5.7.29), University of Sussex.

'the criminal policy . . .' SK to Leonard Woolf (n.d. but 1924), University of Sussex.

The invitation to the interview with Victor Wellesley is in Stoye MSS.

'Her division and "secret sorrow" . . .' SK to Waterlow (12.12.28), Turnbull.

'my resolution to free myself . . .' SK to Waterlow (28.11.24), Turnbull.

'Murry is a *real* writer . . .' Glenavy, 187.

'You will miss him very much . . .' Glenavy, 191.

'your opinions . . .' MM to SK (22.10.22), Stoye MSS.

For SK and Gertler *see* BM Add. MSS 48969 and 48970. There is room for a considerable study.

'Sophistication is the greatest obstacle . . .' SK to Waterlow (25.4.26), Turnbull.

'I am perfectly convinced . . .' SK to Waterlow (25.4.27), Turnbull.

'Mexico and the religion of death . . .' SK to Waterlow (21.9.26), Turnbull.

'There is in Lawrence . . .' SK to Waterlow (21.9.26), Turnbull.

'Personally I think . . .' SK to Waterlow (20.7.26), Turnbull.

'Virginia's *Orlando* . . .' SK to Waterlow (12.12.28), Turnbull.

'Gertler, who loved life . . .' Glenavy, 166.

'For a quarter of an hour . . .' Marjorie Wells to Leonard Woolf (23.1.55), University of Sussex.

The *New Statesman* (5.2.55).

CHAPTER SEVENTEEN

'the literary underworld . . .' Bell, II, 50.

'men who seem never to lose . . .' Sullivan, 9.

'We rushed from the forest . . .' Beatrice was very proud of this poem, which first appeared in *NA* (9.6.10). Twenty-three years later she published it in *ST* for February 1933.

'A writer who has succeeded . . .' O, *Selected Essays*, 190.

'a brave voice . . .' Frieda Lawrence, *Memoirs and Correspondence*, 149.

'The standards of success . . .' Sullivan, 127.

'Thus modern technique . . .' MM, *Defence of Democracy*, 38.

'Radio, it is certain . . .' O, *Selected Essays*, 176.

Bibliography

Contractions for certain frequently used sources are shown against the works to which they refer.

MANUSCRIPTS

Katherine Mansfield's MSS, Alexander Turnbull Library, Wellington, New Zealand.
H. G. Wells's MSS, University of Illinois at Urbana-Champaign.
Herbert Read's MSS, University of Victoria, British Colombia.
Stoye MSS (Koteliansky), in possession of Mrs. Catherine Stoye.
British Museum Additional MSS 48969–48973.

PERIODICALS

	Adam International Review
AD	*Adelphi* (and *New Adelphi*)
AT	*Athenaeum*
NA	*New Age*
NEW	*New English Weekly*
	Open Window
	Rhythm (subsequently the *Blue Review*)
ST and STB	*Straight Thinker* and *Straight Thinker Bulletin*
	Worthing Gazette

BOOKS

Alpers, Antony. *Katherine Mansfield, A Biography*, Cape, 1954.
Archer, William. *The Life, Trial, and Death, of Francisco Ferrer*, 1911.
Bell, Quentin. *Virginia Woolf*, Hogarth Press, 1972 and 1973.
Brodsky, Horace. *Henri Gaudier-Brzeska 1891–1915*, Faber, 1933.
Carco, Francis. *L'Ami des Peintres*, Albin-Michel, 1934.
—— *Bohème d'Artiste*, Albin-Michel, 1940.
—— *La Bohème et mon Cœur*, Editions N.R.F., 1922.
—— *Les Innocents*, Albin-Michel, 1916.
—— *Montmartre à Vingt Ans*, Albin-Michel, 1938.
Clark, Ronald W. *The Life of Bertrand Russell*, Cape and Weidenfeld and Nicolson, 1975.

Bibliography

Crosland, Margaret. *Raymond Radiguet*, Peter Owen, 1976.

Ede, H. S. *Savage Messiah*, Heinemann, 1931.

Ford Madox Ford. *Letters* (ed. Richard M. Ludwig), Princeton University Press, 1965.

Garnett, David. *The Golden Echo*, Chatto and Windus, 1954 and 1955.

Gibbons, T. *Rooms in the Darwin Hotel*, University of Australia Press, 1973.

Glenavy, Beatrice Campbell, Lady. *Today We Will Only Gossip*, Constable, 1964.

Goldring, Douglas. *Odd Man Out*, Chapman and Hall, 1935.

—— and Beadle, Charles. *Artist Quarter*. Reminiscences of Montmartre and Montparnasse in the first two decades of the twentieth century, by Charles Douglas, Faber, 1941.

Haigh, Richmond. *An Ethiopian Saga*, Allen and Unwin, 1919.

Hamnett, Nina. *Laughing Torso*, Constable, 1932.

Hassall, Christopher. *Edward Marsh*, Longman, 1959.

Hastings, Beatrice. *The Maid's Comedy*, Stephen Swift, 1911.

—— *The Old* New Age—*Orage and Others*, Blue Moon Press, 1935. [*TONA*]

—— Apart from the above, and *Woman's Worst Enemy, Woman*, of which I have been unable to locate a copy, Beatrice's writings are embedded in journals under various pseudonyms, usually 'Alice Morning'. The most important are:

> 'Pages from an Unpublished Novel', *NA*.
> 'Impressions of Paris', *NA*.
> 'Tales of a Peri', *NA*.
> 'Peace Notes', *NA*.
> 'Madame Six', *ST* and *STB*.

Hobson, S. G. *Pilgrim to the Left*, Edward Arnold, 1938.

Jacob, Max. *Correspondance*, Editions Paris, 1953–5. Part of a series entitled 'Correspondance'.

Jones, Alun R. *Life and Opinions of T. E. Hulme*, Victor Gollancz, 1960.

Kenney, Rowland. *Westering*, Dent, 1939.

'L.M.' (Ida Constance Baker). *Katherine Mansfield, The Memories of L.M.* Michael Joseph, 1971.

Lawrence, D. H. *The Collected Letters of D. H. Lawrence* (ed. Harry T. Moore), Heinemann, 1962.

—— *Letters to Thomas and Adèle Seltzer* (ed. Gerald M. Lacy), Black Sparrow Press, 1976.

Lawrence, Frieda. Memoirs and Correspondence (ed. E. W. Tedlock), Heinemann, 1961.

—— *Not I, But the Wind*, Heinemann, 1934.

Lea, F. A. *The Life of John Middleton Murry*, Methuen, 1959. [*L*]

Bibliography

Lucas, Robert. *Frieda Lawrence* (trans. Geoffrey Skelton), Secker and Warburg, 1973.

MacDiarmid, Hugh. *The Company I've Kept*, Hutchinson, 1966.

Mairet, Philip. *John Middleton Murry*, Longman, 1958.

—— *A. R. Orage, A Memoir*, University Books, 1966.

The earlier edition (Dent, 1936) contains less information.

Mansfield, Katherine. *The Letters of Katherine Mansfield* (ed. J. Middleton Murry), Constable, 1928. [*KML*]

—— *Katherine Mansfield's Letters to John Middleton Murry 1913–1922*, Constable, 1951. [*KMLM*]

—— *The Journal of Katherine Mansfield* (ed. J. Middleton Murry), Constable, 1967. [*KMJ*]

Mantz, Ruth, and Murry, J. M. *The Life of Katherine Mansfield*, Constable, 1933.

Marsh, Edward. *A Number of People*, Heinemann, 1939.

Martin, Wallace. *The* New Age *Under Orage, Chapters in English Cultural History*, Manchester University Press, 1967.

Morrell, Lady Ottoline. *Ottoline at Garsington. Memoirs of Lady Ottoline Morrell 1915–1918* (ed. Robert Gathorne-Hardy), Faber, 1974.

Muir, Edwin. *An Autobiography*, Hogarth Press, 1954.

Murry, Colin Middleton. *One Hand Clapping, A Memoir of Childhood*, Gollancz, 1975.

Murry, John Middleton. *Between Two Worlds*, Cape, 1935. [*BTW*]

—— *Fyodor Dostoevsky, A Critical Study*, Martin Secker, 1916.

—— *God*. Cape, 1925.

—— *Katherine Mansfield and Other Literary Portraits*, Peter Nevill, 1949.

—— *Keats and Shakespeare*, Oxford University Press, 1925.

—— *Reminiscences of D. H. Lawrence*, Cape, 1933.

—— *Son of Woman*, Cape, 1931.

—— *To the Unknown God*, Cape, 1924.

(There is a very full bibliography of Murry's Works in Lea *op. cit.*)

Murry, Mary Middleton. *To Keep Faith*, Constable, 1959.

Naylor, L. *Culham 1853–1953*, Abbey Press, Abingdon, 1954.

Nehls, E. *D. H. Lawrence. A Composite Biography*, University of Wisconsin Press, 1957.

Norman, C. H. *Essays and Letters on Public Affairs*, Frank Palmer, 1913.

Nott, C. S. *Teachings of Gurdjieff*, Routledge, 1964.

—— *Journey Through This World*, Routledge, 1969.

Odouard, Nadia, *Les Années Folles de Raymond Radiguet*, Seghers, 1974.

Orage, A. R. *Selected Essays and Critical Writings* (ed. Herbert Read and Denis Saurat), Stanley Nott, 1935.

Orton, William. *The Last Romantic*, Cassell, 1937.

Pauwels, Louis. *Monsieur Gurdjieff*, Editions du Seuil, 1954.

Bibliography

Peters, R. F. *Boyhood with Gurdjieff*, Gollancz, 1964.

—— *Gurdjieff Remembered*, Gollancz, 1965.

Plowman, Max. *Bridge into the Future. Letters of Max Plowman* (ed. D.L.P.), Andrew Dakers, 1944.

Read, Herbert. *Annals of Innocence and Experience*, Faber, 1940.

Reckitt, Maurice B. *As It Happened*, Dent, 1931.

Rich, R. W. *The Training of Teachers in England and Wales during the Nineteenth Century*, Cedric Chivers, 1972.

Roberts, Carl Bechhofer. *Let's Begin Again*, Jarrolds, 1940.

Selver, Paul. *Orage and the New Age Circle*, Allen and Unwin, 1959.

Shaw, George Bernard. *Collected Letters* (ed. Dan H. Lawrence), Max Reinhardt, 1965.

Sichel, Pierre. *Modigliani*, W. H. Allen, 1967.

Sullivan, J. W. N. *But For The Grace Of God*, Cape, 1932.

Travis, M. A. *The Work of the Leeds School Board 1870–1902, Researches and Studies No. 8* May 1953.

Wallace, Lewis, (Pseud. 'M.B. Oxon'). *Cosmic Anatomy, or The Structure of The Ego*, Watkins, 1921.

Index

Index

Index

Flecker, James Elroy, 42
Fontainebleau-Avon, 186, 188, 189, 190, 195, 197, 202, 210–11, 213, 215, 220, 228, 231, 261
Ford, Ford Madox *see* Hueffer
Forster, E. M., 109, 157, 200, 265
Foujita, 105
France, Anatole, 41, 46
Free Society, The, 256
Freud, 91, 127, 147
Fry, Roger, 91
Fullerton, Jinnie, 163, 165, 174, 175
Futurism, 91
Fyodor Dostoevsky, 115, 116, 246, 256

Gamble, Mary *see* Murry, Mary
Garden Party, The, 178, 182
Garnett, Constance, 115
Garnett, David, 13, 88, 172
Garnett, Edward, 186
Garsington Manor, 110, 113–14, 130–1, 132, 136, 146, 152, 158, 264, 274, 276
Gaudier-Brzeska, Henri, 49, 76–8, 83, 86, 91, 151, 242, 247, 258
George, W. L., 66
Georgian Poetry, 159
Gertler, Mark, 110, 130, 155, 160, 202, 260, 264, 267
Gibbon, 136
Gide, André, 49
Gill, Eric, 219
Gillet, Louis, 107
Glenavy, Lord and Lady *see* Campbell, Gordon and Beatrice
God: an Introduction to the Science of Metabiology, 181n., 235, 236
Goldring, Douglas, 270
Gorky, Maxim, 89, 179
Gosse, Edmund, 232
Granville, Edward *see* 'Stephen Swift'
Granville-Barker, Harley, 35
Gray, 103, 105, 107
Grayson, Victor, 43–5, 47, 83, 92, 276
Greatham, 108, 109
Green, Doris, 227
Greenwood, Arthur, 156
Grey, Sir Edward, 47

Grieve, Christopher Murray ('Hugh MacDiarmid'), 122, 217
Guild Socialism, 19, 43, 83, 92, 123, 146, 147, 173
Gurdjieff, George, 171, 173, 182, 184–92, 210–16, 219, 220, 248, 249, 262, 276

Haigh, Emily Alice, 28; *and see* 'Hastings, Beatrice'
Haigh, Richmond, 29, 62, 157
Hamnett, Nina, 72
Hampstead, 133, 150, 151, 152, 201, 203, 219, 261
Hardie, James Keir, 19
Hardy, Thomas, 131, 157, 204, 230, 232, 271
Harris, Frank, 169
Hastings, 29
'Hastings, Beatrice' (Emily Alice Haigh), 53, 106, 151; origins and early career, 28–30; and Orage, 19, 28, 30–1, 34, 78–9, 81, 90, 118–19, 146, 169, 224; and Katherine Mansfield, 52, 58–9, 60, 62, 64, 73–5, 102, 104, 107–8, 165–6, 169, 175, 223, 270, 273; and Modigliani, 94–6, 98, 121–2, 134, 167–8; and the *New Age*, 33, 37–8, 41, 45, 49, 50, 65, 75, 117–18, 119–21, 135, 166–7, 224–5; life in Paris, 90, 93–6, 104–5, 117; and the 'Woman Question', 41, 59–60, 63, 79–81, 91, 96; and the War, 104–5, 117–18, 125–6; autobiographical writings, 28, 29, 167–9, 222, 224; other writings, 62–3, 141, 166, 223, 226–7; letters from, 165–6, 181, 221–2; later years, 222–7; retrospect of, 270–6
Heap, Jane, 213
Heaven – and Earth, 229, 251, 252
Hébuterne, Jeanne, 134, 167
Heppenstall, Rayner, 217, 247–9, 251
Higher Tregerthen, 127, 128, 129, 131, 150
Hitlerite Germany, 251, 253, 255
Hobson, S. G., 33, 41, 43, 44, 45, 79, 83

Index

Hogarth Press, 135
Horne, – , 96
'Hudson, Stephen' *see* Schiff, Sydney
Hueffer, Ford Madox (later Ford
   Madox Ford), 157
Hulme, T. E., 36, 91, 123, 125, 144
Huxley, Aldous, 155, 156, 175, 236,
   242, 243, 256, 265, 270
Huxley, Julian, 157, 176n.
Hyndman, H. M., 18, 19

Ibsen, Henrik, 23, 24, 35, 54, 252
Impressionism, 91
In a German Pension, 52, 66, 73
Independent Labour Party, 18–19,
   223, 246, 249, 253, 256
Innocents, Les, 86, 107, 108, 119, 138

Jackson, Holbrook, 21–3, 26, 31–3, 37,
   38, 42, 147, 148, 220, 272
Jacob, Max, 93, 95, 106, 121, 122, 168,
   169
James, Henry, 54
Jameson, Storm, 220
Jesus, 231, 232–3, 240
Joad, C. E. M., 122, 144
John, Augustus, 95, 146, 219
Johnson, Hewlett, 219
Joyce, 211, 271
Jung, 147, 153, 234

Kafka, 216
Keats, 115, 136, 176, 228–9, 257
Keats and Shakespeare, 178, 205,
   228–9, 252
Kennedy, John McFarland ('S.
   Verdad'), 34, 45, 48, 49, 92, 99, 145
Kenney, Rowland, 92, 171, 172
Kenway, P. T., 51
Keynes, John Maynard, 130, 133, 137
'Kingsmill, Hugh' (Hugh Lunn), 61,
   72, 99, 115, 122, 144
Kipling, 275
Knox, Ronald, 133
Koteliansky, Samuel Solomonovich
   ('Kot'), 103, 111, 121, 130, 150, 155,
   196, 268; origins and education,
   88–9; and D. H. Lawrence, 89,

96–7, 100, 131, 153, 165, 201, 202–3,
   265–6, 279; and Katherine Mansfield, 101, 102, 103, 106, 109, 113,
   157, 179–81, 184, 186, 260–2, 267,
   276; and Murry, 110, 114, 138, 151,
   201, 203, 206–9, 228, 236, 257, 258,
   261, 274–5; literary work, 110, 131,
   138, 157, 158, 243; business manager
   of the *Adelphi*, 197, 199, 205–8, 262;
   later years, 259–68, 276, 278; letters
   to, 101–2, 106, 109, 115, 117, 129,
   138, 151, 158, 159, 177, 179, 180,
   183, 190, 195, 200, 235, 236, 278,
   279; letters from, 101, 177, 179,
   187, 194, 208, 230, 261, 264–5;
   retrospect of, 269–76

Labour Party, 44–5
Lady Chatterley's Lover, 236, 244n.,
   266
Landor, 275
Larling, 243, 248, 249, 250, 253–4
Larrouy, Maurice, 68
Lawrence, D. H., 16, 86, 114, 131,
   153, 154, 157, 159, 160, 164–5,
   176n., 184, 237; marriage, 89; walking tour, 96–7, 98; at Chesham,
   100–1, 102; at Greatham, 108–9;
   Signature, 110–11; in Cornwall,
   127–9; New Mexico, 198, 202–3,
   241n.; Café Royal dinner-party,
   201–3; and Murry, 83–5, 164–5,
   196, 198, 200, 201–3, 205, 209,
   230–1, 235–6; and Kot, 265–6;
   letters from, 127–8, 131, 177, 194,
   196n., 198, 200, 201, 209; retrospect, 272, 276, 279
Lawrence, Frieda, 84, 89, 96, 100–1,
   129, 200–3, 217, 236–7, 244, 268,
   275, 276, 279
Leavis, F. R., 258
Leeds, 18–24
Leeds Arts Club, 23, 24
le Maistre, Violet, 200, 203–4; *and
   see* Murry, Violet
letters, Katherine Mansfield's dependence on, 149–50, 161
Levy, Oscar, 21, 45, 124

Index

Index

Scott, Sir Walter, 275
Secker, Martin, 86, 114, 244, 270
Segonzac, 74
Seltzer, Thomas, 203
Selver, Paul, 144, 145, 219
Sharp, Clifford, 41, 91, 171, 222
Shaw, George Bernard, 16, 23, 34, 35, 36, 38, 43, 44, 54, 94, 117, 125, 198, 235; and Orage, 24, 30, 32–3, 37, 41, 42, 219–20; and the Fabians, 25–6, 31, 32; Chesterbelloc controversy, 40
Sheppard, Revd. Dick, 249, 251
Sheppard, John Tressider, 130, 131
Sickert, 49, 91, 146
Signature, 111, 113, 259
Sinclair, Upton, 42
Smith, Joseph, 23, 32
Snowden, Philip, 45
Sobieniowski, Floryan, 58, 76
Social Credit, 147–8, 170, 218–19, 247n.
Socialism, 18–19, 20, 25–6, 31, 38, 39–42, 45, 92, 98, 123–4
Son of Woman, 237, 240–2, 244, 258, 270, 279
Sorapure, Dr. Victor, 156, 158, 184, 186
South Acre, 234, 236, 237, 238, 243
South Africa, 29, 30, 59
Spectator, 35
Spender, J. A., 75, 86
Squire, J. C., 160
Stendhal, 49
'Stephen Swift' (Edward Granville), 62, 63, 64, 66, 75, 76, 81, 82, 117
Stephens, James, 263–4, 268
Sterne, 67, 93, 94
Still Life, 86, 127
Strachey, Lytton, 130, 132, 133, 137, 157, 176n.
Straight Thinker, 167n., 222–3
Straight Thinker Bulletin, 167n., 223–4
Sullivan, J. W. N., 116, 133, 155, 156, 186, 197, 198, 205, 262, 263, 272, 276
Sunwise Turn Bookshop, 211

Swift, 258
Swift, Jonathan, 91
Syndicalism, 124

Tawney, R. H., 24
Taylor, G. R. S., 43
Tchekov, 49, 52, 158–9, 172, 203
teacher training, 16
tea-shops, 34, 122, 216, 217, 263, 276
Thelnetham, 255, 256
theosophy, 20–1, 28, 30, 211
Thomas, Dylan, 36, 217
Thomson, Lachlan, 29, 30
'Thursdayers', 263–4, 276
Times Literary Supplement, 85, 86, 102, 129, 133, 153, 236, 242, 246, 253, 258
Tolstoy, 49, 131, 172
Tomlinson, H. M., 133, 184, 197, 205–7
Tomlinson, Philip, 133, 197, 205–7, 208
'Tonson, Jacob' *see* Bennett
Trades Unionism, 31, 38, 123
Trowell, Arnold, 53, 54, 55
Trowell, Garnet, 55, 57
Turgenev, 49, 131
Turner, W. J., 263
Twyford, 196–7, 235

Van Gogh, 6
Valéry, 49, 176n.

Walker, Alexander, 18
Walker, Jean *see* Orage, Jean
Wallace, L. A. R., 24, 33, 36, 50–1
Wassilieff, Marie, 105, 134
Waterlow, Sydney, 101, 132, 150, 209, 260, 261, 263, 264, 266, 276
Webb, Beatrice, 19, 26, 31, 43, 91, 123
Webb, Sidney, 19, 26, 31, 44, 91
Wells, H. G., 24, 26, 27, 30, 31, 35, 36, 38, 40, 42, 43, 120, 200, 218, 219, 225, 260
Wells, Marjorie, 259, 267
Westminster Gazette, 75, 85, 86, 126
White, Sir George, 29
Whistler, 22